RODALE'S
SUCCESSFUL ORGANIC GARDENING™
PERENNIALS

RODALE'S
SUCCESSFUL ORGANIC GARDENING™
PERENNIALS

TEXT BY SUSAN McCLURE

PLANT BY PLANT GUIDE BY C. COLSTON BURRELL

Rodale Press, Emmaus, Pennsylvania

Our Mission

We publish books that empower people's lives.

RODALE BOOKS

If you have any questions or comments concerning this book, please write:

Rodale Press
Book Readers' Service
33 East Minor Street
Emmaus, PA 18098

Library of Congress Cataloging-in-Publication Data

McClure, Susan.
  Perennials / text by Susan McClure ; plant by plant guide by
C. Colston Burrell.
      p.   cm. — (Rodale's successful organic gardening)
  Includes index.
  ISBN 0–87596–559–8 hardcover — ISBN 0–87596–560–1
paperback
  1. Perennials. 2. Organic gardening I. Burrell, C. Colston.
II. Title. III. Series.
  SB434.M37   1993
  635.9'32—dc20
                                                    92–45809
                                                         CIP

Printed by Tien Wah Press in Singapore on acid-free paper ∞

Rodale Press Staff:
    Executive Editor: Margaret Lydic Balitas
    Senior Editor: Barbara W. Ellis
    Editors: Nancy J. Ondra and Ellen Phillips
    Copy Editor: Carolyn R. Mandarano

Produced for Rodale Press by Weldon Russell Pty Ltd
107 Union Street, North Sydney NSW 2060, Australia
a member of the Weldon International Group of Companies

    Publisher: Elaine Russell
    Publishing Manager: Susan Hurley
    Senior Editor: Ariana Klepac
    Editor: Margaret Whiskin
    Editorial Assistant: Libby Frederico
    Horticultural Consultant: Cheryl Maddocks
    Copy Editor: Kirsten John
    Designer: Rowena Sheppard
    Picture Researcher: Anne Nicol
    Photographers: John Callanan, David Wallace
    Illustrators: Barbara Rodanska, Jan Smith
    Macintosh Layout Artist: Edwina Ryan
    Indexer: Michael Wyatt
    Production Manager: Dianne Leddy

A KEVIN WELDON PRODUCTION

Distributed in the book trade by St. Martin's Press

2 4 6 8 10 9 7 5 3 1 hardcover
2 4 6 8 10 9 7 5 3 1 paperback

Opposite: Cottage garden with delphiniums, foxgloves, and lupines
Half title: Lupines
Opposite title page: Hybrid bearded irises
Title page: Daylily
Opposite contents: Anemone
Contents page: *Hibiscus moscheutos* (left), *Primula vulgaris* (right)
Back cover: *Geranium himalayense* and *Achillea millefolium* (top),
    Iris sibirica and *Chrysanthemum x superbum* (center)

CONTENTS

INTRODUCTION

Gardening with perennials is a joy that everyone can share. Whether your garden is large or small, sunny or shady, wet or dry, a wide variety of perennials will thrive there and provide you with beauty for years to come.

Let's begin by establishing just what we mean by a "perennial." Perennial plants live and bloom for more than two growing seasons. Many will survive a decade or longer if planted in the right location. But even the shorter-lived plants are worth growing. For instance, blanket flowers (*Gaillardia* x *grandiflora*) bloom vigorously for a long portion of the summer, although they seldom return more than 2 years. Other perennials, such as columbines (*Aquilegia* spp.) and hollyhocks (*Alcea rosea*), have a short natural life span but set seed that replaces the parent plant. Occasionally, a biennial plant, like foxglove (*Digitalis grandiflora*) or sweet William (*Dianthus barbatus*), which normally grows foliage the first year and flowers the second, will live on for the third year. Despite their differences in life span, you can call all of these perennials.

Identifying perennials by their 2-year-plus life span may seem reasonably tidy, but the definition of perennials gets more complicated. You see, trees and shrubs also are perennials. However, they are exempted from our definition of perennial plants because they develop woody stems and limbs. With the exception of tree peonies (*Paeonia suffruticosa*) and a few other plants, perennial garden flowers are herbaceous, which means they lack woody stems. In most cases, the foliage of perennials dies back to the underground roots each dormant season. A few perennials, like coral bells (*Heuchera* spp.) and rock cresses (*Arabis* spp.), have evergreen foliage that persists through the winter.

Some tropical plants are perennial in their natural habitat, but we treat them like annuals in cold climates because they perish when the temperature drops to freezing. Geraniums, impatiens, marigolds, and others in this group have the ability to live on if the seasons are mild enough. However, for the purposes of this book, we will concentrate only on herbaceous perennials that have some kind of dormant period.

Now that you know what a perennial is, you can start to explore the many possibilities of incorporating perennials into your garden. You may want to re-create a classic English perennial border, an informal cottage garden, a lush meadow, or a shady woodland garden. With thousands of perennial species and cultivars available, there's a good chance that you'll find a wide range of plant forms, leaf textures, and flower colors to fit any garden you may have in mind.

In most respects, starting and caring for a perennial garden is just like any other type of garden. You need to choose a good spot and to lay out the garden to fit the site and your needs. You'll prepare the soil, plant, water, fertilize, weed, and control pests and diseases— just as you would for a vegetable garden or an annual bed. But in return, you'll enjoy the beauty of your perennials as they grow and flower year after year. *Rodale's Successful Organic Gardening: Perennials* will guide you through the steps of creating and maintaining the best perennial garden you ever thought possible.

Opposite: Showy perennial New England and New York asters (*Aster novae-angliae* and *A. novi-belgii*) add masses of color to late-summer and fall gardens. Include them in formal borders or informal meadow plantings.

HOW TO USE THIS BOOK

Whether you are starting a new perennial garden or renewing an old one, you will more than likely have questions that need to be answered. This book is here to help you.

In the following chapters, you'll become attuned to the climate around you and understand how it influences your choice of herbaceous perennials. You'll learn how to dig into your soil, identifying its physical and chemical, or nutritional, structure. You'll start to make a living organic soil in which your garden will thrive. You'll develop the skills to make well-educated decisions about situating, organizing, and selecting healthy, well-adapted plants for your garden.

You'll discover what care perennials need—and what they do not need—and become familiar with organic growing techniques so you can tend the garden without using synthetic chemicals. You'll learn how to grow more plants from the ones you have as well as the pros and cons of different propagation methods. And when you need to know specific information on a particular perennial, or if you just want to get ideas on different perennials to grow, check out the "Plant by Plant Guide," starting on page 78.

"Understanding Your Garden," starting on page 12, explains how the environment influences your perennial garden. You'll find out how your climate and the topography, soil, and exposure of your garden all affect where you site your garden and which perennials will grow best for you. You can also check out the USDA Plant Hardiness Zone Map on page 154 to determine your area's average annual minimum temperature, which will help you to determine which perennials will thrive in your area.

Once you are aware of your site conditions, you can start designing your garden to fit your site and your needs. In "Landscaping with Perennials," starting on page 22, you'll find out what you need to know about the stages of garden planning. Matching the perennials you want to grow to the conditions available on your site is a key part of planning a successful garden. And if you are looking for ideas on different ways to incorporate perennials into your landscape, you'll find a whole section on different garden styles.

"Choosing Your Plants," starting on page 32, is the place to look when you are ready to buy your plants. Here you'll find an explanation of how perennials are named so you can understand the different names you may see in a catalog or at your local garden center. Tips on selecting and buying the best plants are also included. And if you're looking for a particular perennial to fit that special spot in your design, check out the extensive species charts that start on page 38. They cover many of the most popular perennials, along with their bloom times and colors.

"Cultivating and Planting," starting on page 42, is where you'll find complete information on the all-important stage of a new perennial garden: soil preparation. Adding nutrients is also covered, as well as details on the correct planting techniques for container-grown, bareroot, and field-dug perennials.

Once your perennials are in and growing, there are many steps you can take to keep them healthy and looking good for years to come. "Maintaining Perennials," starting on page 50, covers topics such as mulching, watering, feeding, and composting, as well as staking, deadheading, pinching, and cutting back. If, in spite of all your care, weeds, insects, or diseases get out of hand, you'll find what you need to know to get the problem under control using organic methods.

Once you've experienced the fun of your first

perennial garden, you'll probably want to grow even more perennials. "Propagating Perennials," starting on page 70, shows you how to grow new plants from seed and reproduce plants you already have by layering, division, or cuttings. Once you learn how easy it is to propagate perennials, you'll be able to fill new gardens at a fraction of the cost of buying plants. You'll probably have plenty to share with friends, too!

Plant by Plant Guide

This full-color guide covers complete growing information for more than 120 different perennials. The entries are arranged alphabetically by botanical name. If you only know a certain perennial by its common name, you can easily find its botanical name by looking up the common name in the index.

Each entry is accompanied by a color photograph for easy identification of the plant. You'll also find information on flower color, flowering time, height and spread, temperature requirements, position, and landscape uses, as well as cultivation, propagation, and pest and disease prevention. If a perennial also has cultivars available, you'll find that information here, too.

The "Plant by Plant Guide" is designed to make organic perennial gardening as simple and as fun as possible by providing all of the information you need in a concise, easy-to-use format. The diagram below helps explain what to look for on these practical pages.

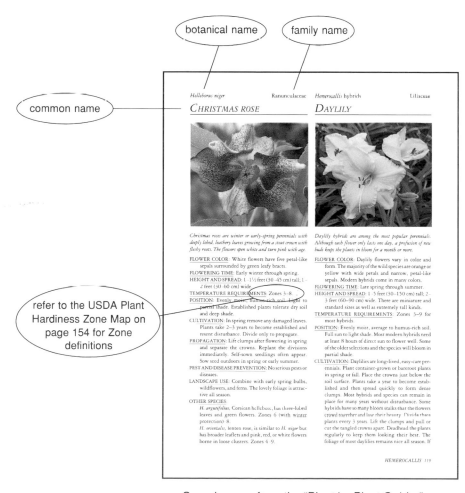

Sample page from the "Plant by Plant Guide."

UNDERSTANDING YOUR GARDEN

You may have some idea of what you want from perennial plants, but do you know what kind of growing conditions you have to give them? A new garden will get off to a successful start if you take stock of your growing conditions, including your climate and your garden's soil, topography, and exposure. These factors will have a great effect in determining which perennials will grow well in your garden, as well as how and where you plant them. In this chapter, you will find out in detail how to identify the conditions that you have in your garden and how they affect which perennials will thrive there.

A good first step in planning your garden is collecting and recording information about your climate and weather. Knowing what hardiness zone you live in is a good place to start. The most commonly used hardiness zone reference is the United States Department of Agriculture Plant Hardiness Zone Map (see page 154). It divides the continental United States and Canada into several numbered zones, from 10 in the South to 1 in the North. Many common perennials grow well in the middle range of hardiness zones. If you live in the very warm and cold climates at either end of the zone scales, it is still possible to have a lovely perennial garden, but you'll need to take a bit more care in selecting plants that can tolerate your extreme conditions. If you want to know if a perennial may be hardy in your zone, look in the "Plant by Plant Guide," starting on page 78. Nursery catalogs also often list hardiness zones for the plants they sell.

While hardiness zones are a good starting point, they are only based on average annual low temperatures. Many other factors, including rainfall and average high temperatures, also affect the growth of your perennials. You can find out about your area's weather statistics from local farm bureaus, agricultural services, or weather forecasters. They can supply you with data on the coldest winter low, the hottest summer high, and the amount of rainfall and its frequency.

To record information on your local weather conditions, keep a journal of daily or weekly weather happenings. You can also use your journal to record how different plants and parts of your yard endure the changing seasons. Note, for instance, when an unusual heat spell strikes in early spring, and which plants suffered when the thaw turned back to ice.

How much sun, heat, and humidity your garden receives will determine whether you need to plant perennials that are sun-loving or shade-tolerant, disease-resistant or drought-tolerant. As you plan your garden, observe when and for how long the sun falls on areas you are considering for perennial beds. Check before and after the trees leaf out, and as the daylength changes with the season. Determine when the summer typically turns hot and dry. Is there a spell when days drip with humidity or nights become cool and moist enough to bring on foliage diseases? Record all of these observations in your garden journal, and use what you've learned to help you choose perennials that are well adapted to the conditions your garden has to offer.

Opposite: Once you understand the growing conditions that your yard has to offer, you're on your way to creating an effective garden design. As you plan, remember to combine plants that have similar needs, like this yellow yarrow and blue-purple sage for a site with average, well-drained soil in full sun.

Many perennials, such as this sedum, can adapt to hot or cool climates. Sedums are also drought-resistant.

Climate and the Perennial Garden

When do you go on vacation? Does that say something about your climate? If you go to the mountains in the summer, you may be escaping sweltering heat that is as hard on perennial flowers as it is on you. If you fly to warmer locations in the winter, you may be fleeing bitter cold that your plants can't avoid.

Of the two extremes, perennials are best suited to take the cold. They avoid winter's worst by going dormant—shedding their aboveground growth and hiding beneath the insulating earth. Heat, however, affects them while they are actively growing. Heat, especially at night, forces plants to respire (burn energy) more quickly. This limits the amount of food perennials can put into growing strong tissues and storing winter reserves. Consequently, in warm climates many perennials will grow faster and taller, but not as sturdy. They flower earlier and more briefly and may need staking to support the stems. Perennials growing in

Purple coneflowers (*Echinacea purpurea*) are showy perennials native to prairies and open woods. These plants are extremely heat- and drought-tolerant, due to their thick, deep roots that store moisture for leaner times.

Consider Your Climate

Understanding your climate will help you choose perennials that are best adapted to the conditions available in your garden. If you're not sure what kind of climate you live in, review the list of temperate and subtropical climates below. Find out which applies to your location, and how your climate will influence the perennials you can grow.

Cool summer and cold winter (Southern Canada and New England): You'll need to look for cold-hardy perennials that emerge after spring freezes subside and that bloom early enough to escape fall freezes.

Hot summer and cold winter (Midwest and Northeast): You can grow a wide range of perennials that are hardy and moderately heat-tolerant.

Cool summer but mild winter (Northwest coast): Many perennials will thrive and bloom here, flowering longer than they would in warmer areas.

Mild winter and hot summer (South Central and Southeast): These areas have enough cold for a dormant period, but their long, hot summer may stress perennials. If the summer is humid, fungal diseases can plague susceptible plants, so look for disease-resistant cultivars. Winter rains may leave the soil wet for long periods, increasing the potential for rotting; consider growing plants in raised beds.

Arid climates (Southwest): Periods of drought can stress plant growth, so grow drought-tolerant plants in sunken beds with good irrigation. Salt buildup may damage plant roots; look for salt-tolerant species like sea lavenders (*Limonium* spp.).

Subtropical (Southern Florida and Texas): Where a cold dormancy period is limited or lacking altogether, select suitable tropical and subtropical plants for your garden. Or, if you want to grow more common perennials, you can take special measures, like planting in fall or giving plants a rest period by cutting foliage back.

Some daylily cultivars are suited to hot climates; others can't take the heat. Ask your local nursery for advice.

warm climates are more prone to fungal rots and may have a shorter life span.

Some Southern gardeners get around these problems by growing heat-sensitive perennials as annuals, pulling them out and replanting with something else when they are through flowering. This treatment goes a long way toward avoiding diseases or winter losses that are common in warm-climate areas. But not all perennials suffer in warm climates. Heat tolerance will vary from species to species and cultivar to cultivar. With careful plant selection, warm-climate gardeners can have wonderful perennial gardens based on heat-tolerant plants like gaura (*Gaura lindheimeri*), purple coneflowers (*Echinacea purpurea*), and daylilies.

Cold-climate gardeners have their challenges, too. Even though the perennials go dormant, they can be damaged by severely cold temperatures. Periods of alternate freezing and thawing can cause the surface soil to shift, breaking plant roots and pushing the crowns of dormant perennials out of the soil (a process called frost heaving). A thick, consistent layer of snow is the best natural insulator for keeping the soil at an even temperature. If you can't rely on snow cover, you may need to protect your plants with a layer of mulch to help them survive the winter.

Keep these limiting factors in mind as you try to decide which perennials to grow, and look for ones that can tolerate the temperature and humidity extremes in your garden. Even if you can't grow all the plants you long for, the perennials you can grow will reward your efforts with lush growth and lovely flowers for years to come.

The Ups and Downs of Topography

The topography of your yard—whether it slopes or is uniformly flat—will influence how plants grow, when they bloom, how long the display lasts, and how you'll design your garden. Each kind of topography has its own advantages and disadvantages for perennial gardening.

Gardening on a Flat Area

If your yard is as flat as a cornfield, you have your own particular design opportunities and growing considerations. Actually preparing the site is usually fairly easy, since you don't have to worry much about soil erosion, although you may have drainage problems if your soil is high in clay. A major design challenge is often the lack of a background for your garden. As part of your landscape design, think about installing fences or planting shrubs and trees to "frame" your perennial gardens. Another option is to regrade the site, creating gentle, natural-looking rises that will add visual interest.

Gardening on a Hilltop

A garden on a hilltop will face different conditions than gardens just down the slope. The soil on a hilltop may be thin due to erosion, and is often very well drained. Hilltop sites are often windswept as well. Strong winds can topple tall plants, so you'll either need to stake your perennials or stick with shorter plants. Winds can also dry out plants quickly, so you may have to water more

If you live in a valley, you may have a pond or wet spot where primroses, hostas, and irises will thrive.

often. The stunning views available from many hilltop sites turn all of these problems into minor inconveniences, however. When planning a landscape for a hilltop site, you may want to design your perennial gardens to frame a particularly nice view of the surrounding countryside. If excessive wind is a problem, you can decrease the velocity by setting a fence, hedge, or vine-covered trellis between the prevailing wind direction and your garden.

Gardening on a Slope

A hilly yard has great potential for interesting settings for your perennials. It also has more microclimates—the slight variations in growing conditions that will affect plant displays. In general, soils on slopes tend to be well drained, but the topsoil may be thin because of erosion. Perennial gardens on slopes are less prone to late-spring and early fall frosts, as the cold air tends to settle down in the valley and the warm air rises up over the slope.

Slopes are ideal sites for rock gardens. If the slope isn't naturally rocky, you can add groupings of large boulders or layers of flat rock that resemble natural outcroppings. Leave pockets of soil between the rocks to grow small perennials like sweet violets (*Viola odorata*), primroses (*Primula* spp.), and candytuft (*Iberis sempervirens*), along with small bulbs and dwarf conifers.

If you have a steep slope, though, think twice before

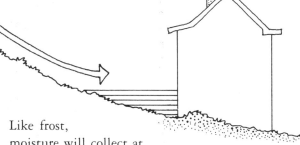

Frost pockets form when obstacles block the flow of cold air down a slope. The other side of the obstacles can trap warmth, providing good growing conditions.

stripping the existing vegetation to plant a perennial garden. The soil might wash away before most of the perennials can root and stabilize the slope. One way to handle slopes is by planting them with perennials that take root and spread aggressively, such as daylilies, bugleweed (*Ajuga repens*), and geraniums (*Geranium* spp.). Space the plants closely for more rapid stabilization of the bank, and use burlap or straw to hold the soil in place until the roots do their job.

If you don't want to rely on plants alone to control erosion, you can terrace the hill or install a retaining wall to moderate the slope. A beautiful rock or timber retaining wall will give your landscape interesting structure and let you grow perennials that do not root strongly enough to survive on a slope.

Gardening in a Valley

At the base of a slope, perennial gardens are more prone to late-spring and early fall frosts. Frost and cold air inevitably concentrate in low-lying areas, known as frost pockets, slowing or damaging spring growth and fall flowers. The same frost may miss plants growing in warmer areas slightly uphill. Gardeners in low-lying areas may want to wait a little later than others to remove protective winter mulches.

Like frost, moisture will collect at the base of the slope. Valleys are rich in rainfall runoff and, often, natural water features like ponds and streams. Topsoil eroded from surrounding slopes tends to collect here, but if the soil is clayey, it may not drain well. A common way to deal with this drainage problem is to plant perennials in raised beds. If poor drainage is really a problem, you could install drainage tiles to channel the excess water into another area.

In valleys and flat terrain, the best solution to poor drainage often is to use the moisture around creeks, ponds, and lakes to your advantage. Let a bubbling brook or the reflective surface of a pond become the focus around which you plant water-loving perennials. Clothe the banks with the flashiest of the moisture-lovers like Japanese primroses (*Primula japonica*), red-spiked cardinal flowers (*Lobelia cardinalis*), broad-leaved, golden-flowered ligularia (*Ligularia dentata*), or astilbe-like rodgersia (*Rodgersia pinnata*).

Valley gardens often collect water from surrounding areas. If drainage is poor, try planting in raised beds.

Slopes tend to be well drained and are natural sites for rock gardens. A wide range of plants thrive there.

All about Soil

Developing and maintaining healthy garden soil is a critical part of establishing a thriving perennial garden. You must balance the mineral and organic components of your soil to provide the air, water reserves, and nutrients needed by plants and other living organisms.

Soil Composition

Sand, silt, and clay—the mineral elements that make up your soil—are categorized by size. Sands are the largest mineral particles. A coarse grain of sand can be as large as 1 millimeter in diameter; finer sand may dwindle down to one-tenth that size. Sand particles sit irregularly in the soil. They leave loose, air-rich pockets, called pore spaces, that allow water and dissolved nutrients to drain away. Consequently, sandy soils tend to be dry and infertile. Clay particles, the ultrafine elements, are about 1,000 times smaller than sand. They can pack together to make a tight, water- and nutrient-rich but low-oxygen soil. Between sand and clay are the medium-sized silt particles, from 0.05 to 0.002 millimeters in diameter. They are intermediate in their effects on water retention and aeration.

The Ribbon Test

You can make a rough estimate of your soil's texture by making a fist of moist soil and squeezing out a ribbon of earth between your thumb and forefinger. Sandy soils will break up immediately. Clayey soils hold together, forming a ribbon 1 inch (2.5 cm) long or more. Loamy soils fall somewhere in between.

Soil Texture Soil texture refers to the sand, silt, and clay content of a particular soil. The relative proportions of the three particle types vary widely among soils. The ideal soil texture for most perennials is a loam, which contains a balanced mixture of sand, silt, and clay. A loam with 30 percent or more clay is a clayey loam, ideal for heavy feeding, moisture-loving perennials like astilbes, or for perennials grown in warm, dry climates. Drier and less-fertile sandy loams, with at least 35 percent sand, are ideal for slowing the growth rate of vigorous plants and reducing root or crown rots on susceptible plants.

Soil Structure Another important characteristic of your soil is its structure. Soil structure refers to the way that the sand, silt, and clay particles join together

Earthworms are a key part of good garden soil. If your soil has few worms, try adding more organic matter.

to form clumps (known as aggregates). A soil with high amounts of sand or clay will usually be too loose or too dense to support good plant growth. A well-balanced soil tends to form crumbly, granular clumps. Unlike soil texture, which is very difficult to change, soil structure can be improved by adding organic matter on a regular basis.

Organic Matter Organic matter is a critical component of the soil. The organic particles—the remains of plants, manure, and other animal products—increase water retention, improve drainage, and increase fertility. Organic matter can hold up to twice its weight in moisture, releasing water to plant roots and improving moisture retention in sandy soils. It encourages fine clay particles to clump together into larger pieces, improving soil aeration. Organic matter

If you have room, work up a patch of soil for a nursery bed, where you can raise more perennials for the garden.

Soil preparation is critical for good plant growth. Roots and other organisms thrive in loose, rich soil.

is continually decomposing, so you must continue to add more to replace the decaying particles.

Soil Organisms

There is abundant life in a healthy soil. Among the beneficial organisms are fungal mycelia, strands of fungus that run through the soil. They can bind small soil particles into larger ones and improve soil structure. Beneficial bacteria decompose organic and mineral elements, freeing nutrients for your perennials to use for growth. Earthworms tunnel through the soil, consuming and breaking down organic matter, and leaving behind nutrient-rich castings. All of these organisms thrive in the same conditions that the roots of most perennials prefer: a loose, moist but well-drained soil with plenty of organic matter. Soil that is compacted, low in organic matter, or excessively wet is generally low in soil organisms, and your perennials probably won't flourish there either.

Soil pH

Soil pH—the measurement of your soil's acidity or alkalinity—is another factor that can determine which perennials grow well for you because it affects the availability of nutrients in your soil. Chemically, pH is the measure of hydrogen ions in the soil. It is measured on a scale of 1 to 14, with 7 as neutral. Soils that have pH ratings below 7 are acidic, and as the pH drops, the soil becomes increasingly more acidic. Soils with pH ratings above 7 grow increasingly more alkaline. For most perennials, a slightly acid pH—5.5 to 6.5—is ideal. But a few perennials, such as pinks (*Dianthus* spp.) and baby's-breath, need a soil that is more alkaline, or rich in limestone. Their ideal pH is slightly above neutral, at around 7.5.

You can determine your soil pH yourself with a simple home test available at your local garden center, or send a sample to a soil-testing laboratory for analysis. (For details on taking a soil sample, see "Adding Organic Nutrients" on page 46.) If the soil test shows you need to adjust the pH level, begin by adding extra compost when you are preparing the bed or as a top dressing. If that is not sufficient to moderate excess acidity, add calcitic limestone (calcium carbonate) or dolomitic limestone (which contains both calcium and magnesium) for magnesium-deficient soils. Organic matter also helps lower the pH of overly alkaline soils. If it is not enough, you can also add powdered sulfur. The quantity of pH amendments you use will vary with how far you need to adjust the pH and what type of soil you have. For more on preparing soils for planting, see "Planting Your Perennials" on page 47.

In most cases, it's best to choose perennials that will thrive in your soil conditions rather than to change the soil to fit the plants. If you want to grow plants that need different conditions, consider grouping them in one bed, where you can more easily adjust the soil to fit their needs.

Soil forms as solid bedrock weathers into smaller and smaller mineral pieces. Organic matter, from compost or decaying roots, gives the surface soil a darker color.

Sun or Shade?

Sunlight provides the energy plants need to grow and flower, so it's an important factor to consider when choosing a site for your garden. Many perennials prefer full sun: at least 6 hours of direct light. Some, like coral bells (*Heuchera* spp.), can grow well in partial sun, with between 4 and 6 hours of light. Others, including foamflowers (*Tiarella* spp.) and bleeding hearts (*Dicentra* spp.), need partial shade. In cool-season areas, some shade-loving plants can tolerate more sun. In warm areas, sun-lovers may do better in a little shade.

These fall-blooming plants, including asters, grasses, and coneflowers (*Rudbeckia* spp.), thrive in full sun.

The amount and intensity of the sunlight that reaches your plants will vary, depending on the time of the year, the cloud cover, and by the trees and buildings around your garden. The direction your garden faces also has a great impact on the quality and quantity of light it receives. A garden facing east is exposed to cooler morning sun. A garden facing south receives more intense sun all day, while one facing west is exposed to the warm afternoon sun. Beds that face north have limited sun, staying cool, moist, and dark.

The trick to perennial gardening is finding and combining plants that will thrive in your particular conditions.

South-facing Sites Gardens planted along the south sides of buildings or on south-facing slopes warm quickly in spring. Because these sites are touched by early spring sun, perennials growing there bloom extra early, a wonderful sight for winter-starved eyes. But their early arrival makes new shoots more susceptible to frost kill. South-facing gardens will be hot in summer, especially if planted against a reflective white wall or backdrop. Make use of southern exposures to grow heat-loving perennials in cool summer areas. However, where full sun combines with a warm climate, perennials will drop their flowers faster, and the soil will dry out more quickly. You should add extra organic matter and mulch the area to help keep plant roots cool and evaporation to a minimum. Irrigate often or plant drought-tolerant perennials.

A southern exposure can wreak havoc on perennial gardens during winter. The sun thaws the soil despite below-freezing temperatures. When night falls, the soil refreezes. The thawing/freezing sequence makes the soil contract and expand, or heave. It can rip roots or throw new plantings and shallow- or delicate-rooted perennials like coral bells (*Heuchera* spp.) out of the ground. Mulch in early

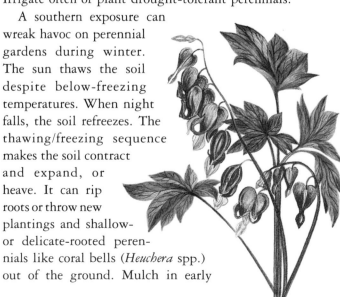

Don't despair if you have shade! Many colorful perennials, including irises and primroses, thrive in shade.

winter with evergreen boughs, salt hay, or other fluffy materials to help keep frozen soil frozen.

North-facing Sites Gardens planted facing north are just the opposite. These gardens are on the shady side of trees, shrubs, or structures. They will warm slowly in spring. They are the last to lose their protective snow cover and to show signs of life. North-facing beds remain cooler in summer, so you can expect a longer blooming season. In winter, the soil is less prone to frost heaving. Use these sites to grow plants that love shade and moist soil.

East- and West-facing Sites Gardens that face east have cool morning sun. Use this exposure to grow sun-loving perennials in warm climates. Or lengthen the bloom season of a species by planting the same plant here and on the warmer west-facing slope. The same kind of plant sited on the two exposures often flowers a week or two apart, giving you an extended bloom period. Flowers that bloom in a garden with an eastern exposure tend to have more vivid flower colors than those bleached by the bright afternoon sun from the west.

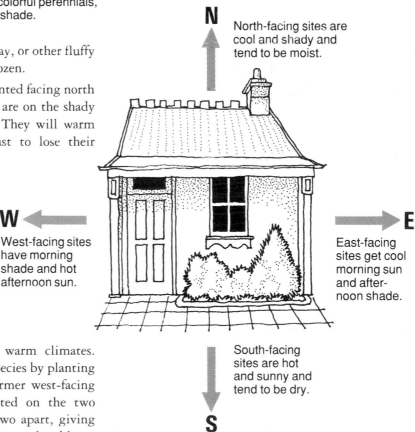

N

North-facing sites are cool and shady and tend to be moist.

W

West-facing sites have morning shade and hot afternoon sun.

E

East-facing sites get cool morning sun and after-noon shade.

South-facing sites are hot and sunny and tend to be dry.

S

Each side of your house offers different growing conditions. These areas, called microclimates, let you grow a wide range of perennials, even on a small site.

LANDSCAPING WITH PERENNIALS

Any yard—large or small, sunny or shady—can be accented with perennials. A few clusters of perennial flowers will bring colorful highlights to drab corners; a garden full of perennials will become a landscape highlight. You can use perennials as accents, focal points, masses of color, or intriguing scenes of constant change. In this chapter, you'll learn how to create a functional design for a new perennial garden and how to choose plants that will grow well in the conditions your site has to offer. You'll also find lots of tips for creating eye-catching plant combinations, which can turn a jumbled collection of plants into an attractive and effective landscape feature.

As you create your garden design, don't make the mistake of thinking your flowering perennials should be separate from the rest of the landscape. To get the most enjoyment and the greatest effect from these plants, you first need to establish a garden size and shape that looks natural in your landscape and fits in well with the existing elements, like buildings and trees. Then choose perennials with colors, textures, and forms that enhance your entire landscape.

Use large sweeps of bold perennials in beds and borders beside the lawn, beneath openings in trees, and in front of hedges and shrub plantings. Put smaller clumps of dramatic perennials in strategic locations to highlight the entrance to walks, the location of a door, or the view out a window. Consider nesting a trio of three gold-centered, broad-leaved hostas (such as *Hosta* 'Gold Standard') at either side of the entrance of a woodland path. Or use a large clump of red-hot poker (*Kniphofia uvaria*) to frame the top of a drive. A stand of elegant irises or plumed astilbe is an attractive feature near a Japanese bridge and water garden.

One of the most delightful features of perennials is their ability to change throughout the season—growing and spreading, passing into and out of bloom, and sometimes coloring up nicely in fall or producing seed heads to stand over winter. The changeable quality of perennials can add life to an otherwise boring planting, such as a row of evergreens or a mass of annuals.

Succession of bloom is one reason the changeable nature of perennials is so appealing. By selecting plants carefully, you can have perennials blooming throughout the growing season, from early spring to late fall. Arrange your garden so some flowers, seed heads, or foliage is of interest at any time during the growing season. Let the beauty of the flowers create a shifting sequence of harmonies and contrasts. Spring might be rich with golden daffodils, yellow primroses, and purple violets. In early summer, the garden could be ripe with pink peonies and violet-blue Siberian iris (*Iris sibirica*). In late summer this might change to purple coneflowers (*Echinacea purpurea*), ivory chrysanthemums, and pink Japanese anemones (*Anemone* x *hybrida*).

Before and after the bloom, let the show continue with the beauty of foliage and form alone. Enjoy the excitement of watching the plants grow, from the first shoots to the much-anticipated bloom. Note how the flower stalks rise gracefully over the foliage or peep from between the stems. Watch the leaves late in the season, as they ripen to bronze or lemon, then disappear.

Opposite: When designing your garden, use perennials to accent existing structures. By itself, this well might appear utilitarian and uninviting; surrounded by perennials, it becomes a charming garden feature.

Planning a Perennial Garden

Don't jump into perennial gardening without sufficient planning. To end up with a beautiful, healthy, easy-care garden, you really must do some homework before you begin. By following the steps below, you'll create a garden that suits your landscape and requires the least possible upkeep.

Look at Your Landscape Before you start digging, walk around your yard and look at it from all angles—from the street, from the back door, from the side yard. Think about where a perennial garden would look good and enhance your yard. You could have the garden edge your shrub borders, run along the perimeter of the patio, or radiate out from the back door or picture window. In short, you want to give the garden a reason for being wherever it is. For ideas of different ways to use perennials around your home, see "Garden Styles" on page 28.

Put Your Ideas on Paper Once you've chosen a site and style for your garden, you can start putting your plans down on paper. Measure the length and width of the area you have targeted for your garden. Determine an appropriate outline and draw it to scale on a piece of graph paper. For example, if you decide to use a perennial border that is 7 feet wide and 20 feet long, you could draw a replica plan with a scale of 1 inch on the paper to 2 feet in the garden. The resulting scale drawing would be 3.5 inches wide and 10 inches long. To fit a larger garden plan onto your graph paper, you could adjust the scale, with 1 inch on paper equaling up to 5 feet of garden. If you compress more than about 5 feet of garden space to an inch of graph paper, your plan may be too small to include details you need.

Draw in the major features that surround your garden, such as buildings, trees, shrubs, and existing paths. This is also a good place to jot down notes about the soil conditions in the area (is it frequently wet, often dry, or evenly moist?), as well as the amount and type of sunshine available (does it get full sun, just a few hours of morning or afternoon sun, or no direct sun at all?).

Pick Your Plants Once you've chosen a site, you can start identifying the perennials you want to grow. A fun way to do this is to keep a wish list of plants that you've admired in catalogs, read about in books, or seen in neighbors' gardens. For each species or cultivar, write down flower color, shape, height, season of bloom, foliage appearance, and cultural requirements so you can compare all the perennials side by side. Then you can start matching up the plants you want with the conditions you have available. For more specifics on choosing appropriate perennials, see "Picking the Right Perennials" on page 26.

Putting Plants into Your Plan As you finalize your plant list, start thinking about how to organize the different perennials in the garden. To create a pleasing, balanced garden, you'll need to consider factors like flower and foliage colors, plant sizes, and bloom seasons. To visualize possible color combinations, cut circles representing each group of flowers out of colored paper, matching the paper color to the flower color. Juggle these around until you find combinations that you like. Another way to approach the plan is to sketch in the locations of edgings, mid-border groupings, and tall plants, noting where you want certain colors, flower shapes, or seasonal bloom. Then go through your plant wish list to find the best perennial for each spot. See "Design Rules for Your Garden," on page 25, for a summary of the factors

Garden planning is a fun wintertime activity, and it's an easy way to try out different design options. It can also help you spot possible problems before you start digging!

Liven up mass plantings with a focal point. A bird bath, for example, adds interest to this bed of mums.

Large masses of plants in single colors add unity to a garden design and avoid a "spotty" look.

you'll want to keep in mind as you plan your garden.

Before you finalize your plan, make overlays on tracing paper for every season the garden will be in bloom. Color in the groupings that will be flowering at the same time. See whether the colors will be compatible and the garden will be balanced, or whether there

will be too much of a color at any particular place or time. Once you have your planting scheme figured out, it's time to bring your garden plan from paper into reality. See the chapter "Cultivating and Planting," starting on page 42, for complete instructions on soil preparation and planting techniques.

Design Rules for Your Garden

While designing a garden is a very personal and creative activity, following some basic design rules will give your finished garden a very polished or natural look. The key rules are to create balance and rhythm and to add a dominant feature to tie the garden together.

First, keep the garden in balance. Include plants with a mix of heights and sizes throughout your plantings. Don't plant all of the tall or massive flowers on one side, with a group of low, delicate plants at the other end. In formal gardens, you may balance one side of the garden by planting the same design on the other, making a mirror image. For an informal garden, you can vary the plantings, perhaps matching a large blue-flowered perennial on one side with a lower-growing plant that has bright red flowers. In this case, you are balancing brighter color with larger size.

Second, create a rhythm, or a sense of continuity, throughout the entire garden. You

can repeat groupings of the same plant or use other plants with identical colors or similar flower shapes. Let a middle-of-the-border plant drift from the foreground to the background, giving a sense of movement and uniting the different layers of the garden.

Third, establish a dominant feature. This focal point can be as simple as a spectacular long-blooming perennial. But since perennials come in and out of bloom fairly quickly, you will have to establish a new focus when the first bloom ends. For a more permanent accent, you can feature a path, sculpture, birdbath, or tree as your center of interest, and build the garden around it. This brings you back to the concept of making the perennial garden part of the overall landscape. The perennials can brighten existing permanent structures, and the structures can bring stability and focus to the continually changing display of foliage and flowers.

Trailing plants, such as bellflowers (*Campanula* spp.), are ideal for softening walls and other hard edges.

Picking the Right Perennials

Even experienced perennial gardeners can be a little overwhelmed by the thousands of perennials available. How do you begin to tell which are best for your garden? When you choose, you'll want to weigh criteria such as height, color, shape, and sunlight and soil requirements. Here are some considerations to keep in mind.

Coordinating Heights and Habits

Mix perennials of varying heights to add visual interest to your garden design. Organize heights to progress from short to tall so no flowers will be hidden behind taller plants. If you view a garden from the front, put the tallest plants toward the back of the garden. Or with a bed that you see from all sides, cluster the tall plants near the center, and let the lower plants taper down in height toward the edges.

Many perennials have shapes or growth habits that make them particularly useful for certain purposes. Low-growing plants like common thrift (*Armeria maritima*), pinks (*Dianthus* spp.), and coral bells (*Heuchera sanguinea*) have neat foliage and make attractive edgings. Try full or tall types like boltonia (*Boltonia asteroides*) or black snakeroot (*Cimicifuga racemosa*) to hide unattractive views or to serve as a background for large beds and borders.

Some perennials are excellent groundcovers. They can squeeze out weeds, provide attractive

foliage, and give you a more interesting alternative to English ivy and pachysandra. Use perennial groundcovers individually, one species per bed, or blend several with different foliage textures and colors but similar growth rates. Try creeping phlox (*Phlox stolonifera*), ajuga (*Ajuga reptans*), spotted lamium (*Lamium maculatum*), and heart-leaved bergenia (*Bergenia cordifolia*), among others.

Combining Compatible Colors

When you're designing a perennial garden, approach it as you would your living room decor. Limit yourself to two main colors and possibly a third for accent. Also add some minor colors for small touches of diversity. If possible, match flower or foliage colors with other landscape elements, like walkways, shutters, or flowers or berries on nearby shrubs. But keep the color scheme simple. If you use too many colors, the garden will look fragmented and chaotic.

Bolder colors such as red, orange, and gold stand out in a landscape. Use them to make a distant border appear closer. Place pale blues, soft pinks, lavender, and dark violet up close where the colors won't fade into the background. Use white and ivory to brighten up dark combinations or to act as highlights in a night garden.

Be especially careful about color compatibility. Colors have many different hues, and they don't all look good together. Typically, the following rules hold true:

Color theme gardens are fun to plan. If you like soft colors, try a pink-and-blue garden.

- Warm and cool combinations are surefire. Mix blue and pink, green and red, blue and orange, or purple and yellow.
- Take advantage of foliage color—add plants with silver, blue, gold, or variegated leaves if they work well with surrounding flowers.
- Magenta is hard to mix, but it works with cream or pale yellow.
- Muted colors can look washed out against strong, clear tones. Stick with one or the other.
- Reddish blues may not work beside yellowish blues.
- Orange-pink flowers will clash next to purple-pink flowers.
- White flowers do not look good next to cream.
- Mix orange-red with scarlet, salmon with yellow, or pure pink with lavender only in cool climates or partially shady sites where the colors will stay vivid. In heat or full sun, these colors can fade to less compatible combinations.

Varying Shapes and Textures

In addition to their flowers, perennials have many different shapes and textures. Blend perennials with creeping, mounding, and upright habits to make your design more interesting. For a more natural and informal arrangement, use creepers to edge the bed. Then emphasize mounded plants, using the occasional upright spikes at strategic locations.

The lacy leaves of this artemisia combine well with different flower forms and provide season-long color.

Considering Sun and Shade

Because perennials need a certain amount of sun or shade to grow well, you must group them with other species that have similar light requirements. If your garden includes both lightly shaded and sunny areas, you have great design freedom because you can pick from a wide range of suitable plants. Or if you want to blend some perennials that need partial shade into a sunny bed, you can plant them on the shaded north side of taller plants or in the filtered sunlight that reaches near the base of lanky plants. For instance, you could put Siberian bugloss (*Brunnera macrophylla*) in the northern shadow of a daylily. Or grow clumps of sweet violet (*Viola odorata*) below a tall purple coneflower (*Echinacea purpurea*).

Studying Soil Preferences

As you choose your perennials, you also need to consider their preferred soil conditions and group those with similar needs. For instance, you can combine prairie-type perennials, like thread-leaved coreopsis (*Coreopsis verticillata*), New York aster (*Aster novi-belgii*), and common sneezeweed (*Helenium autumnale*), in a well-drained soil without excessive fertility. Likewise, group plants that take a more moist, more fertile soil, like sun-loving delphiniums and garden phlox, or perennials for light shade, like bleeding hearts (*Dicentra* spp.), astilbes, and coral bells (*Heuchera* spp.).

If you enjoy bright colors, consider planting a yellow-and-orange theme garden.

Garden Styles

Now you need to take what you have learned about sites, climate, and design, and apply this knowledge to the many traditional and nontraditional design styles for flower gardens. These include formal gardens, cottage gardens, herbaceous borders, island beds, cutting gardens, and other specialty gardens.

Formal Gardens

Historically, formal gardens were found on large estates. But today, this style of garden is spreading into smaller yards. Formal beds mimic the prevailing angles of houses and patios, blending in where space is too limited to soften the scene with curving lines.

Formal gardens are usually laid out in squares or rectangles with low hedges of clipped boxwood, hollies, or other evergreens. Plant the beds symmetrically, using the same sequence of perennials and edging plants on either side of a central axis. Make your own patterns with lines, angles, and curving rows. Choose plants carefully—limit your selection to perennials that will stay in place and maintain uniform height. Try new cultivars developed for uniformity such as 'Moonbeam' thread-leaved coreopsis (*Coreopsis verticillata* 'Moonbeam'), 'Stella de Oro' daylily, and 'Blue Clips' tussock bellflower (*Campanula carpatica* 'Blue Clips').

If the classic formal garden is too rigid for your taste, you also can take a more modern approach. Plant sections of the garden with a touch of informality by maintaining the basic geometric shapes but softening the angles with creeping and trailing edgers.

This delightful garden blends the casual feeling of a cottage garden with the structure of a double border.

Cottage Gardens

The classic cottage garden is an eclectic collection of plants, including perennials, annuals, herbs, and roses, allowed to ramble and intertwine. Cottage gardens usually are at least partially enclosed within walls, hedges, or fences, making them a natural choice for a small suburban house or a contemporary townhouse with an enclosed yard. You might allow the plants to spread unchecked or to self-sow, letting the seedlings arise where they may. For this to work well, though, you must be willing to do some rearranging if the plants pop up where they're not wanted. Unify the scene with a permanent focal point, such as a path that marches through the garden's center to a door, patio, or bench.

Perennial Borders

Borders are the most popular and versatile of all ways to grow perennials. A border is a planting area that edges or frames another feature of the garden. It may separate the lawn from a hedge, fence, deck, or wooded area; set off a path from the lawn or driveway; or divide the vegetable garden from the lawn. Look at the transition areas in your property to find potential areas for borders.

Most perennial borders are designed to be seen primarily from the front, allowing you to set the shorter plants in the foreground and the taller plants in the back. You can plant a border exclusively with perennials

This tiny cottage garden combines a variety of plants for season-long interest.

to produce what is known as an herbaceous border. Or add structure, excitement, and four-season interest by creating a mixed border of woody plants, bulbs, and annuals as well as perennials.

Borders typically are long, rectangular areas. Generally, the longer a border is, the wider it should be—to a point. This will keep you from making awkward-looking squares. A rectangle extends the garden and maintains enough depth for varying plant heights. In a small suburban yard, you could make a border that is 4 feet (1.2 m) wide by 14 feet (4.2 m) long. Or in a larger yard, extend the border to 5 feet (1.5 m) wide by 21 feet (6.3 m) long. However, there is no reason why you can't make a border any length and width you want, as long as it complements existing structures. If you want a really wide border, put an access path through it so you can maintain the middle without walking on the garden soil. If a border must be small to fit a small yard, give it more power by placing it close to the house and using small but effective groupings of flowers. Especially in a small garden, every plant must be attractive for as long as possible, so look for plants that have a long bloom season and attractive foliage.

Island Beds

Unlike borders, which are usually seen from only one side, island beds are designed for you to walk around them and see them from all different angles. Because they are located away from structures like houses and fences, island beds are exposed to maximum sun and air penetration. As a result, plant stems are stockier and need less staking, and the garden tends to be healthier and easier to maintain.

Locate your island bed in some open situation, but don't just plunk the bed down in the middle of the lawn. Like a border, you must tie it in with existing permanent structures to make it look good. Use an island bed to form an oasis of color in the back corner of the property, to echo the shape of shrub groupings elsewhere in the lawn, or as a "welcome garden" at the foot of the drive.

As a general rule, make island beds three times as long as they are wide for the most natural effect. You also can make one end wider than

A patterned grouping of beds is a fun way to display your plants. The paths allow easy access to all sides.

the other so you can grow taller flowers there. But be sure to balance the extra bed width by putting an appropriate group of bold plants in or near the narrower side. Since you can view an island bed from all sides, put the tallest plants in the center. If, on the other hand, you will view it primarily from one angle, perhaps from the house or patio, make the highest point in the back. Then you can add extra tiers of midborder plants and still have some low-growing perennials on the far side.

For a formal look, try a classic single border. A hedge or fence provides a good background; a solid edging strip makes for easy maintenance.

The Cutting Garden

Many perennials produce flowers and foliage that are ideal for indoor use in arrangements. You can snip a few flowers from your perennial borders, but if you take too many the garden will look bare. To have lots of flowers for picking, grow a utilitarian garden just for cutting. You don't need a fancy design or a particular shape— just pick a suitable spot and line up your plants in rows as you would vegetables. Cage the stems of floppy perennials like delphiniums and dahlias with a wire grid to keep them supported and straight. Add annuals to your cutting garden to round out your choice of materials for arrangements.

Specialty Gardens

Depending on the conditions your site has to offer, you may want to showcase different perennials in your garden designs. Whether your site is dry or wet, sunny or shady, there's a garden style that's just right for you.

Meadow Gardens Natural gardens combine the beauty of local wildflowers with an informal, often low-maintenance, design. The most popular of these are meadow gardens that feature durable, sun-loving flowers. If you don't have room for a whole meadow, you can create a meadow look in a smaller garden by using plenty of reliable cultivated perennials and mixing in meadow flowers and grasses among them. Common perennials that are natural choices for most meadow gardens include butterfly weed (*Asclepias tuberosa*), New England aster (*Aster novae-angliae*), purple coneflower (*Echinacea purpurea*), and bee balm (*Monarda didyma*). Look in wildflower gardening books

If you enjoy bringing flowers like delphiniums and dahlias into the house, consider a cutting garden.

or check with local wildflower societies to find out which plants grow best in your area.

Once you've chosen the plants that will be in your meadow, you'll need to help them gain a roothold by preparing a good seedbed. You can't just scatter seed in a lawn or open piece of ground and expect good results. You'll also need to keep the soil moist while the seeds are germinating, and weed regularly for the first few years. Once the meadow is established, a yearly mowing in late winter will help control woody plants that would otherwise eventually overwhelm the perennial flowers. Beyond that, you can let these perennials grow and mingle as they will.

Container Gardens Take a break from those petunias and grow perennials in containers. Potted perennials are great as accents for steps, decks, and patios, especially in small gardens. Compact, long-blooming, and drought-tolerant perennials are good choices for containers. Some perennials for containers include 'Stella de Oro' daylily and the Galaxy series of yarrow (*Achillea* Galaxy Series). Or try spring-blooming bleeding

Meadow and woodland gardens are excellent options for brightening up out-of-the-way corners.

Many perennials, including asters and campanulas, adapt well to life in containers.

Perennials are perfect complements to rock gardens, adding beautiful foliage and seasonal color.

This charming cottage garden combines perennials with annuals, shrubs, and trees for season-long interest.

heart (*Dicentra spectabilis*); when it goes dormant in summer, cover it with annuals. Containers dry out more quickly than gardens, so you may need to water them daily during hot and dry parts of the summer.

Rock Gardens Some perennials are particularly attractive grouped among rocks in a wall or rock garden. They grow best in full sun and soils that have exceptionally good drainage and low fertility. Some, such as perennial candytuft (*Iberis sempervirens*), wall rock cress (*Arabis caucasica*), and basket-of-gold (*Aurinia saxatilis*), cascade gracefully over the rock surface. Others, like the more petite Labrador violets (*Viola labradorica*) and primroses (*Primula* spp.), as well as a host of unusual alpine plants, nestle between the rocks. All of these plants are delightful choices for planting on rocky slopes, in raised beds, or in dry stone retaining walls.

Bog Gardens Some perennials have an affinity for wet ground and will thrive at the edge of a pond or in

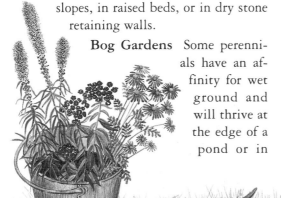

boggy or marshy areas. Perennials for low, moist areas include Japanese iris (*Iris ensata*), goat's beard (*Aruncus dioicus*), marsh marigold (*Caltha palustris*), and cardinal flower (*Lobelia cardinalis*).

If you do not have a naturally wet area but enjoy the beauty of bog plants, you can create your own bog. Dig a trench at least 12 inches (30 cm) deep and line it with a heavy plastic pond liner. Put a soaker hose on the top of the plastic and refill the trench with humus-rich soil. The open end of the hose should protrude slightly so that you can attach it to your garden hose and fill the "bog" with water. Repeat as necessary to keep the soil moist.

Woodland Gardens If you have a wooded lot, take advantage of the shade to create a woodland garden. To brighten the area in early spring (before the trees leaf out and shade the area), try early blooming woodland wildflowers like wood anemone (*Anemone nemorosa*), wild columbine (*Aquilegia canadensis*), Virginia bluebell (*Mertensia virginica*), and common bleeding heart (*Dicentra spectabilis*). To extend the season of interest, add ferns and shade-tolerant perennials that retain their handsome foliage all season. These include hostas, lungwort (*Pulmonaria saccharata*), Lenten rose (*Helleborus orientalis*), Siberian bugloss (*Brunnera macrophylla*), and Solomon's seal (*Polygonatum odoratum*).

Growing a perennial garden gives you the luxury of having fresh cut flowers at a moment's notice. To keep flowers in good condition, carry a bucket of cool water and insert stems as you cut the flowers.

CHOOSING YOUR PLANTS

For many people, choosing and buying perennials is one of the most pleasurable aspects of creating a new garden. In the frenzy of shopping, it's easy to get carried away and go home with lots of plants you don't really need. But with a little preparation, you can take your time and get the right plant at the right price.

In this chapter, you'll learn lots about selecting the right perennials for your garden. Knowing a bit about how plants are named will help you make sure you're getting exactly the plants you ask for. You'll also need to know what to look for before you buy, so you get vigorous plants that are free of insects and diseases. When you are ready to buy, you can make an informed decision and choose strong, healthy plants that will settle into your garden with a minimum of trouble.

Begin your search in the depths of winter by browsing through the colorful and informative mail-order catalogs. But remember, they are biased toward making sales. You may have to look elsewhere to get honest information on growth rate, disease susceptibility, and other potential problems like invasiveness. When the planting season comes, go to plant sales, nurseries, garden centers, and greenhouses that sell perennials.

There are a few common temptations to avoid. First of all, don't fall for every pretty flower. A perennial plant blooming in the protected environment of a greenhouse may be lovely, but its beauty does not tell you whether it is prone to problems or whether it will be suited to your garden conditions. If you see a plant you love but know little about, take a 24-hour cooling-off period. Do a little research on its preferred growing conditions, seasonal appearance, and potential problems. If you find it will grow well in the conditions your garden has to offer, determine if you have a place for it.

Second, use the same frame of mind to shop for perennials as you would to expand your wardrobe. When you need a new shirt or skirt, you look for one that fits with the rest of your clothes. Likewise, buy only those perennials that will work into your garden plans. If you use a plant that clashes with its neighbors, you may wish you had a closet to hide it in. If you like a little garden spontaneity, you can leave openings here and there for trial plants in different colors. Work them into a coordinated framework of proven perennials.

Third, evaluate gift plants carefully before setting them loose in your garden. A perennial from a friend's garden may be insect-infested or diseased and better suited to the compost heap than your perennial border. Also, when a plant produces enough extra divisions to be shared with great generosity, it's probably an aggressive spreader. Find out if it can be difficult to keep under control. Then ask yourself if this plant will enhance the garden design or clutter it. If it passes all these tests, enjoy a great bargain. If not, put it in the wildflower meadow, grow it in a container, or compost it.

Finally, if you simply cannot resist buying or saving every plant that catches your eye, perhaps you are a candidate for a casual cottage garden rather than a more formal perennial bed or border. Or you could create a special nursery bed in an out-of-the-way spot, where you could stick in all different kinds of plants to see how they grow and bloom.

Opposite: A key part of selecting perennials is choosing plants that will thrive in your climate and garden conditions. Columbines (*Aquilegia* spp.) are adaptable to many climates but need light, evenly moist soil.

Name That Perennial

One of the tricks to growing perennials successfully is to learn their names. Members of your neighborhood plant society may understand common names, like bee balm for instance. But if you go to an out-of-town nursery and ask for bee balm, you may only get puzzled stares. Perhaps they call the plant Oswego tea, based on the fact that American pioneers used it as herbal tea. Or if you are looking for bee balm in a catalog, you may only find it listed under its botanical name, *Monarda didyma*.

You can see from this example that one plant can have several common names. Likewise, one common name can apply to several different plants. For instance the common name loosestrife can refer to a creeping perennial with golden flowers known by the botanical name *Lysimachia nummularia*; to a tall perennial with white flowers in a swan-necked spike, *Lysimachia clethroides*; to its less invasive counterpart, *L. ephemerum*; or to a spreading, long-blooming purple-flowered plant, *Lythrum salicaria*. If you order "loosestrife" by mail without using a botanical name, you have a good chance of receiving the wrong plant.

Get to know botanical names so you know exactly which plant you are talking about, planting, or ordering. Most botanical names are based on Latin, so they can be a mouthful. However, they will be the same in America, Japan, and Europe, despite differences in the native language. Botanical names change rarely, usually

This diagram identifies some of the most common plant parts. Knowing a bit of botanical jargon will help you understand the plant descriptions you read in books and catalogs.

only when scientists update the name to better reflect what they have discovered about the plant's heritage. If you have learned an older name, you will usually find it listed beside the newer names in nursery catalogs. For instance, hollyhock has changed from *Althaea rosea* to *Alcea rosea*. Both may be listed for the same plant.

As you've probably noticed by now, botanical names are usually given as two words. The first word, the

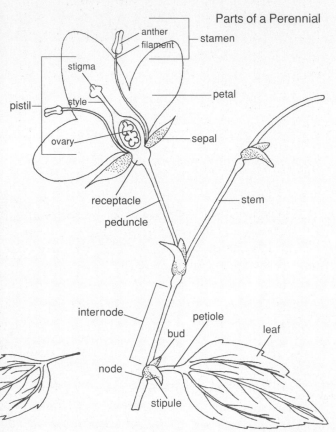

Parts of a Perennial

name of the genus, refers to a group of closely related plants. The second word indicates the species, a particular kind of plant in that genus. You may end up growing several different species from the same genus. *Achillea millefolium* and *Achillea tomentosa*, for example, both belong to the genus *Achillea*, commonly known as yarrow. But *Achillea millefolium* refers to a species with finely cut leaves, while *Achillea tomentosa* refers to one with particularly fuzzy leaves.

Botanical names can be easier to remember if you determine what they tell about the plant. Some refer to the person who discovered the plant or to what part of the world it was discovered in. For instance, *Sanguisorba canadensis* is Canadian burnett, native to Canada and the Eastern United States. Other botanical names are descriptive. *Viola odorata* is sweet violet, which bears an especially fragrant flower.

Horticulturists and botanists recognize two other classifications of plants that you will often encounter:

As you may guess, Siberian irises (*Iris sibirica*) are native to Russia, as well as areas of central Europe.

Sweet violet (*Viola odorata*) bears charming spring flowers that are delightfully fragrant.

varieties and cultivars. Although the names are sometimes used interchangeably, plants that develop a natural variation in the wild are called varieties, and the varietal name is included as part of the botanical name after the abbreviation "var." This is the case, for example, with the white-flowered, peach-leaved bellflower (*Campanula persicifolia* var. *alba*). In this case the species, which normally has blue flowers, produced plants with white ones. Cultivars, whose names are set in single quotes after the botanical name, are plants that gardeners or horticulturists have selected and propagated as part of a breeding program or from a chance mutation in a garden. For example, *Aster novi-belgii* 'Professor Kippenburg' is a dwarf type of lavender-blue Michaelmas daisy.

You may also come across hybrids, blends of two species or, more rarely, two genera. One example is *Anemone* x *hybrida* — the "x" indicates that this plant is a hybrid. A few hybrids come from two different but related genera, such as x *Heucherella tiarelloides*.

In this book, you will find perennials listed by the most widely used common name. But to avoid confusion, we will follow it with the botanical name in parentheses. When we use "spp." we are discussing several related species in the same genus. For *Iris* spp., this could include bearded, Siberian, and Japanese irises. Take note of both common and botanical names for your garden planning.

Perennials have a variety of root structures. Bulbs, corms, and rhizomes are actually underground stems.

What's in a Name?

Learning botanical names may seem intimidating at first, but you'll be surprised at how easily you pick them up as you read. Besides being a tool for accurately communicating about plants, a botanical name can often tell you something about the plant it identifies, such as its flower color or growth habit. Listed below are some words that commonly appear in botanical names, along with their definitions.

Albus: white
Argenteus: silver
Aureus: golden yellow
Caeruleus: blue
Luteus: yellow
Nanus: dwarf
Niger: black
Palustris: swampy, marshy
Perennis: perennial
Prostratus: trailing
Punctatus: dotted
Purpureus: purple
Reptans: creeping
Roseus: rosy
Ruber: red
Sempervirens: evergreen
Speciosus: showy
Spinosus: spiny
Stoloniferus: with stolons
Tomentosus: with thick, short hair
Variegatus: variegated
Viridis: green
Vulgaris: common

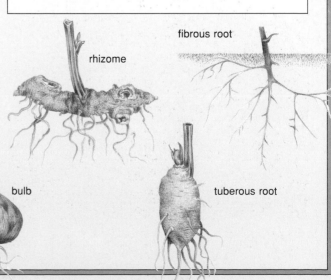

fibrous root

rhizome

corm

bulb

tuberous root

Selecting and Buying Perennials

As you shop by mail and at a variety of garden centers, nurseries, and farms, you will find that there are several ways to sell the same plant—in a container, bareroot, or field-dug. Here are some specifications that will let you evaluate how to use your plant budget most wisely.

Container-grown Perennials

Perennials are most commonly sold in containers. Container-grown perennials are convenient and easy to handle. You can keep the pots in a well-lit location until you are ready to plant. Then you can slide the root ball out and plant it in the garden with minimal disturbance. However, there is a catch. Horticultural researchers are finding that roots tend to stay in the light, fluffy "soil" of synthetic mixes, rather than branching out into the surrounding garden soil. But you can avoid this problem by loosening roots on the outside of the ball and spreading them out into the soil as you plant. (For more information on dealing with container-grown plants, see "Planting Your Perennials" on page 47.)

Container-grown perennials come in different sizes, so their prices vary widely. Larger-sized pots, usually 1- and 2-gallon (4.5 to 9 liter) containers, are generally more expensive. The cost may be worthwhile if you need immediate garden impact. On the other hand, you can buy younger plants inexpensively in multicell packs or small pots. These sizes work fine if you don't mind waiting a year or more for them to fill out and bloom with abandon. In fact, young plants tend to become established in the garden faster than older ones, catching up to the bigger plants in a short time.

Bareroot Perennials

You will come across many species of dormant bareroot plants for sale early in the growing season. In late summer or early fall, you can also find bareroot items such as bearded irises, common bleeding heart (*Dicentra spectabilis*), peonies, and oriental poppies. You may choose to buy bareroot plants to save money—they usually are less expensive than large container-grown plants—or you may receive them unexpectedly. Mail-order companies often send plants bareroot to save on space and shipping. You open the box to find long spidery roots and—at best—a small tuft of foliage. These plants look more dead than alive, but fortunately, in this case looks are deceiving. If you keep the roots moist and cool and plant them quickly and properly, most plants will recover and thrive.

When the plants arrive, tend to them promptly. Open the box to let some air in. Your plants' roots should be wrapped in a protective medium like shredded newspaper, excelsior, or sphagnum moss. Keep this medium moist but not soggy. When it's time to plant, soak the roots in a bucket of lukewarm water for a few hours, then plant as detailed in "Planting Your Perennials" on page 47. If you can't plant right away, keep the roots moist and store them, in their original package, in a cool location for a day or two. If you need to wait longer than that to plant, pot up the roots or set them into a nursery bed until you are ready.

Field-dug Perennials

You may be able to find a farmer, hobbyist plant breeder, plant collector, or nursery owner who will sell you mature plants dug from the field. If you handle the root ball carefully, you can move field-dug perennials much later into the summer than bareroot plants because the roots are protected by soil. Set the root ball, surrounded by soil, in a firm wooden flat or sturdy bucket. Cover it with a moist towel, damp peat moss,

Before you buy, look at the leaves. Off-color leaves may indicate nutrient deficiencies or pest problems.

Healthy plants have strong, evenly colored leaves. Check leaf undersides to make sure no pests are lurking.

Container-grown perennials may cost more but give instant effect.

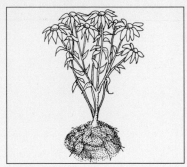

Field-dug plants usually adapt quickly to a new site.

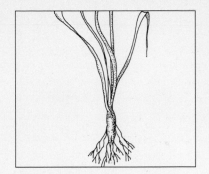

Bareroot plants take a bit of care but are often less expensive.

or compost to keep the roots and soil moist. Replant it as soon as you get home.

Buying Healthy Plants

Before you pull out your wallet to buy a new perennial, follow this checklist to make sure you verify the plant's quality:

1. Look to see if the plant is tagged with its botanical and cultivar name. If not, or if it's labeled only by common name or color, chances are that it's not an improved type and you may not want it.

2. Test for root-bound plants, which may have been sitting around for a long time in a small pot. Give the plant a soft tug from the top and see if the root ball pops out of the pot readily. If the roots are packed into a solid mass or are circling around the inside of the pot, the plants are root-bound and may be slow to adapt to garden conditions.

3. Look at the roots. Firm, white roots are a sign of good health. If you can't pull the plant out of its pot to see the roots, check where the shoots emerge from the soil. Emerging stems should not be brown, soft, blemished, or wilted—symptoms of rots and other diseases.

4. Give the same thorough inspection to the stems and foliage. Look for signs of diseases such as brown or black leaf spots, white powdery mildew, or tiny orange spots of rust. You don't want to bring these problems home to infect plants in your garden.

5. Check the color of the foliage. If it is a deep and uniform color, the plant is most likely healthy and well fed.

6. Be on the lookout for weed shoots emerging through or near the crown (base) of the perennial. Although the weed leaves may have been clipped off in a presale grooming, grasses and perennial weeds will reemerge and can invade your newly planted garden.

7. Last, check for insect pests. Look beneath the leaves, along the stems, in shoot tips, and on flower buds for soft-bodied aphids, cottony mealybugs, and hard-shelled scale insects. Spider mites, another common pest, will make leaves stippled or turn them yellow or bronze. If pests are on one plant, they may be on every plant in that greenhouse or garden center. Consider shopping elsewhere.

Gently slide a plant from its pot to check the roots before buying. Avoid plants with massed or circling roots.

Good-quality plants will have healthy white roots that are still growing through the soil ball.

Species Chart

Choosing exactly which perennials to grow out of the thousands that are available can be a real challenge. For easy reference, this species chart offers some of the most important information for over 50 of the most popular perennials. The chart covers bloom season, flower color, sun or shade requirements, and vital statistics such as hardiness zone and maximum height. Use the chart to identify perennials that fit your needs and your growing conditions. For more detailed information, look up specific plants in the "Plant by Plant Guide," starting on page 78.

Bloom Season These are the approximate bloom times of many favorite perennials. If you want to extend the blooming season, look for cultivars that bloom extra early or late—they can stretch the normal limits shown here. The weather will also influence season of bloom; warmth will bring flowering on faster and coolness

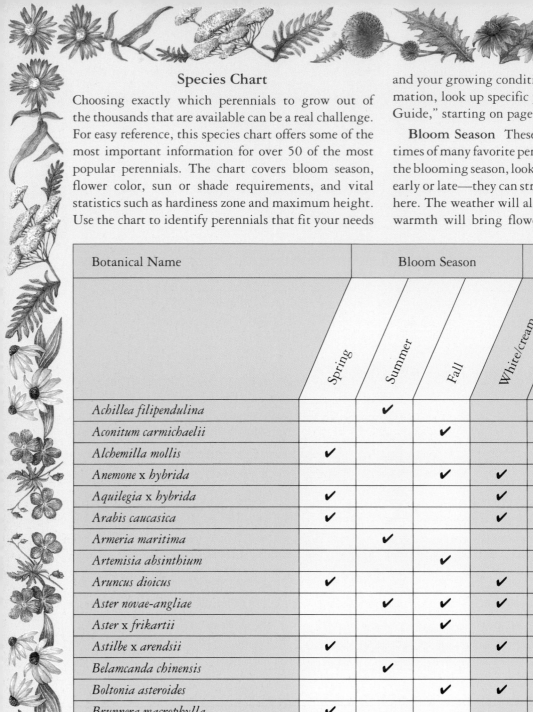

Botanical Name	Bloom Season			Flower Color				
	Spring	Summer	Fall	White/cream	Yellow/gold	Orange	Blue	
Achillea filipendulina		✔			✔			
Aconitum carmichaelii			✔				✔	
Alchemilla mollis	✔				✔			
Anemone x hybrida			✔	✔				
Aquilegia x hybrida	✔			✔	✔		✔	
Arabis caucasica	✔			✔				
Armeria maritima		✔						
Artemisia absinthium			✔		✔			
Aruncus dioicus	✔			✔				
Aster novae-angliae		✔	✔	✔			✔	
Aster x frikartii			✔				✔	
Astilbe x arendsii	✔			✔				
Belamcanda chinensis		✔				✔		
Boltonia asteroides			✔	✔				
Brunnera macrophylla	✔						✔	
Caltha palustris	✔				✔			
Campanula glomerata		✔					✔	
Campanula persicifolia		✔					✔	
Chrysanthemum x morifolium			✔	✔	✔	✔		
Chrysanthemum x superbum		✔		✔				
Cimicifuga racemosa		✔		✔				
Coreopsis verticillata		✔			✔			
Delphinium x elatum		✔		✔			✔	
Dianthus plumarius		✔		✔				
Dicentra spectabilis	✔							
Echinacea purpurea		✔						
Gaillardia x grandiflora		✔			✔	✔		

will encourage the flowers to stay open longer.

Flower Color Most perennials come in a large range of flower colors. For convenience, we have indicated which species have flowers of white and cream, gold and yellow, orange, blue, purple, pink, or red. In the garden, colors may vary widely depending on the cultivar and the growing conditions. If you want a specific color, try to see the plant in bloom before you buy.

Exposure You can choose from dozens of perennials that grow in full sun or shade. Some also take conditions that are in between both extremes. The information in the chart will help you to begin selecting the right plant for the right place.

Vital Statistics A number of perennials can grow in warm and cool climates. As their growing conditions vary—and as you choose cultivars bred to grow taller or shorter—their height will differ. This chart shows hardiness zones and average height.

Flower Color			Exposure			Zone	Height	Height (metric)
Purple	Pink	Red	Sun	Partial shade	Shade	Hardiness zone	Height	Height (metric)
			✔			3–9	3–4 ft	90–120 cm
			✔	✔		3–7	2–3 ft	60–90 cm
			✔	✔	✔	4–8	8 in	20 cm
	✔			✔		5–8	3–5 ft	90–150 cm
✔	✔	✔	✔	✔		3–9	2–3 ft	60–90 cm
	✔		✔			3–7	10 in	25 cm
	✔		✔			4–8	14 in	35 cm
			✔			3–9	3 ft	90 cm
				✔		3–7	3–6 ft	90–180 cm
✔	✔	✔	✔			3–8	3–6 ft	90–180 cm
✔			✔			5–8	3 ft	90 cm
	✔	✔		✔		3–9	2–4 ft	60–120 cm
			✔			4–10	4 ft	1.2 m
			✔			3–9	4–6 ft	1.2–1.8 m
				✔	✔	3–8	18 in	45 cm
			✔	✔		2–8	2 ft	60 cm
✔			✔	✔		3–8	1–3 ft	30–90 cm
			✔	✔		3–8	3 ft	90 cm
	✔	✔	✔			3–9	1–5 ft	30–150 cm
			✔			3–10	1–3 ft	30–90 cm
			✔	✔		3–8	7 ft	2.1 m
			✔			3–9	1–3 ft	30–90 cm
✔			✔			4–7	6 ft	1.8 m
	✔		✔			3–9	2 ft	60 cm
	✔			✔		2–9	30 in	75 cm
✔	✔		✔			3–8	2–4 ft	60–120 cm
		✔	✔			4–9	2–3 ft	60–90 cm

Botanical Name	Bloom Season			Flower Color				
	Spring	Summer	Fall	White/cream	Yellow/gold	Orange	Blue	
Gaura lindheimeri		✔	✔	✔				
Geranium endressii		✔						
Helenium autumnale		✔	✔		✔			
Heliopsis helianthoides		✔			✔			
Helleborus niger	✔			✔				
Hemerocallis hybrids		✔		✔	✔	✔		
Heuchera x *brizoides*	✔	✔		✔				
Hosta hybrids		✔	✔	✔				
Iris sibirica		✔		✔	✔		✔	
Liatris spicata		✔						
Lobelia cardinalis		✔						
Mertensia virginica	✔						✔	
Monarda didyma		✔						
Nepeta x *faassenii*	✔	✔					✔	
Paeonia lactiflora	✔			✔				
Papaver orientale		✔						
Phlox paniculata		✔		✔				
Platycodon grandiflorus		✔					✔	
Primula x *polyantha*	✔			✔	✔	✔	✔	
Rudbeckia fulgida		✔	✔		✔	✔		
Salvia x *superba*		✔					✔	
Scabiosa caucasica		✔		✔			✔	
Sedum spectabile		✔						
Stokesia laevis		✔					✔	
Thalictrum aquilegifolium	✔			✔				
Tiarella cordifolia	✔			✔				

Flower Color			Exposure			Zone	Height	Height (metric)
Purple	Pink	Red	Sun	Partial shade	Shade	Hardiness zone	Height	Height (metric)
			✔			5–9	4 ft	1.2 m
	✔		✔	✔		4–8	18 in	45 cm
			✔			3–8	3–5 ft	90–150 cm
			✔			3–9	3–6 ft	90–180 cm
				✔	✔	3–8	18 in	45 cm
	✔	✔	✔	✔		3–9	1–5 ft	30–150 cm
	✔	✔	✔	✔		3–8	30 in	75 cm
✔				✔	✔	3–8	6–36 in	15–90 cm
✔	✔		✔	✔		3–9	3 ft	90 cm
✔			✔			3–9	3 ft	90 cm
		✔			✔	2–9	4 ft	1.2 m
	✔			✔		3–9	2 ft	60 cm
		✔	✔			4–8	2–4 ft	60–120 cm
✔			✔	✔		3–8	3 ft	90 cm
	✔	✔	✔			2–8	3 ft	90 cm
		✔	✔			2–7	3 ft	90 cm
✔	✔	✔	✔			3–8	4 ft	1.2 m
✔			✔			3–8	2–3 ft	60–90 cm
✔	✔	✔		✔		3–8	1 ft	30 cm
			✔			3–9	3 ft	90 cm
✔			✔			4–7	18–40 in	45–100 cm
✔			✔			3–7	2 ft	60 cm
	✔		✔			3–9	2 ft	60 cm
			✔			5–9	2 ft	60 cm
✔			✔	✔		5–8	2–3 ft	60–90 cm
					✔	3–8	10 in	25 cm

CULTIVATING AND PLANTING

Once you have fine-tuned your plan and selected your perennials, you can have the pleasure of turning your garden idea into reality. As you prepare the soil and plant, you can anticipate the satisfaction of watching the garden grow and develop. Putting it all together will take work, but if you prepare the soil thoroughly and plant carefully, you can feel confident that you've given your plants the best possible start in life. You will enjoy the garden more with each passing year.

You are getting close to completing your perennial garden, but you still have several critical steps to take: The first is soil preparation, which may include making compost. (For information on creating your own compost, see "Making and Using Compost" on page 58.) The second is getting the perennials into their places and taking one last look to reevaluate your plan before you plant. The third is to get the plants in the ground so they can grow. In this chapter, you'll learn all you need to know to get your new garden off to a good start.

Soil preparation is a key part of creating a lush, healthy perennial garden. Loose, adequately fertile soil will promote good root growth, so your perennials will be able to get the water and nutrients they need. Your plants will thrive, and these stronger plants will be naturally more pest- and disease-resistant. They will grow better, live longer, and flower more profusely, all without a lot of fertilizing or reworking. If you skimp on this stage, you're asking for sickly perennials and major rescue work.

Once the soil is ready, look again at the bed and take a moment to fine-tune your design. When you were sitting in front of your books and catalogs in midwinter making plans, you may have missed subtle details that could make the garden arrangement even better. A great idea may strike when you actually see the plants together. You should allow yourself enough flexibility to maneuver them as you see fit. However, don't disregard your plan entirely. It represents the purpose of the garden, coordination of the plants, and elements of design that you carefully worked out before this point.

As you set out your plants on the prepared soil, determine the spacing within each group of plants and between groupings. Check the mature width of each plant in the "Plant by Plant Guide," starting on page 78, so you're sure to leave enough space between plants for all your perennials to spread without crowding each other. Or to get a fuller look faster, space plants closer together, but expect to buy more plants and to divide them earlier to relieve overcrowding. Once you determine the spacing, you'll be ready to plant your perennials and get your garden growing.

Opposite: The time you put into good soil preparation will be amply rewarded by the health and beauty of your plants. Imagine the pleasure of strolling down this lush, lavender-lined pathway on a warm summer evening.

Preparing the Planting Bed

Along with proper plant selection, preparing a good planting bed is critical to the success of your perennial garden. If you do a thorough job here, you will be rewarded by quicker plant establishment and less weeding to do later.

Timing

If possible, start digging your new perennial garden a season or a year before you plant. That way, you can do a really thorough job of preparing the soil, and the soil will have a chance to settle before you plant. If spring typically is too wet to work the soil in your area, dig the garden in fall instead. If you can't prepare the soil ahead of time, you can usually get the bed ready and start planting in the same season. See "Planting Your Perennials" on page 47 for suggestions on the best time to actually plant.

Making New Beds

When you're digging a garden bed in a lawn, begin by marking the bed outline with rope, a garden hose, or string and stakes. Strip off the sod with a flat spade by cutting long, spade-width strips across the width of your garden. Slide your spade under the strips to sever them from the soil. Roll up the turf as you go, or remove it in rectangles, and take the bundles to the compost pile. As an alternative, you can kill the grass by covering it with black plastic. However, this can take several weeks or more than a month depending on the weather—the hotter it is outside the faster the plastic works. Till in the turf when it has decayed.

Working the Soil Once you've cleared the beds, it's time to break up the soil. Consider your choice of tools carefully. Decades ago, gardeners turned the soil with shovels, garden spades, forks, and other hand tools. In recent years, many have turned to rotary tillers. These machines can churn the top 5 to 6 inches (12.5 to 15 cm) of soil with much less effort on your part. However, tillers aren't always the best choice. Excessive tilling, or tilling when the soil is too wet or too dry, will break up the granular soil structure into tiny particles and lead to soil compaction. If you choose to use a rotary tiller, make sure you work the soil when it's evenly moist. (For details on

rotary tiller

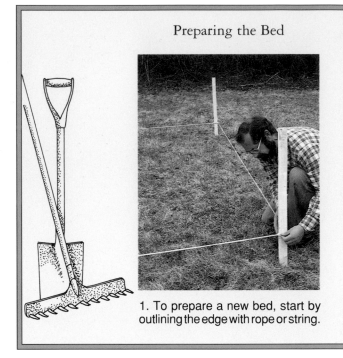

Preparing the Bed

1. To prepare a new bed, start by outlining the edge with rope or string.

determining soil moisture, see "Squeeze Your Soil to Test Moisture" below.)

If you have a small garden and are willing to dig with hand tools, you can usually loosen the soil to a depth of up to 6 inches (15 cm). Or you can make the bed 12 inches (30 cm) deep if you double dig. Double-digging increases drainage in heavy soils and is a great way to encourage deep-rooting plants. For complete instructions on this technique, see "Double-digging".

Add compost before planting so you can work it in throughout the bed. For a heavy clay or light sandy

Squeeze Your Soil to Test Moisture

Walking on or working wet soil can quickly destroy the porous, open structure you're trying so hard to build. So before you break out your shovel and work boots, try this simple test: Take a handful of soil and squeeze it. If moisture runs out between your fingers, the soil is too wet to work. If it does not, open your hand. The soil should be in a ball in your palm. If it will not cling together, it is too dry to work. In that case, water the bed thoroughly, let it sit for 24 hours, and evaluate again. If the soil stays in a ball, tap it lightly with a finger. The soil should break apart easily. If it stays tight, it is still too wet. Wait a few more dry days and try again.

2. Use a spade to strip off the sod and expose the soil.

3. If a soil test indicates the site is too acid, apply lime to the soil.

4. Spread a layer of compost over the surface and work it into the bed.

loam that is low in organic matter, lay a 4-inch (10 cm) thick layer over the entire area and work it into the top 8 inches (20 cm) of soil. Use less compost if you want to grow yarrows, artemisias, and other perennials that grow best in dry, sunny sites. Add even more compost in warm climates—where organic matter seems to "burn up" in a few weeks—to make up for the the fast rate of decomposition.

While you are working through the soil, pull out all perennial weed roots. You may have to follow those like docks (*Rumex* spp.) and bindweeds (*Convolvulus*

In poor soil, double-digging can help give your perennials the best possible conditions for root growth.

spp.) for quite some distance to get the entire root system. If you merely snap off the top, the root will probably resprout.

Double-digging Double-digging is hard work, but it can be worthwhile if you are gardening in heavy clayey soil or if you want to encourage perennials to root extra deeply in drought-prone areas. Remove the sod and weed roots first. Starting at one end of the bed, dig a trench 12 inches (30 cm) wide and as deep as your spade across the width of the bed. Put all the topsoil you unearth into a wheelbarrow and move it to the far end of the garden. Now loosen up the exposed subsoil with a garden fork or your spade. Then back up to dig the next 12-inch (30 cm) wide strip. Shift that topsoil, with some extra compost or other organic matter, into the first trench and then loosen the new area of subsoil. Continue in this fashion until you reach the far end of the bed. Finish the last strip with the topsoil from your wheelbarrow and rake the bed smooth. Once you've prepared the bed, avoid stepping on it; otherwise, you'll compact the soil and undo all your hard work. If you can't reach in from the sides to plant, lay a board across the soil and step on that. Remove it when you're done.

Some perennials, like thread-leaved coreopsis (*Coreopsis verticillata*), grow best if the soil isn't too rich.

Adding Organic Nutrients

As you prepare your new perennial garden for planting, you should also think about adding any nutrients your plants may need. The right nutrients in the right balance will help ensure that your perennials get off to a good start.

The availability of soil nutrients is as important to plant health and vigor as vitamins and minerals are to people. Three elements are especially critical—nitrogen, potassium, and phosphorus. These are called macronutrients and are represented on fertilizer bags in ratios tagged by their elemental initials: N, P, and K. Nitrogen (N) powers growth and protein formation; phosphorus (P) is essential for root and fruit development and for photosynthesis; and potassium (K) is key to root and flower development as well as water and sugar flow. All three must be present in the right balance for your perennials to grow and thrive.

Start with a Soil Test

Before you invest in a big bag of organic fertilizer to add nutrients to your soil, find out what's in your soil to start with. It may already contain everything your plants need to grow beautifully. The best way to find out is to send soil samples to a lab for testing before you plant. You can use home test kits instead, but they may not be accurate. To have your soil analyzed by a lab,

contact your local Cooperative Extension agent, land-grant university, or professional soil-analysis laboratory for information or directions.

Applying Nutrients

How you actually apply organic nutrients to your garden depends on several different factors. If you're starting a new bed, for instance, you can spread compost, fertilizers, and other amendments (like lime or sulfur) over the surface and work the materials in before you plant. Once your perennials are established, you can supply them with nutrients by working fertilizer materials into the soil around the base of each plant and by mulching with organic materials like chopped leaves or compost. If they need a midsummer nutrient boost, you can spray the plants with a liquid fertilizer like compost tea or seaweed extract. For more details on how to select and apply fertilizer materials, see "Fertilizing" on page 56.

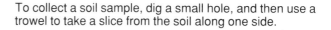

To collect a soil sample, dig a small hole, and then use a trowel to take a slice from the soil along one side.

Perennials That Grow Best Lean and Light

If you think more nutrients are always better, think again. Many perennials, including coreopsis (*Coreopsis* spp.), yarrows, and common thrift (*Armeria maritima*), are sun-loving and drought-tolerant. They grow best where soils are not lush. If you overfeed them, they become soft and succulent—too tender to stand upright without staking. On disease-susceptible plants like garden phlox (*Phlox paniculata*), this soft, succulent tissue is more prone to mildews and other diseases. Rich soil also gives an extra boost to plants that spread by rhizomes or stolons, like bee balm (*Monarda didyma*). These creeping stems will run all over the place instead of staying in more controlled clumps. Excess fertility will also make silver- and gray-leaved perennials such as artemisias and lavenders fade to green.

Your newly planted garden may look a little sparse, but don't despair—it will fill in surprisingly fast!

Planting Your Perennials

Once you've prepared the soil in your garden, it's finally time to get your carefully chosen plants in the ground so they can start growing. Planting your perennials at the right time of year is an important factor in giving them a good start. Although you may have been anticipating the moment of planting for months, don't rush when it arrives. Planting properly takes time and a lot of bending. Work slowly and deliberately to save wear and tear on your body and to get each plant settled as well as possible. Try not to compact the soil. Lay boards across the bed when you need to step in it. This spreads your weight across a broad area instead of concentrating it in one spot.

When to Plant

Time your planting efforts so your new perennials will start growing in a period of abundant rainfall and moderate temperatures—usually spring or fall. In cool climates, like Zone 5 and colder, concentrate your planting efforts in spring. (If you aren't sure what zone you live in, see the USDA Plant Hardiness Zone Map on page 154.) Spring planting allows the new plants time to establish strong root systems before winter. You can chance late-summer planting for very hardy or seasonally available perennials. In warmer climates with mild winters, such as Zones 9 and 10, plant in fall so perennials will be well established before the long, hot summer. In areas where summer isn't too hot and winter isn't too cold—Zones 6 through 8—you can plant perennials in fall or spring. If your climate has periods of drought, plant whenever there is abundant

natural rainfall and temperatures are between about 40° and 70°F (4.4° and 21.2°C).

Plant Spacing

Before you actually plant the perennials, set them in place to see how they look. If you are grouping several of the same kind of plant, mark the outside edge of the mass on the soil surface with a hoe, a trickle of limestone, or a row of pegs. Then set the plants, still in pots, inside the marks. Move them into a natural-looking arrangement—clustered unevenly rather than lined out in geometrical rows. Be certain each plant has enough space. If you crowd plants, they will grow weakly and be more susceptible to disease.

Double-check spacings with a tape measure—eyeballing distances is not always effective. Check lines and masses of a single species of perennial to be sure the spacing is even. Leave more space between the faster growers. Let difficult-to-move plants like peonies, blue false indigo (*Baptisia australis*), and gas plant (*Dictamnus albus*) have enough elbow room to mature to their full size. You can use tighter spacings for smaller, slow-spreading plants like coral bells (*Heuchera* spp.), since

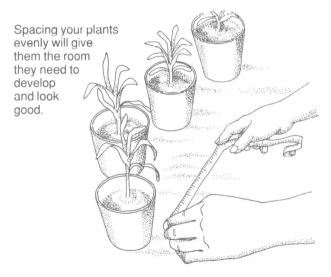

Spacing your plants evenly will give them the room they need to develop and look good.

When planting bearded irises, keep the tops of the rhizomes even with the soil surface—don't bury them.

they are easy to move when the plants need more room.

As you work out the spacings, decide if you want to leave some open areas here and there within the garden to let air circulate and sun penetrate. A more open garden lets you enjoy the attractive silhouettes of plants. However, a tightly packed garden will be an ocean of color and texture—a more intense display.

Stand back and study the appearance of the bed from different angles to get some idea how the finished garden will look. Readjust as needed. When you are satisfied, start planting.

Planting

In most cases you'll set new plants in the ground at the same depth at which they are growing presently. Re-planting at the same depth keeps the crown—the point from which shoots emerge—from being buried in damp soil, where it is likely to rot. However, if you have just prepared the soil, it will settle 1 to 2 inches (2.5 to 5 cm) over the coming months. In a new bed, plant slightly deeper so the perennials' roots and crowns do not stick out of the soil when it has settled. Exactly how you plant depends on whether you are using bareroot, container-grown, or field-dug stock.

Container Plants If you are planting a potted perennial, you can easily see how deeply to plant it. Dig deeply enough so the surface of the container soil will be at the top of the hole (adjusting accordingly for new beds). Fill the hole with water to moisten the soil.

Now, prepare the plant. Slip the roots out of the pot. Most larger plants are root-bound enough to slide out easily. If not, you can gently squeeze the base of a plastic pot to loosen the root ball. Break up the edges of the root ball so the roots will have more contact with the surrounding soil.

If the roots are wrapped around them-selves, they may not break free and root into the soil. You will have to work them loose. You can quarter the roots of fibrous-rooted perennials like chrysanthemums. Although the process may seem harsh, it will encourage new root growth. Make four deep slices, one on each

Planting a Container-grown Perennial

1. Dig a planting hole that is larger than the root ball.

2. If desired, add a handful or two of compost to the hole.

3. Add water to moisten the soil before planting.

4. Gently slide the perennial out of its container.

5. Use your fingers to loosen the soil mix around the roots.

6. Set the plant in the hole. Backfill with soil; firm lightly.

side of the root ball, or make a single cut two-thirds up the center to divide the ball in half. Mound some soil in the center of the planting hole. Open the root quarters out from the cuts and spread them out over the mound. Cover the rest of the roots up to the crown. Don't try this technique on perennials with taproots like monkshoods (*Aconitum* spp.).

After planting, firm the soil gently around the plant, water it well, and mulch. Mulching your bed with organic materials like compost, straw, or shredded leaves will conserve moisture and reduce weed competition. (New beds are especially weed-prone, since turning the soil exposes weed seeds.) For more information on choosing and using mulches, see "Selecting and Using Mulch" on page 52.

Field-dug Plants Plant field-dug perennials that have a large amount of soil still around the roots in a hole the same size as the root ball. If much of the soil has fallen off the roots, make the hole slightly larger so you can move the roots into the best position. Drench the hole with water and set in the perennial at the same depth it was growing. Work any exposed roots into the surrounding soil as you refill, then firm the soil gently.

Bareroot Plants When you start with bareroot plants, you will have to take more time settling the plants into the ground. This process can be tricky the first few times, but be patient and don't be afraid to work with the roots. You'll soon get it right.

Quartering

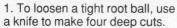

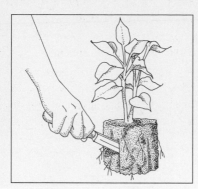

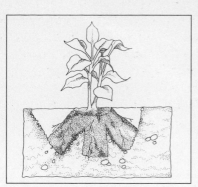

1. To loosen a tight root ball, use a knife to make four deep cuts.

2. Spread the quartered root ball over a mound of soil and backfill.

First, soak the roots in a bucket of lukewarm water for a few hours to prepare them for planting. When you are ready to plant, identify how deeply the plants had been growing in the nursery. The aboveground portions—green foliage tufts, leaf buds, or dormant stems—usually emerge from the root system above the former soil line. Plant so that these structures will stay slightly above the soil in your garden. (Peonies are an exception, since their shoots will emerge through the soil from about 1 inch [2.5 cm] underground.)

Next, make a hole that is deep and wide enough to set the plant crown at the soil surface and stretch out the roots. Form a small mound of soil in the bottom of the hole. Set the root clump on it with the crown resting on top of the mound. Spread the roots gently in every direction and fill in around them with soil. Then firm the soil gently, water, and mulch. Keep the soil evenly moist for the next few weeks.

Planting a Bareroot Perennial

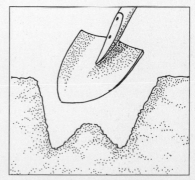

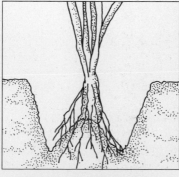

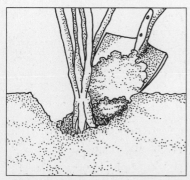

1. Dig a hole large enough to hold the roots without bending them.

2. Set the crown in the hole. Spread the roots over the mound.

3. Backfill with soil, firm gently, and water well.

MAINTAINING PERENNIALS

If you have chosen plants that match your site, prepared the soil thoroughly, and planted carefully, you will probably find your perennial garden demands less maintenance than your lawn. However, low maintenance isn't no maintenance. Even the toughest perennials will need a little pruning, weeding, and watering. But these tasks need not be a chore. Whenever you wander by your garden, carry your garden scissors or pruners in one hand and a hand weeder in the other. You can deadhead or weed as you admire new developments that unfold. A few minutes each day can save hours of labor on the weekends!

In this chapter, you'll find all the information you need to keep your perennials healthy and beautiful. Mulching, watering, and fertilizing provide the moisture and nutrients plants need to grow and flower beautifully. Staking, deadheading, pinching, and other plant-grooming tasks will keep perennials looking neat and well maintained. Controlling weeds, pests, and diseases is also a critical part of growing healthy, attractive perennials.

Many gardeners believe that mulching—layering organic or inorganic material over your garden's soil—will eliminate all their gardening chores. Mulch's great reputation is based on its many benefits, such as retaining soil moisture, controlling weeds, and moderating soil temperatures. But while it can reduce chores, even

it can't produce a work-free garden. Spend some time selecting the right mulch for your needs. If you apply an organic mulch, you'll need to add new layers as the material breaks down into the soil. In some climates, mulch can keep the soil too wet or provide a hiding place for plant pests. Managing your mulch is a critical part of good garden maintenance.

Regular watering and fertilizing are also important for keeping your perennials in top shape. You can increase your soil's moisture-holding capacity and add nutrients at the same time by mulching with generous amounts of compost. Making and using compost is a great way to recycle kitchen scraps and garden trimmings into a free source of mulch and fertilizer.

Once your perennials are growing vigorously, there are a few tricks you can use to keep them looking their best. Tall-growing or sprawling plants may benefit from staking. Deadheading removes spent flowers, which makes plants look neater; it can also extend the bloom season or encourage a second flush of bloom later in the season. And pinching or cutting plants back will encourage more compact, bushy growth.

Sometimes, despite your best efforts, weeds, pests, and diseases can get out of hand. Preventing and controlling problems organically will help you keep your plants healthy while maintaining the natural populations of beneficial organisms in your garden.

Opposite: With a little help from the gardener, common foxgloves (*Digitalis purpurea*) can be real showstoppers in the border. To keep plants vigorous, remove spent flower stalks and divide plants after blooming.

Selecting and Using Mulch

Mulching is an important aspect of producing healthy plants in almost any climate. Mulch helps keep out weeds by preventing weed seedlings from getting a foothold. It protects the soil, slowing evaporation and keeping it moist longer after each rain or watering. Organic mulches add nutrients and organic matter to the soil as they decay.

If you use mulch on frozen soil during the winter, it will keep the earth evenly frozen; this reduces the rapid freezing-and-thawing cycles that can damage plant roots and push plant crowns out of the soil (a process known as frost heaving). In hot-summer climates, mulch will slow the rapid decay of organic matter in the soil so each application will last longer. In any climate, mulch can work double duty as an attractive background for your perennials.

Mulching with compost is a good way to add nutrients to your garden. It may be all you need to fertilize light feeders, such as coreopsis (*Coreopsis* spp.), yarrow, and common thrift (*Armeria maritima*). Compost mulch will conserve moisture, but will not do much to squeeze out weeds.

As useful as mulch is in most gardens, there are situations when mulching can actually cause garden problems. If slugs and snails are your garden's major

A generous layer of organic mulch will help moderate soil temperatures and conserve moisture.

pests, an organic mulch can provide them with the cool, dark, moist conditions they prefer. If you're trying to garden in heavy, wet clay, mulch can slow evaporation even more, contributing to root rot.

In cold-climate areas with short growing seasons, mulch will keep the soil cool longer in spring, giving your plants a late start. In this case, mulch in summer, when plants are up and the soil has warmed, then remove and compost the mulch when you clean up the garden in fall.

If you mulch your garden with uncomposted sawdust or wood chips, keep in mind that these materials can rob your

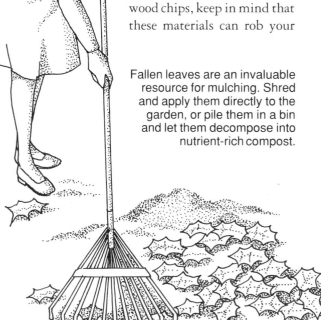

Fallen leaves are an invaluable resource for mulching. Shred and apply them directly to the garden, or pile them in a bin and let them decompose into nutrient-rich compost.

In cold climates, winter mulching with evergreen branches can help protect dormant plants from drying winds.

Mulches come in a variety of colors. Choose one that is
similar to your soil color for the most natural effect.

plants of soil nitrogen as they decompose. If you must
mulch with these woody materials, top-dress the soil
with a high-nitrogen material like bloodmeal or
cottonseed meal before adding the mulch.

Choosing a Mulch

The time you take to choose the right mulch for your
needs is time well spent. You want a mulch that looks
good and is free of weeds. Cost and availability may also
be important factors in your choice.

Many kinds of organic mulches are available for the
perennial garden. Shredded leaves make a useful mulch
and they are free, so the price is right. Cocoa bean hulls
have an attractive dark color and chocolatey aroma but
are not widely available. Dark-colored, fine-textured,
well-decomposed compost can also give the soil a rich,
healthy look as well as improve soil fertility.

Grass clippings or straw may make a fine mulch for
vegetables, but they may look too utilitarian for most
flower gardens. Chunks of bark or wood may be suitable for large, bold perennials, but they are hard to
work through without gloves and they will dwarf
small, fine-textured alpines and creepers.

Try to choose a mulch that won't pack down into
dense layers. Dense layers of fine-textured or flat materials, like grass clippings or an extra thick coat of
shredded bark, tend to shed water. Rain and irrigation
water will run off the bed instead of trickling down
into the soil. If you want to use these kinds of mulches,
create air pockets between the particles by mixing in
coarse, fluffy material like shredded leaves, small bark
chunks, or ground corncobs.

If you use a mulch that won't pack down and
your garden has well-drained soil, you can lay the

mulch as much as 4 to 6 inches (10 to 15 cm) deep to
get maximum weed control. On soils that tend to stay
wet or in gardens that do not have a big weed problem,
reduce the mulch layer to 2 to 3 inches (5 to 7.5 cm)
deep. Leave 4 to 6 inches (10 to 15 cm) of unmulched
ground around the base of each perennial plant; this
way, the crown stays drier and is less likely to rot.

Organic mulches will gradually decompose over
a period of weeks or months, so you need to replace
the mulch layer often to keep the soil covered. You
will have to reapply softer mulches like compost or
grass clippings more often than harder wood chips or
shredded leaves, which decompose more slowly.

When applying mulch, leave several
inches of bare soil around the base
of each plant. Otherwise, the mulch
would hold moisture around the
plant stems and encourage rot.

Whenever possible, avoid overhead watering. It wastes water and can encourage the spread of diseases.

Watering

A garden that is actively growing and flowering will need a source of moisture at all times. If water is in short supply, flowers and flower buds are the first to suffer damage; if water is overly abundant, perennial roots will rot. You will have to fine-tune your watering depending on several factors, including the type of soil you have, the amount of natural rainfall, the plants you grow, and the stage of growth the plants are in.

Consider Your Soil

If you do not already know how moisture-retentive your garden soil is, find out. For instance, will it

provide reserves of water for 1 week after a good drenching or will most of the moisture drain away within a day? To answer this question, water a portion of the garden thoroughly. After 48 hours, dig a small hole 6 inches (15 cm) deep. If the soil is reasonably water-retentive, the earth at the bottom of the hole will still be moist. If it is not, you can improve its water-holding capacity by working in lots of compost. This organic matter acts like a sponge, holding extra moisture reserves that plant roots can draw on if needed. If you do add a great deal of compost, shredded leaves, or other organic matter, you can water less frequently. But when you do irrigate, water extra thoroughly to saturate the organic matter.

Keeping Track of Rainfall

Monitor the rainfall in your garden and vary your irrigation schedule accordingly. Overwatering can be as disastrous as underwatering, especially in heavier soils. You can tell how much rain has fallen if you leave out a rain gauge, which is like a narrow

Hand-watering with a watering can is often the most realistic option for irrigating small gardens or for spot-watering thirsty plants.

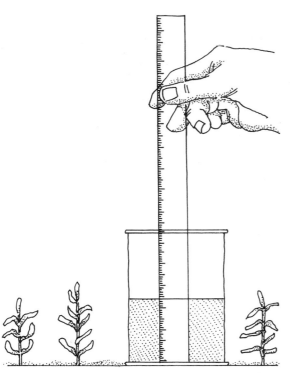

Use a commercial or homemade rain gauge to keep track of how much rain your garden receives each week.

When rainfall is not sufficient for plant needs, you'll need to irrigate. Supply moisture gently so it will seep down instead of running off. Whenever possible, use a drip or trickle irrigation system or a soaker hose that releases droplets of water onto the soil without wetting plant leaves. Keeping the leaves and flowers dry reduces disease problems. Also, letting the water trickle into the ground is efficient because little is lost to evaporation.

Water conservation is even more effective if you organize your network of "leaky" tubes or soaker hoses so they irrigate only the perennials, not the weeds or open areas. But don't expect perennials to grow roots in areas of the garden that remain dry. Since perennial root spread may be limited to irrigated zones, be sure to soak the soil deeply where you do water so the root systems can grow big enough to support the plants.

You also can apply water to individual plants with a trickling hose or watering can. To reach extra deeply in the soil or to supply additional water to a wilting plant on a hot day, sink a water reservoir into the soil. This can be a plastic drainage tube, clay pot, or leaky plastic bucket filled with water. For slower release in sandy soils, plug the largest holes on pots and tubes and let the moisture slowly seep out of small, pin-prick openings.

Overhead sprinkling, which wastes lots of water through evaporation, is not a good choice for perennial gardens. It waters weeds, helping them grow, and wets foliage and flowers, increasing disease problems.

measuring cup with inches of rainfall marked on the side. If you don't want to buy a rain gauge, you can set a small, clean can in an open part of the garden and use a ruler to measure how much rain water it collects. Check once a week to keep track.

A good rule of thumb is that your garden should get an inch (25 mm) of water a week. This amount of water wets the soil deeply, encouraging roots to grow farther underground. Of course, some perennials need more moisture and some need less, so you'll have to adjust your supplemental irrigation depending on the needs of your plants.

Different Plants Have Different Needs

Some perennials thrive in moist soils. Others will grow weakly or rot where water is abundant. Water more often if you grow perennials that need evenly moist soil. These include delphiniums, astilbes, and moisture-loving bog plants like Japanese primroses (*Primula japonica*) and marsh marigolds (*Caltha palustris*).

Let the soil dry more between waterings for drought-tolerant plants, such as lavender, perennial candy-tuft (*Iberis sempervirens*), Cupid's dart (*Catananche caerulea*), and torch lilies (*Kniphofia* hybrids). These perennials probably need no more than ½ inch (12 mm) of water per week.

Expect to coddle newly planted perennials until their roots spread far enough to support the plants. If the weather is warm and dry, you may have to water daily until a drenching rain comes. If the season is cool and rainy, you can let nature handle the irrigation.

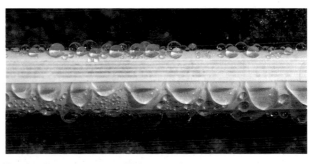

Soaker hoses are an efficient and easy way to water your perennial garden. They wet the soil—not your plants.

Garden phlox (*Phlox paniculata*) needs an ample supply of nutrients throughout the season to look its best.

Delphiniums thrive in humus-rich soil. Work in lots of compost before planting, and use it as a mulch, too.

Fertilizing

Supplying your perennials with the nutrients they need is a critical part of keeping them healthy and vigorous. How much fertilizer you should add to your garden will depend on how fertile the soil is and which perennials you're growing.

How Soil Affects Fertilizing

The texture and natural fertility of your soil will have a great impact on how much and how often you need to add supplemental nutrients. A sandy soil will hold fewer nutrients than a clayey soil or a soil that's high in organic matter, so you'll need to fertilize a sandy soil more frequently. If you prepared the soil thoroughly before planting and corrected nutrient shortages (as explained in "Preparing the Planting Bed" on page 44 and "Adding Organic Nutrients" on page 46), you may not have to fertilize a new perennial garden for a year or more.

Nutrient Needs Vary among Plants

Fertilizer requirements vary widely among different perennials. Some are light feeders, including common sneezeweed (*Helenium autumnale*), oxeye (*Heliopsis helianthoides*), and daisy fleabane (*Erigeron speciosus*). A light layer of compost applied once or twice a year should meet their nutrient needs. Other perennials are heavy feeders; these include delphiniums, astilbes, and garden phlox (*Phlox paniculata*). They need more frequent fertilizing to stay in top form.

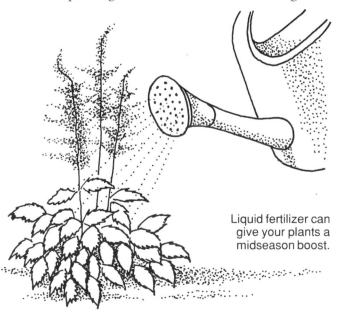

Liquid fertilizer can give your plants a midseason boost.

Making Compost Tea

If you want to turn your compost from a solid nutrient source into a quick-acting liquid fertilizer, make it into tea. Add one or two shovelsful of compost (or farm manure) into a burlap or woven-mesh bag. Tie the bag securely and submerge it into a large bucket or barrel of water. Let it steep for 1 week, then remove the bag. Dilute the remaining liquid until it is the color of weak tea if you plan to spray or sprinkle it directly on your perennials, or use it full strength to drench the ground around the base of the plants.

A Sampler of Organic Fertilizers

A wide variety of organic materials is available for correcting nutrient deficiencies. Before you buy any fertilizer, check the label for the nitrogen, phosphorus, and potassium content. This is indicated by a series of three numbers, such as 5-10-5. This means that 100 pounds (45 kg) of a fertilizer with this formulation contains 5 pounds (2.25 kg) of nitrogen, 10 pounds (4.5 kg) of phosphorus, and 5 pounds (2.25 kg) of potassium. Use this information to compare the nutrient contents of different fertilizers and to figure out how much of a given material you need to add to your garden based on your soil test results. Compost is one source of many plant nutrients. Listed below are some other commonly used organic fertilizers, along with their nutrient contents.

- Bloodmeal, 12-0-0 to 14-0-0, contains nitrogen plus iron.
- Bonemeal, 1-10-0, contains about 20 percent calcium. If processed with some meat or marrow, bonemeal can contain higher percentages of nitrogen.
- Fish emulsion, 3-1-1 to 5-2-2, releases most of its nitrogen quickly. It is often sprayed onto leaves for a fast-acting nutrient boost.
- Fish meal, 5-3-3, contains both immediately available nitrogen and a slow-release form that supplements the soil for up to 2 months.
- Seaweed extract, 1-0.5-2.5, usually made from kelp, provides trace elements and natural growth hormones. Use liquid kelp as a foliar spray. Kelp meal is a concentrated form high in potassium and boron.

Daisy fleabane (*Erigeron speciosus*) grows best in lean soil. A light mulch of compost is all it needs.

as not enough, leading to weak stems, rampant sprawling growth, and disease problems.

Liquid Fertilizers Commonly used liquid fertilizers include fish emulsion, liquid seaweed, and compost tea (see "Making Compost Tea" for complete instructions). Use a single dose of liquid fertilizer for a quick but temporary fix of a nutrient shortage, or apply it every 2 weeks for a general plant boost. You can spray these materials directly on the plants, which will absorb the nutrients through their foliage.

Dry Fertilizers Dry fertilizers are released to plants more slowly than liquid fertilizers. Scratch them into the surface of the soil in a circle around the perimeter of the plant's foliage, so the nutrients are released gradually as they dissolve in soil moisture. This encourages roots to extend outward.

Small or spindly perennials may benefit from a dose of organic fertilizer.

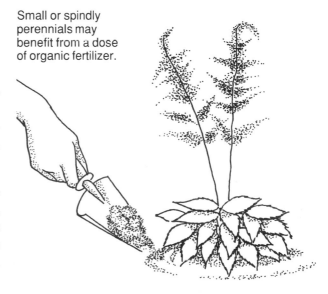

You may want to give your perennials a little fertility boost to encourage new growth or rejuvenation. Fertilize in spring as plants begin growing, after planting or dividing, and after deadheading or cutting back.

Applying Fertilizers

When you fertilize, you can eliminate deficiencies by applying either liquid or dry fertilizer or both. If you decide to use a combination of fertilizers, make sure you don't apply more total nutrients than your plants need. Remember that too much fertilizer can be as bad

Making and Using Compost

Making and using compost is the key to success in any kind of gardening. Compost is a balanced blend of recycled garden, yard, and household wastes that have broken down into dark, crumbly organic matter. The time you spend making compost and applying it to your garden will be more than returned by improved soil and plant health.

Creating Your Own Compost

Making compost is a lot like cooking—you mix together ingredients, stir them up, and let them "cook." But with a compost pile, the source of heat isn't electricity or gas—it's decomposer organisms like bacteria and fungi that live in soil and break down dead plant and animal tissues. These organisms work best when given warmth, moisture, plenty of oxygen, and a balance of carbon and nitrogen.

You can add a wide variety of materials to your compost. Vegetable scraps from the kitchen, grass clippings, fallen leaves, and soft plant trimmings are all appropriate choices. If you have access to manure from animals like chickens, rabbits, cows, or horses, you can add that also. There are some things you should avoid, including fats, bones, and meat scraps, which can attract scavengers to your pile. Also avoid composting manure from humans, dogs, and cats—this material can carry disease organisms.

Choose a shady, well-drained spot for your compost pile. For your convenience, put it as close to your garden as possible. If you're concerned that a loose compost pile would be unattractive, you can contain it in a bin. Make a homemade bin from wire fencing, wood, or concrete blocks, or buy a commercially available bin.

A wood-and-wire bin is a good way to keep your compost contained but easily accessible.

Most kinds of kitchen scraps are great ingredients for compost. Avoid bones and fat, which can attract animals.

Circular woven wire bins are easy to make and use. The large stick helps direct water to the center of the pile.

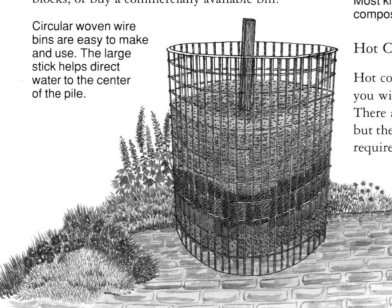

Hot Composting

Hot composting takes some work, but it will provide you with high-quality compost in a matter of weeks. There are many different systems of hot composting, but they tend to have some elements in common. Most require building a large pile of different layers of high-nitrogen and high-carbon elements, along with some soil or finished compost to make sure the right decomposers are present. Turning or fluffing the pile every few days or weeks, to provide the decomposer organisms in the pile with oxygen, is another critical part of encouraging fast breakdown.

To create a hot-compost pile, blend both soft and green (high-

If you have some extra space, you don't need a bin for your compost—just pile it in an out-of-the-way spot.

nitrogen) plant scraps, like lawn clippings, lettuce scraps, and dandelion leaves, and tough and brown (high-carbon) scraps, like fallen leaves, straw, and woody flower stalks. The moist, green items provide the decomposers with the nitrogen they consume as they break down the high-carbon materials.

Chop up the debris you plan to compost, and combine about 1 part of high-nitrogen elements with 2 parts high-carbon material in a pile about 3 feet (90 cm) high and wide. Pile up these elements in layers or just jumble them together. Add a shovelful of soil or finished compost in between each layer and enough water to keep the pile evenly moist. Turn or fluff the pile with a pitchfork every few days to add oxygen.

If all goes well, your compost should be ready in a few weeks. The material may break down more quickly in hot weather or more slowly in cold weather. When your compost is fairly cool and most of the original materials are unrecognizable, it is ready to use.

Cold Composting

Making "cold" compost is easier than making hot compost, but it takes longer. (A cold-compost pile won't really feel cold; it just doesn't get warm as a hot-compost pile does.) Since the decomposition period is extended up to a year or more, more nutrients can wash away in rainwater. You'll have to leave more space for the slower decomposing piles, and you'll have to wait much longer until it's ready. Cold compost will not heat up enough to kill seeds or disease organisms, so don't add mature weeds or diseased plant material to the pile.

To create a cold-compost pile, just choose a shady, well-drained place to drop your organic scraps. Let them build up to a pile about 3 feet (90 cm) wide by 3 feet (90 cm) high and then begin again in a new location. After a year or so, the original materials should be broken down, although the compost will probably still be fairly lumpy. Use the compost as it is, or screen out the lumps and leave them to break down for a while longer.

Using Compost

There are many different ways to add compost to your garden. If you are preparing a new bed, you can work it in as you dig. In an established garden, use compost as a mulch. As a general rule, cover the bed with 2 inches (5 cm) a year to maintain a fertile soil. Use more if you are growing moisture-loving perennials like astilbes or if you want to control weeds. (For more on mulching for weed control, see "Selecting and Using Mulch" on page 52.) Use less around perennials such as yarrow that prefer drier, less-fertile soils. Compost breaks down gradually over the growing season—add more as needed.

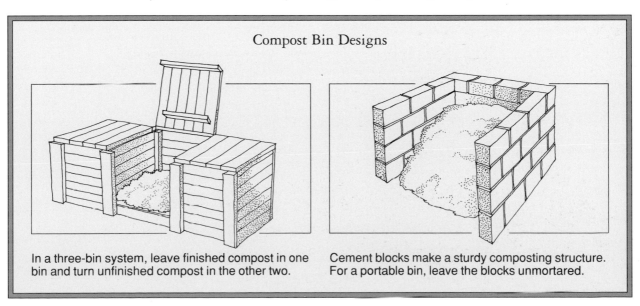

Compost Bin Designs

In a three-bin system, leave finished compost in one bin and turn unfinished compost in the other two.

Cement blocks make a sturdy composting structure. For a portable bin, leave the blocks unmortared.

Staking

Some gardeners routinely stake all their perennials; some gardeners refuse to do it at all. In all probability, you'll find yourself somewhere in the middle—staking a few and letting others grow as they may.

As you consider growing tall plants that need staking, you can equate the work involved with that entailed in growing longer hair. Short hair stays in place with little fuss, while you may need to curl or sweep back long hair. That takes time to do properly, but the end result can be magnificent if you use care. Plan ahead and encourage a natural look with discreet staking that blends in rather than sticking out obviously. Here are some guidelines to help you.

Staking Secrets

The key to successful staking is to support plants as they grow. Don't wait until the stems are sagging to tie up the plant; you can easily break the stems when you wrap them with string and prop them up with a stake. And you interrupt the beauty of the garden with the artificiality of the staking—it can look worse than letting the plants flop in the first place.

Instead, make a note on your calendar to set out your supports as the perennials are emerging from the ground. For bushy plants, use something the plants can grow up through, which they'll then fill out and hide.

Form a 6-inch (15 cm) high bridge of wire mesh and set it over an emerging perennial. You can make it higher for taller types. You can also buy prefabricated grow-through rings with adjustable heights. These can become an internal backbone for yarrows, peonies, common bleeding hearts (*Dicentra spectabilis*), Shasta daisies (*Chrysanthemum* x *superbum*), and coreopsis (*Coreopsis* spp.). Another option is to place strong, green, well-branched twigs around the perimeter of bushy plants. These twigs should be about three-quarters as tall as mature plant height and sturdy enough to support the bulk of the perennial.

If the foliage of your perennials is not full enough to hide the supports, you can plant low-growing annuals or perennials in the front. They will fill in quickly and hide the staking for the rest of the season.

Support individual upright flowering stems with bamboo stakes as tall as the flower will be. These work well with large-flowered dahlia hybrids, delphinium, hollyhock (*Alcea rosea*), lilies, or foxgloves (*Digitalis* spp.). Set the stake securely in the ground in spring. Tie the flower stem to it as it grows with strips of nylon hose or flexible florist's tape. Unfortunately, you will have to look at the barren stake as the plant grows, but if you use green bamboo against a backdrop of other greenery, it is much less obvious.

In the cutting garden, you may want to use a system of wire and stakes to keep flower stems straight.

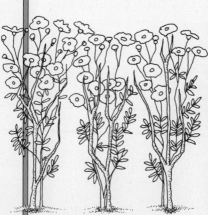

Stake leggy coreopsis (*Coreopsis* spp.) with branched twigs.

Individual stakes can help support tall stems. For a more formal effect, use less visible, green stakes.

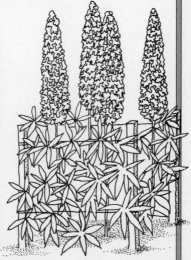

Stakes and string can support bushy lupines (*Lupinus* spp.).

Deadheading

Deadheading—removing spent flowers—is an essential part of perennial gardening. When you deadhead, you can enjoy a garden unmarred by brown or drooping petals. Your plants will be free from rots and other diseases that invade the decaying blossoms. And since deadheaded perennials don't waste energy on seed production, they have more strength for flower production and plant growth.

The following perennials may bloom longer or rebloom if you remove the faded flowers promptly: baby's-breath, bellflowers (*Campanula* spp.), thread-leaved coreopsis (*Coreopsis verticillata*), red valerian (*Centranthus ruber*), daylilies, delphiniums, pinks (*Dianthus* spp.), foxgloves (*Digitalis* spp.), blanket flowers

Pruning shears are handy for snipping off spent flowers that have thick or wiry stems.

(*Gaillardia* x *grandiflora*), phlox (*Phlox* spp.), sages (*Salvia* spp.), and yarrows. To reduce disease problems, be sure to remove the old blooms from disease-susceptible plants such as phlox, common sneezeweed (*Helenium autumnale*), and peonies.

Deadheading Made Easy

You can handle deadheading with a quick snip or a series of calculated cuts. Make individual cuts with a clean pair of hand clippers, sharp scissors, or a garden knife. These tools will cut cleanly, leaving healthy tissue and a quick-healing wound. However, with very soft-stemmed perennials, such as bleeding hearts (*Dicentra* spp.), the work may go faster if you pinch off old flower heads between your index finger and thumb.

No matter what tools you use, cut back to a leaf, bud, or another stem. Stubs of flowering stems are unattractive, as well as an open invitation for diseases. The exceptions are perennials with fine, wiry stems topped with flowers like thread-leaved coreopsis and mat formers like perennial candytuft (*Iberis sempervirens*) and moss pinks (*Phlox subulata*). When the flowers fade, you can shear off the top layer with grass clippers. The foliage and flower buds quickly fill in to hide the cut stems.

Special Tips

Some of the most beautiful garden flowers—the double-flowered pinks (*Dianthus* spp.), daylilies, and bearded irises—are also the most difficult to deadhead. These perennials bear their short-stemmed blooms in clusters at the end of each main flower stalk. Since the spent blooms are often packed tightly against the new buds, you need to clip off the old flowers carefully so you don't damage the buds.

Other perennials like phloxes and yarrows bear their flowers on longer flowering stems. They do not require as much detail work. Once the flowers fade, simply cut the entire stem back to the next cluster of flower buds developing. Often these are nestled at the base of a leaf or branch lower on the stem. If there are no more buds waiting to flower, cut the old flower stalk back to the ground or to a leafy portion of the stem.

When Not to Deadhead

Despite the advantages of deadheading, you may have good cause to skip it on occasion. Spare the seedpods of perennials that you want to self-sow, like wild columbines (*Aquilegia canadensis*) and foxgloves (*Digitalis* spp.). You may also want to leave attractive seedpods or cones, which can extend the beauty of certain perennials through the dormant season. Try this with the velvety black or orange-brown cones of coneflowers (*Rudbeckia* and *Echinacea* spp.), the glossy, dark seed clusters of blackberry lilies (*Belamcanda chinensis*), the dry, feathery plumes of astilbes, the russet pods of 'Autumn Joy' sedum (*Sedum* 'Autumn Joy'), and the papery "flowers" of Lenten roses (*Helleborus* x *orientalis*). You also may want to spare the plume-like seed heads of ornamental grasses that you grow with your perennials.

Pinching

Pinching is another form of pruning that can help keep your perennials looking their best. By removing the growing tip of the stem, you cut off the source of hormones that make that branch elongate; this frees buds lower on the stem to develop into side branches. It will make leggy perennials more bushy and compact, with better branching and more (although often smaller) blooms. Perennials like common sneezeweed (*Helenium autumnale*), boltonia (*Boltonia asteroides*), or 'Autumn Joy' sedum (*Sedum* 'Autumn Joy') that otherwise need staking will be able to stand on their own if you pinch them back.

Pinching and Flowering

The effect of pinching on plant shape is reliable. What you may have trouble determining is what pinching will do to the time of flowering. Usually it delays flowering by 1 or 2 weeks, which generally isn't a problem. For example, pinching a plant like Frikart's aster (*Aster* x *frikartii*), which begins to flower in late summer, will give the plant a better form and probably a better show of flowers. But pinching could cause a problem if you grow a late bloomer in a cold climate area with early fall frost. For instance, a late-September-flowering New York aster (*Aster novi-belgii*), pinched in June, might not bloom until early October. In this case, the flowers could open just in time to be hit by frost. Keep this flowering delay in mind when you decide which plants to pinch and when.

Carefully pinching the growing tip out of clumping perennials will promote more bushy growth.

Pointers for Easy Pinching

You want to pinch the plant when it is young enough to develop a full shape but not so early that later growth becomes scrawny over the shapely base. Also, pinch before flower buds develop. Otherwise, you could remove them all and lose the season's bloom.

For chrysanthemums and asters, you may need to pinch twice. Make the first pinch when shoots are about 6 inches (15 cm) tall. Repeat the pinching at 8 inches (20 cm), but not later than the end of June.

Pinching generally removes the top 1 or 2 inches (2.5 to 5 cm), down to just above a leaf or bud. Use a sharp pair of pruning shears or a garden knife to make clean cuts. If the stems are soft and pliable enough, you can also pinch with your finger and thumb.

If you tire of the pinching routine, look in nursery catalogs for newer cultivars that are shorter and bushier, needing little extra fuss on your part.

Cutting Back and Thinning

Like giving your plants a haircut, you can cut back long or straggly stems to make a plant tidier and to encourage it to produce healthy new growth. Cutting back (also known as shearing) differs from pinching because it is done after flowering and from deadheading because it can be more radical. Thinning involves removing whole stems, giving the remaining stems more room to expand and improving air circulation around the plant.

Cutting Back Perennials

If you have a small number of plants, use hand clippers to cut back each stem to just above a leaf or bud. You should remove one-third to one-half of the stem length, encouraging a neater shape and rebranching, while deadheading at the same time. For large gardens, some landscape contractors use a string trimmer. This method is certainly fast, although it might be too rough for more delicate or disease-prone perennials like pinks (*Dianthus* spp.).

Besides making them look neater, cutting plants back can also help control insect and disease outbreaks. Simply cut back diseased or insect-infested plants to the ground and dispose of the trimmings with household trash. The shoots may reemerge with clean and healthy

If your perennials look tattered after blooming, cut them back; they'll produce a fresh clump of foliage.

Columbines (*Aquilegia* spp.) are beautiful in bloom but decline after flowering. Cut them back to get new leaves.

foliage. This technique works well for controlling powdery mildew on bee balm (*Monarda didyma*), leafminers on columbines (*Aquilegia* spp.), and galls on goldenrods (*Solidago* spp.). Plants probably will not reflower during the year in which they have been subjected to this drastic treatment, but their foliage will look much more appealing for the rest of the season.

Fall cleanup is another common time to cut plants back severely. Remove old stems and leaves near the ground, eliminating pests' hiding places and making the plants look tidier. A few perennials, such as coneflowers (*Rudbeckia* and *Echinacea* spp.) and 'Autumn Joy' sedum (*Sedum* 'Autumn Joy'), are an exception to this rule. Their seed heads remain attractive during winter, so you may want to spare them during the fall cleanup and wait until spring to cut them back.

Thinning

Some mature clump-forming perennials send up such a thick crop of stems that they crowd and shade each other out. As a result, they flower sparsely, and the poor circulation within the clump makes them more susceptible to diseases. Thinning—removing about half of the crowded stems—can help such mildew-prone perennials as garden

Crowded clumps of stems may be more prone to disease. Removing some of the stems allows air to circulate.

phlox (*Phlox paniculata*), bee balm (*Monarda didyma*), and common sneezeweed (*Helenium autumnale*).

If your phlox has been mildewed in previous seasons, try radical thinning, leaving only four or five of the strongest stems. Prune the weaker shoots back to the ground when you can see how dense the clump will be but before it expends much energy in growth. The remaining strong stems should be more vigorous and often are less disease-prone as a result. Dividing large clumps is another way to encourage strong new growth.

Bee balms (*Monarda* spp.) are prone to powdery mildew. Cut back affected stems; clean ones will sprout.

Weeding

Like insects and diseases, weeds can pop up in even the most-well-cared-for gardens. The trick is to take care of the problem early, before the weeds get large enough to compete with your perennials for space, light, water, and nutrients.

How to Be Weed-wise

Weed control starts while you are preparing the bed for your new perennial garden. Removing the sod from the area and composting it will remove many of the existing weeds. As you dig, keep an eye out for the long white roots of spreading weeds. Thoroughly remove any of these roots; if you leave little pieces, roots can quickly sprout into new plants.

Once your perennials are established, you can control most weeds if you mulch and weed conscientiously for the first year or two. By the third year, your perennial clumps should be well filled in, leaving little room for weed invasion.

Perennial Weeds

Like the perennial flowers you're growing in the garden, perennial weeds will live for many years once they are established. What separates the weeds from the desirable plants is often the speed with which the weeds can spread. Many perennial

A key part of weed control is removing them before they set seed. A hand fork helps dig out stubborn weeds.

weeds, like bindweed and Canada thistle, have creeping underground stems, called rhizomes. These rhizomes can spread quickly in the loose, rich soil of your perennial garden, quickly engulfing your desirable plants. Other perennial weeds, like dandelions, have long, tough taproots. If you break off the top of the plant, a new one will quickly sprout from the root.

Thoroughly removing the roots of perennial weeds as you prepare the soil for planting will go a long way toward keeping these weeds at bay. Mulching and regular weeding will help prevent new perennial weeds from getting started.

If perennial weeds get out of control despite your best efforts, it's often easiest to just start the bed over. Dig up your good perennials and set them aside until you dig through the bed and remove all the fleshy roots of the weeds. Before you replant your perennials, make sure their clumps are free of weed roots, too; otherwise, the weeds will have an easy time reinvading your garden.

One of the most common weed problems in perennial gardens is lawn grass, which will creep in along the edges of beds and borders. Block invasion of grass by cutting along the garden's edge often with a sharp spade or edger, removing the errant sprigs of grass. Or take preventive action when you dig the bed: Add a metal, wood, stone, brick, or plastic edging to form a barrier around the perimeter of the garden. Sink the edging at least 4 to 6 inches (10 to 15 cm) deep to block creeping grass stems in their underground movement.

Annual Weeds

Annual weeds may not have the invasive roots of their perennial counterparts, but they will reproduce themselves hundreds of times over from seed, often growing fast and spreading far. The key to controlling annual weeds is to remove them from the garden before they set seed. Cut them off or scrape them out of the soil with a hoe or hand weeder. If the soil is soft or damp, you can easily pull the entire weed, root and all, by hand. Snip weeds with scissors if you suspect pulling would damage small or newly planted perennials that are nearby. Throw the weeds, as long as they are seed-free, into your compost pile.

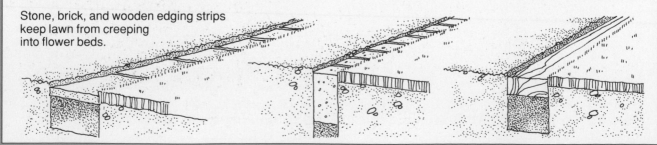

Stone, brick, and wooden edging strips keep lawn from creeping into flower beds.

Preventing and Controlling Pests and Diseases

Pests and diseases generally are not a big problem on perennials. You may never have to spray if you seek out the most disease-resistant species and cultivars and then plant them where they will thrive. Strong, healthy plants do not make easy targets for pests or diseases. Just as we are constantly exposed to cold and flu germs, plant pests, fungi, viruses, and bacteria are all around. They will infect weaker or stressed plants before harming vigorous perennials.

Pests and diseases are easiest to control if you catch them before they get out of hand. Inspecting your plants regularly will help you spot problems before they spread. If you do find a pest or disease problem, you'll need to properly identify it. Only then can you decide how to treat it: by handpicking, trapping, or by some other organically acceptable control.

Identifying Some Common Pests

Knowing about the most common perennial pests will help you notice and identify infestations on your perennials. You can identify insects by how the larvae or adults look and also by the kind of damage they do to the plant.

Aphids Aphids are tiny, soft-bodied, pear-shaped insects that feed on a wide variety of perennials. They tend to cluster near the growing tips and on the undersides of leaves. Large groups of aphids can cause the foliage, flowers, or shoots of perennials to twist, pucker, or drop, and they leave a trail of sugary excrement (called honeydew), which is sticky and often harbors a black, sooty mold. Aphids also can spread viral diseases as they feed.

Japanese Beetles These shiny, metallic blue-green beetles with bronze wing covers feed on many different perennials, including hollyhocks (*Alcea rosea*), New York asters (*Aster novi-belgii*), foxgloves (*Digitalis* spp.), and purple coneflowers (*Echinacea purpurea*). They will eat the green part of leaves, so that only the leaf veins remain, and will also chew on flowers. The grubs are white with brown heads; they feed mostly on lawn grass roots.

Leafminers Leafminers are the tiny larvae of small flies. The larvae tunnel within perennial foliage, leaving light-colored trails that you can see from the top of the leaf. Leafminers can be a problem on columbines (*Aquilegia* spp.), chrysanthemums, and delphiniums.

Mites These tiny, spider-like pests will attack many perennials, especially when the weather becomes hot and dry. The brown, red, or green mites suck the plant sap from the underside of a leaf, causing it to curl and its upper surface to turn speckled, pale, and dull-looking.

Plant Bugs Tarnished plant bugs are green or brown with yellow triangles on their forewings; four-lined plant bugs are yellowish green with four black stripes down their back. Both of these insects will leave irregular holes or sunken brown spots in the middle of leaves. They also cause distorted growth on the leaves or growing tips of many perennials.

Slugs and Snails Slugs (slimy mollusks) and snails (slimy mollusks with a coiled shell) can be a problem anywhere the soil stays damp, especially in shady gardens. They crawl up on perennials and chew ragged holes into the leaves, stems, and flowers. They can eat the entire plant this way.

Thrips Thrips are minute, quick-moving insects that feed on several kinds of flowers and leaves, giving the plant tissue a pale, silvery look in damaged areas. Eventually the infected plant parts can wither and die.

Other Pests You also may find mealybugs (slow-moving, soft-bodied insects hidden beneath a white,

Found on stems, leaves, and buds, aphids are common perennial pests.

Japanese beetles chew holes in leaves. They are fond of hollyhocks.

Spider mites make tiny webs and suck plant sap, causing stippled leaves.

cottony shield) under the leaves and along stems; leafhoppers (which look like tiny grasshoppers) on stems and leaves; borers (fat pink caterpillars), which tunnel down the leaves of bearded irises and eat large cavities into the rhizomes; and cutworms (fat, dark-colored caterpillars), which chew through the stems of young seedlings. For more information on pests of other perennials, check the "Plant by Plant Guide," starting on page 78.

Controlling Pests

Once you have figured out the identity of a problem-causing pest, you can choose the best method for controlling it.

Handpicking If you only find a few pests among your perennials, you can pick them off the plants by hand and crush them under your heel. This is effective for large, slow-moving pests like slugs and snails, Japanese beetles, borers, and cutworms.

Grapefruit rinds make great slug traps. Lift the rinds daily and remove any slugs that you find.

Traps and Barriers Avoid garden damage by catching pests in traps or deterring them with barricades. Sticky traps are very effective for some pests: Yellow sticky traps will attract aphids, while white traps will catch tarnished plant bugs. You can either buy premade sticky traps at a garden center or make your own by painting pieces of wood or cardboard the appropriate color and coating them with petroleum jelly. Hang the traps on stakes throughout your garden and clean or replace them as needed to keep them effective.

You can trap slugs with a shallow container of beer set in the soil so the top rim is at ground level; the slugs will crawl in and drown. Surrounding plants with a ring of diatomaceous earth (a powdery material composed of tiny, spiny-shelled algae) will also keep slugs and cutworms at bay; renew the barrier after each rain.

Biological Controls You can use biological weapons like Bacillus thuringiensis (BT), a bacterial disease, and milky disease to eliminate pests without harming people, animals, or beneficial insects. To control damage by many different kinds of caterpillars, spray or dust foliage with BT. (Don't use this material if you want to encourage butterflies in your garden, though; it will kill the larvae of attractive butterflies as well as those of pests.) Another bacterial disease, known as milky disease, attacks Japanese beetle grubs. Apply this granulated material over your lawn and water it into the soil, where it will infect the grubs.

Beneficial Insects When you plant a number of

Spittlebugs (nymphal froghoppers) suck plant sap, causing stunted growth.

Leafminer larvae feed within leaves, causing winding tunnels.

Tiny thrips attack leaves and flowers, giving plant parts a silvery appearance.

Praying mantids devour many other insects—pests and beneficials alike. They even prey on each other!

Lady beetle larvae are voracious predators of aphids and other soft-bodied pests. The adults are also beneficial.

different perennials, most of which produce nectar and pollen, you will attract many beneficial insects that will eat or parasitize pests. In a healthy garden, natural populations of beneficial insects will go a long way in keeping pests under control.

Organically Acceptable Insecticides

If, after you've tried other options, you still can't control a pest, you can try some of the less toxic insecticides that come from natural sources. These tend to break down faster than chemical pesticides and leave less environmental residue. Make sure you apply these products according to package directions and at the susceptible time in the pest's life cycle.

Insecticidal soaps, made of the potassium salts of fatty acids, will kill soft-bodied insects such as aphids, leafhoppers, mealybugs, and plant bugs. You can also spray with new highly refined horticultural oils to coat

plant leaves and to smother insects like aphids, mealybugs, leafminers, mites, and leafhoppers. Read the label carefully and apply only when the weather is cool. Before spraying a whole plant with either soap or oil, spray just a few leaves and wait a few days. If the leaves show any sort of damage, such as discoloring or spotting, find another control method.

Among the botanicals, which are insecticides derived from plants, pyrethrins are effective on some beetles, caterpillars, aphids, and bugs. Rotenone will control beetles, borers, aphids, and red spider mites. Ryania is effective against caterpillars and beetles. Sabadilla, another botanical, is a powerful insecticide; use it as a last resort for tough pests like thrips. Botanical pesticides have broad-spectrum activity, meaning that they will harm beneficial as well as pest insects.

Slugs and snails chew large holes in leaves. Hostas are a favorite target.

Cutworms live in the soil. They chew through the stems of young seedlings.

Mealybugs commonly attack leaves and stems, but they also feed on roots.

Plant viruses cause discolored foliage and distorted growth. Remove and destroy infected plants.

Identifying Some Common Diseases

Perennials that are sited in ideal growing conditions seldom suffer much from diseases. Sometimes, though, the weather or other influences beyond your control will provide the right conditions for fungal, bacterial, or viral diseases to attack your plants. Being aware of the most common diseases will help you take the appropriate prevention and control measures for your conditions.

Fungal Diseases Many different fungi attack perennials, causing a variety of symptoms. Rot fungi can affect perennial roots, crowns, stems, and flowers, usually making them turn soft and mushy. You will see rot most commonly on perennial roots growing in wet, heavy soil or on crowns planted too deeply in the garden. Among the most susceptible perennials are baby's-breath, balloon flowers (*Platycodon grandiflorus*), coreopsis (*Coreopsis* spp.), delphiniums, irises, and garden phlox (*Phlox paniculata*).

Botrytis blight is another common fungal disease. It attacks flowers that open during wet weather, making them blacken and curl downward. Peonies, irises, and dahlias are especially susceptible.

Fungal leaf spots infect perennials such as chrysanthemums, columbines (*Aquilegia* spp.), daylilies, peonies, and asters. These leaf spots disfigure foliage and, if not caught, can cause widespread defoliation and even plant death.

Downy mildew and powdery mildew are fungal diseases that form a furry, white coating on the leaves of perennials like garden phlox, bee balm (*Monarda didyma*), asters, poppies, dahlias, and delphiniums. These diseases are unattractive and can cause severely infected leaves to drop.

Rust diseases also attack perennials, including hollyhocks (*Alcea rosea*), chrysanthemums, and asters. They turn the foliage a rusty color, often stunting growth and distorting leaf development.

Bacterial Diseases Bacteria also can cause diseases characterized by wilting, rotting tissues, or root or lower-stem galls. Peonies and poppies can get a bacterial blight, which causes black spots on the leaves, flowers, and stems. Dahlias and baby's-breath can be infected with bacterial crown gall, which stunts growth and can kill the plants. Coral bells (*Heuchera sanguinea*) can be attacked by a bacterial stem rot.

Viral Diseases Viruses can cause perennial leaves or flowers to turn yellow or mottled yellow and green. They cause stunted growth and poor flowering or sudden wilting and death. Viruses are carried from plant to plant by sucking insects, such as aphids and leafhoppers, or by garden tools like pruning shears.

Stem rot usually starts at the base of the plant and works upward.

Downy mildew produces white spots on the undersides of leaves.

Powdery mildew is a common fungal disease causing a dusty white coating.

Viral mosaic can attack chrysanthemums, dahlias, delphiniums, pinks (*Dianthus* spp.), peonies, and poppies. Aster yellows, a similar disease, infects baby's-breath, balloon flowers, bellflowers (*Campanula* spp.), chrysanthemums, coreopsis, and delphiniums.

Controlling Diseases

Good garden hygiene and proper plant selection go a long way toward preventing and controlling diseases. If you remove faded foliage in fall and cut back flowers after they bloom, you'll remove common sites of disease attack. If soilborne disease is a particular problem in your area, grow perennials in well-drained soil to reduce root diseases. Also, try not to damage the plant roots when you work the soil or weed.

Careful watering can help reduce disease outbreaks. Whenever possible, avoid wetting plant leaves. If foliage stays wet overnight, fungal spores can germinate and attack leaves. Overhead watering and even walking through wet foliage can transfer disease from plant to plant. Use a ground-level irrigation system, like trickle or drip irrigation, and don't work in the garden when plants are still wet from rain.

If the weather is cold and wet or hot and humid—conditions encouraging disease—and if you grow susceptible plants, you may get an outbreak of diseases in the garden. When a disease does strike, remove damaged parts promptly—before the disease can spread—and throw them away with the household trash. This simple technique can go a long way in controlling diseases.

If your garden has had problems with diseases in past years, you may want to make a preventive treatment with organically acceptable materials. Antitranspirants—leaf coatings ordinarily used to protect broad-leaved evergreens during winter—may reduce fungal disease problems. Try dusting foliage with powdered sulfur to prevent mildew, rust, and leaf

Leaf spots can be caused by either fungi or bacteria. Removing affected foliage may stop the spread of disease.

spots. A baking soda spray (1 teaspoon of baking soda to 1 quart [1 l] of water) can prevent and control some fungal problems. Seaweed-based fertilizer sprays and compost tea can also help prevent diseases. If a disease becomes rampant and even sprays do not help, replace the plant with something that is not susceptible—a different species or resistant cultivar.

In most cases, diseases are not a big problem in the perennial garden. Choosing the right plants, preparing the soil thoroughly, and planting at the proper spacing all contribute to problem-free perennials. Inspect new additions carefully for any signs of disease before setting them loose in the garden. If you have any doubts, consider throwing the plant away or plant it in an isolated spot in the yard. If it seems all right at the end of the season, move it into the garden. If it's diseased, dispose of it.

Rusts produce orange or yellowish spots on leaves and stems.

Fungal wilts cause leaves and stems to droop, giving a wilted appearance.

Crown gall is a bacterial disease that causes swollen growths on stems.

PROPAGATING PERENNIALS

If you have enjoyed planting and maintaining your perennial garden, then you probably will like starting your own plants as well. Propagation is a great way to start or expand a garden on a tight budget. In this chapter, you'll learn how to propagate most perennials easily and with minimal equipment.

Depending on which propagation method you choose, you can end up with a few to a few hundred new perennials from a single plant. Create several good-sized new plants from one large specimen by division. By taking stem or root cuttings, you can get dozens of new plants. Or start perennials from seed and you may end up with hundreds of plants from a single packet.

When you're considering a method, decide how important it is that the offspring resemble the parent plant. With vegetative methods of propagation, such as division, layering, and cuttings, you will obtain an exact clone of the parent plant in nearly every case. This is especially important when you want to propagate cultivars or hybrids, which usually produce variable offspring when grown from seed.

Seed is a good way to propagate perennials when you want species or varieties. There are also a few cultivars that come true from seed, including 'Snow Lady' Shasta daisy (*Chrysanthemum* x *superbum* 'Snow Lady'), 'Nora Barlow' columbine (*Aquilegia* x *hybrida* 'Nora Barlow'), 'Purple Cascade' rock cress (*Aubretia* 'Purple Cascade'), and Pacific Giant hybrid primroses (*Primula polyantha* 'Pacific Giants'). Use seed-grown plants in informal gardens where differences in height, foliage and flower color, and bloom time don't matter or can even be considered an advantage. When uniformity matters in a formal garden, a row, or an edging, use vegetatively propagated plants to get the best results.

When you are looking for perennial seed, you will find two types—open-pollinated and hybrid seed. There are natural hybrids, such as the Lenten rose (*Helleborus* x *orientalis*), and there are commercial hybrids, the result of controlled breeding. Hybrids tend to be more uniform than open-pollinated plants, but they are not always as consistent as vegetatively propagated plants. If you buy the seed of a hybrid and want more of that plant, you must buy more seed from the company or propagate the originals vegetatively. It will not come true from seed that you collect from your own plants.

Another important issue in choosing a propagation method is how long each method takes to produce flowering plants. Perennial seedlings and (to a lesser extent) cuttings will take a season or more—sometimes several years—to reach flowering size. Even when they do flower, the display may be sparse until the plants reach substantial size. If you want quick results, use the division method or choose fast-growing perennials that may flower during their first year of life if you start them early indoors. Divisions generally recover quickly and often bloom the same season they're planted. For fast-maturing cuttings, try asters and chrysanthemums. Perennials that could bloom from seed the first year after a winter sowing include columbines, delphiniums, 'Snow Lady' Shasta daisy, (*Chrysanthemum* x *superbum* 'Snow Lady'), and purple coneflowers (*Echinacea purpurea*).

Opposite: You can propagate many perennials by more than one method. Root cuttings and division are two ways to increase oriental poppies (*Papaver orientale*), depending on the season and how many plants you want.

Perennials from Seed

Seed starting is a great way to stretch a tight budget if you don't mind waiting for a show. Growing your own seedlings allows you to select unusual species and choice varieties that you can't buy at greenhouses and nurseries. However, if you buy seed of a cultivar, like 'Goldsturm' coneflower (*Rudbeckia fulgida* 'Gold-sturm'), the seedlings will be variable and may not all live up to the high performance values of vegetatively propagated stock.

Always use high-quality seed, packed for the current year. Buy from a reputable seed company that offers high germination rates. You can find out the rates from the percentage of viable (live) seeds listed on the package. If you have any seed left over from last year or home-collected seed, try sprouting a few before you sow a whole packet. Roll the seeds in a moist paper towel and enclose the rolled towel in a plastic bag. Keep the bag warm and watch for germination in the next several weeks. If only half of the seeds sprout, you will know you need to sow twice as much seed to get the number of plants you want.

Sowing Seed

Just as wild and self-sowing perennials do naturally, you can sow seed directly outdoors in a well-prepared bed. Cover seed to the depth indicated on the package in loose soil and keep the soil moist until the seedlings begin to emerge.

Although direct sowing is certainly the easiest technique, you will probably discover that it is not the most dependable. When planted directly into your garden, your seed can be eaten by birds or insects or attacked by fungi. They may get too cold or too hot, too wet or too dry. For a better survival rate

Create a minigreenhouse by covering a container with clear plastic.

and an earlier start than direct seeding offers you, start seedlings indoors under fluorescent lights or in a sunny, south-facing window.

Depending on the size of the seed and the speed of growth, you should start easy-germinating seed indoors 6 to 12 weeks before the last spring frost. In warm climates, start fast-germinating seed in summer to set out in the cool of fall and winter.

Potting-up Seedlings

1. Gather your materials together in a clean, shady spot.
2. Put some moist potting mix in the base of the new pot.
3. Squeeze the container gently to loosen the roots.
4. Carefully slide the plant from the container.
5. Center the plant in the new pot and fill in with moist potting mix.

1

2

3

4

5

Shallow trays (also known as flats) are excellent containers for starting lots of seedlings.

Other perennials will take much longer to germinate. You may need to expose the seed to a chilling period by placing the sown seed in the refrigerator for a certain number of weeks. If a perennial needs special treatment, it will be indicated on the seed packet or in the "Plant by Plant Guide," starting on page 78.

Sow your perennial seed in a thoroughly moistened, sterile, peat-based seedling mix. This lightweight medium encourages rooting and discourages root diseases. Start seed in small individual pots or peat pots, or save space by sowing seed in rows in flats (shallow plastic or wooden trays). Sprinkle tiny seeds lightly on top of the seedling mix and press them gently into the surface. Push larger seeds into the soil as deeply as they are wide. Cover the container with clear plastic wrap to keep the soil evenly moist until the seeds germinate, but make sure the plastic doesn't touch the soil.

After sowing, keep the medium moist and between 60° and 75°F (15.5° and 30°C). Warmth-loving perennials will come up most quickly at the higher end of the temperature range while cool-season perennials may germinate faster at the lower end. Avoid rapid temperature changes, which can stunt growth.

It's easy to start plants in peat pots. When seedlings are garden-size, pop them in the ground, pot and all.

With a little patience, you can have nursery-size plants for seed-packet prices.

Caring for Seedlings

When your seedlings emerge, move them into bright light and remove the plastic. Water as often as necessary to keep the soil moist and to prevent wilting. When you water, set the container of seedlings in a tray of water so the growing medium can soak up moisture without disrupting the seedlings. If you water from overhead, you may wash the seedlings away.

If you have sown seed in flats or trays, move seedlings to their own pots when they have two sets of true leaves in addition to the bottom set of fleshy seed leaves. You can move most perennials into 4-inch (10 cm) pots if you intend to plant them outdoors in a couple of weeks. If not, you should keep moving the plants up to larger containers to prevent roots from binding. Feed the young plants lightly with compost tea or liquid seaweed. If the weather is cold or hot, leave the transplants indoors under lights or in the window. If it is relatively mild, move the plants out into a cold frame or another sheltered area.

Layering

Some plants are easy to root while still attached to the mother plant, a technique called layering. Burying a section of the stem encourages roots to form at each buried leaf node (the place where a leaf joins the stem). Layering does take up some space, since you need to bury the attached stem close to the parent plant. You won't get many new plants from this method (usually only one per stem), and it can take weeks or months for the stem to root. But layering is easy to do, and the resulting plants will be exact duplicates of the parent plant.

You can use this technique with plants that have flexible stems or a creeping habit and the ability to root at the leaf axils. Good candidates for layering include pinks (*Dianthus* spp.), cranesbills (*Geranium* spp.), wall rock cress (*Arabis caucasica*), snow-in-summer (*Cerastium tomentosum*), and bellflowers (*Campanula* spp.). Layering will not work on daylilies, ornamental grasses, hostas, irises, peonies, or other bushy perennials.

How It Works

The first step to successful layering is finding a suitable stem. If the plant is upright, look for one or several long stems that bend easily to the ground; if the plant has a creeping habit, any stem is suitable. Leave the top three sets of leaves on the stem to nourish the plant, but remove the leaves from the stem for 2 to 7 inches (5 to 17.5 cm) below the top greenery. Strip the leaves from at least two nodes (leaf joints), carefully leaving the dormant buds undamaged. Bend the stem down and see where the stripped area will contact the soil. Loosen the soil in that area about 4 inches (10 cm) deep and water it. Bury the stem in the loosened soil, holding it in place with a bent wire pin, and firm the soil over the stem. The stem should be buried 2 to 3 inches (5 to 7.5 cm) deep with the leafy tip still exposed. If you are layering an upright shoot, encourage the tip to return to its upright position by tying it to a stake if necessary.

Keep the area moist and mulched while the buried stem roots. Depending on the temperature and species, it will take several weeks to several months. The easiest way to layer is to leave the plant in place until the following season. If you want faster results, check its progress by gently uncovering the stem and looking for roots or tugging lightly to see if the shoot has become more secure in the ground. Once the roots reach about 1 inch (2.5 cm) long you can cut the shoot free from the mother plant. Wait several weeks for more rooting, then dig and transplant the new plant.

Reproduction by Division

Many perennials flower best when they're young, and their flower production drops as they mature. To keep them flowering well, you must divide them—dig them up and split the root mass into pieces. In addition to reviving older plants, division is the easiest and fastest technique for propagating perennials. It's also a good way to keep fast-spreading perennials under control. Plus, you'll have lots of extra plants to share with friends and neighbors.

Simple Layering

Layering is an easy way to propagate many perennials, especially those that naturally tend to creep along the soil. Spring is a good time to start a layer, although it can work anytime during the growing season.

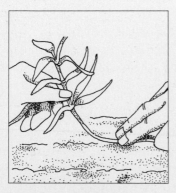

1. Select a flexible stem and bend it down to the soil.

2. Use a wire pin to secure the stem, then cover it with soil.

3. Dig up the rooted layer and transplant it to another spot.

Step-by-step Division

Division is a fast and reliable way to propagate many clump-forming perennials, including daylilies, chrysanthemums, and irises. It may not work well with more sensitive perennials, like sea hollies (*Eryngium* spp.) and gas plant (*Dictamnus albus*).

1. Use shears or your hands to divide the perennial clump into several smaller pieces.

2. Make sure each new piece has its own roots as well as some top growth.

3. Replant the pieces immediately, water them well, and apply a light layer of mulch.

How often you need to propagate depends on why you're dividing. If you're using division to propagate, it depends on how many new plants you want and how fast the plant is growing. Divide annually to retard aggressive spreaders like bee balm (*Monarda didyma*), bigroot geranium (*Geranium macrorrhizum*), obedient plant (*Physostegia virginiana*), and yarrows. If you want to rejuvenate your perennials, you can divide them whenever flowering starts to decline. To keep performance high, you can divide asters and painted daisies (*Chrysanthemum coccineum*) every year or two. Some perennials, including peonies, daylilies, Siberian irises (*Iris sibirica*), and astilbes, can go for years without division.

To divide a big clump, try prying it apart with two spading forks. If that doesn't work, try a saw or ax.

How to Divide

Begin dividing by digging up the root system. Shake off as much loose soil as possible and remove any dead leaves and stems. You may also want to wash most of the soil off the roots and crown so you can see the roots and buds clearly.

Perennials with fibrous roots, such as chrysanthemums and asters, are the easiest to dig and divide. You can pull them apart with your hands or cut them with a spade. Others, like daylilies and astilbe, can grow woody with age. You may have to pry these roots apart with a crowbar or two garden forks held back to back or cut them with a saw or ax. Discard the woody parts, which will not reroot well.

To renew an existing planting, slice the plant into halves, thirds, or quarters. Discard the old, woody growth from the center of the clump and replant the vigorous outer portions.

When you want to build a larger stock of new plants, you can divide perennials into smaller pieces. Just make sure you keep several buds or growing shoots on the sections you will replant. Look for the buds growing along the length of the roots or clustered together in a central crown.

Work compost and other soil amendments back into the soil before replanting. Reset divisions at the same level at which the original clump was growing.

Cuttings

Cuttings—small pieces of stem or root—are another way to propagate many perennials. Cuttings take more care than other methods, like layering and division. But if you like a challenge, you can use cuttings to create many new plants from your existing perennials. Cuttings are a good way to propagate perennials that are difficult to divide and cultivars that don't come true from seed.

Stem Cuttings

Stem cuttings are effective for many kinds of perennials. Try perennials such as wall rock cress (*Arabis caucasica*), chrysanthemums, common sneezeweed (*Helenium autumnale*), garden phlox (*Phlox paniculata*), pinks (*Dianthus* spp.), showy stonecrop (*Sedum spectabile*), and spike speedwell (*Veronica spicata*).

Taking Cuttings You should take stem cuttings when perennials are in vegetative growth: either in spring before blooming or after flowering is finished for the season. You should select a healthy medium-soft stem—one that is not soft, new growth or hard, old growth—from the lower portion of the plant, where shoots are more likely to root quickly. Cut the stems free with a sharp, clean knife or pair of shears.

Preparing the Cuttings Slice the stem into sections between 2 and 4 inches (5 to 10 cm) long, so that each cutting has two or three sets of leaves on the top and a couple of nodes (leaf joints) stripped of leaves on

Taking Stem Cuttings

1. Select a strong young shoot. Use sharp pruning shears to make a clean cut just below a node.

2. Snip the leaves off the bottom half of the cutting, exposing two to three leaf nodes.

3. Insert the bottom half of the prepared cutting into a container of moist potting mix.

4. Cover with an upended jar or with plastic to hold in moisture. Set in a bright place out of direct sun.

Taking Root Cuttings

Root cuttings are a bit trickier than stem cuttings, but they can work just as well with a little care. As you collect the roots, place them in a plastic bag to protect them from drying winds. Use a clean, sharp knife to minimize damage to the root tissue as you prepare the cuttings. Avoid overwatering.

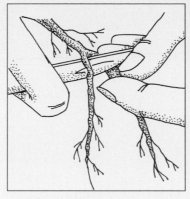

1. Cut a healthy-looking, pencil-thick root piece.

2. Make a straight cut at the end that was closest to the crown.

3. Make a sloping cut at the other end of the cutting.

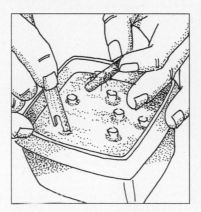

4. Carefully insert cuttings, pointed end down, in a pot.

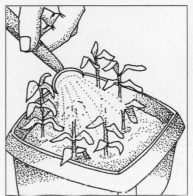

5. Keep cuttings evenly moist until they start to grow; then transplant.

the bottom. These nodes will produce roots when you insert them into a pot of moist, sterile peat-based growing mix.

Some stem cuttings, like those from blue false indigo (*Baptisia australis*), will root more easily if you dip their lower ends in a commercially available rooting hormone powder. However, if you find the right moisture, light, and warmth levels, most perennials will root without this treatment. Make a hole in the mix with a clean pencil and slide the cutting in. Firm the mix around it and water to settle the cutting into the soil.

Caring for Cuttings Cover the container with a clear plastic-wrap tent. Prop the plastic above the plant foliage to avoid rot. Keep the cuttings in a warm place and in indirect light until they root, about 2 to 4 weeks. When they begin to grow, remove the plastic and move the plants into brighter light.

To determine if the cuttings have rooted, look to see if roots are emerging from the pot's drainage hole. You can also tug gently on the stem—if you meet resistance, the cuttings have rooted. Transplant the rooted cuttings into larger containers or a nursery bed to grow them to garden size.

Root Cuttings

Less common than stem cuttings, root cuttings are another way to produce new plants that are usually identical to the parent plant. Root cuttings are suitable for several kinds of perennials, including Siberian bugloss (*Anchusa azurea*), oriental poppies (*Papaver orientale*), and garden phlox (*Phlox paniculata*).

Take root cuttings from fall to early spring, while the parent plant is dormant. Carefully lift the plant from the garden and wash the soil from the roots. Using a sharp, clean knife, cut off a few pencil-thick roots close to the crown. Cut each root into 2- to 4-inch (5 to 10 cm) pieces, making a straight cut at the top (the end that was closest to the crown) and a slanted cut at the bottom. Insert the cuttings into a pot filled with moist, sterile potting mix, so that the flat top of each cutting is level with or slightly below the surface of the mix. Place the cuttings in a cold frame until they root and then pot them individually. Once the plants reach the desired size, move them into the garden.

PLANT BY PLANT GUIDE

The "Plant by Plant Guide" is arranged in an easy-to-use, quick-reference format. This handy alphabetical listing contains everything you need to know to successfully plant and maintain a wide variety of perennials. (See "How to Use This Book" on page 10 for further details on how to use the "Plant by Plant Guide.")

All the perennials are listed alphabetically by their botanical names with their common names displayed prominently. Each perennial is also illustrated with a full-color photograph to make identification easy.

The entries include information on the ideal climatic zone for each perennial. You need to refer to the USDA Plant Hardiness Zone Map on page 154 to find out which zone you live in. It's important to choose perennials that grow well in your area. There is also information on the ideal position for your perennials—whether they prefer sun or shade and also what type of soil conditions they need.

For each plant, you'll find details on flower color, flowering time, and height and spread—essential information to make garden planning easier. You'll also learn about the cultivation requirements, including when to divide or thin plants, whether they need staking, and when to fertilize.

Each entry gives details on how and when to propagate, so you'll have lots of perennials to fill your gardens and share with friends. Seed sowing times are given, and other propagation methods like root cuttings, division, and stem cuttings are also covered.

In addition, the entries tell you how to deal with pests and diseases using organic methods. Being able to identify common problems will help prevent pests and diseases from becoming a big problem.

"Landscape Use" will help you with your garden planning. This is where you'll find details on how to use each perennial in your overall garden design as well as the names of other plants that are attractive and compatible companions.

To get the most out of this guide, refer to it regularly throughout the year. If you're planning a new garden or sprucing up an existing one, browse through the entries to get ideas for different plants to try and to see if they will adapt to the conditions you have available. During the growing season, look up plants you already have to remind yourself about their maintenance needs. By selecting appropriate plants and providing the right care, you'll be rewarded with a beautiful perennial garden that will grow and thrive for years to come.

Opposite: With so many wonderful perennials to choose from, how do you decide which are best for you? First, remember the conditions your garden has to offer, and then look for plants adapted to those situations. Have a sunny, well-drained spot? Try these colorful bearded irises for early summer color.

Acanthus mollis Acanthaceae	*Achillea filipendulina* Compositae

BEAR'S-BREECH

FERN-LEAVED YARROW

Bear's-breech is a robust plant with lustrous evergreen leaves, 1–2 feet (30–60 cm) long and edged with jagged teeth. It grows from a stout crown with thick, fleshy roots.

Fern-leaved yarrow bears flat-topped heads of tiny flowers on dozens of tall, leafy stems. This aromatic herb grows from fibrous roots and has deeply incised, ferny, olive green leaves.

FLOWER COLOR: Unusual 1-inch (2.5 cm) flowers with three white petals and overarching purple hoods carried in tall spikes.

FLOWERING TIME: Late spring or summer; flowers open sequentially up the spike.

HEIGHT AND SPREAD: 2½–4 feet (75–120 cm) tall; 3 feet (90 cm) wide. Spreads to form broad clumps.

TEMPERATURE REQUIREMENTS: Zones 8–10. Sensitive to winter frost and to hot, humid weather. Produces foliage in colder zones but the flower buds are usually killed.

POSITION: Evenly moist, humus-rich soil. Full sun to partial shade.

CULTIVATION: Mulch after the ground freezes in winter and remove mulch gradually in spring to protect plants from heaving. Keep moist; dry soil will reduce the size of the leaves.

PROPAGATION: Divide plants in spring when they first emerge or take root cuttings in spring or late fall. Roots left in the ground when plants are divided will form new shoots.

PEST AND DISEASE PREVENTION: Deter slugs with barrier strips of diatomaceous earth; bait them with pans of beer set flush with the soil surface.

LANDSCAPE USE: Use bear's-breeches as foundation plantings or as bold accents in formal and informal gardens. Combine with fine-textured plants like yarrow for added contrast.

FLOWER COLOR: Dozens of tightly packed golden yellow flowers cluster in heads 4–5 inches (10–12.5 cm) across.

FLOWERING TIME: Summer. Flowers last for several weeks; plants rebloom if deadheaded.

HEIGHT AND SPREAD: 3–4 feet (90–120 cm) tall; 3 feet (90 cm) wide. Forms broad, tight clumps.

TEMPERATURE REQUIREMENTS: Zones 3–9. Thrives in low to moderate summer humidity.

POSITION: Average, dry to moist, well-drained soil. Full sun to light shade. Overly rich soil promotes luxuriant growth but weak stems.

CULTIVATION: Fern-leaved yarrow is a tough, easy-care perennial. Plants spread rapidly and need frequent division. Lift and divide clumps every 3 years to keep plants vigorous.

PROPAGATION: Take tip cuttings in spring or early summer. Divide in early spring or fall. Replant strong, healthy divisions into soil that has been enriched with organic matter.

PEST AND DISEASE PREVENTION: Plants develop powdery mildew, a cottony white coating on the leaves, especially in areas with warm humid nights. Rot causes stems to blacken and topple over. Remove and destroy all affected parts and dust plants with sulfur.

LANDSCAPE USE: Plant fern-leaved yarrow at the front or middle of formal perennial borders or with

AZURE MONKSHOOD

Summer-blooming common yarrow offers finely cut, deep green foliage and colorful flowers. It can be invasive in the border; try it in a meadow or informal garden.

Azure monkshood is a graceful plant with lush, three-lobed, dissected leaves, sturdy stems, and hooded flowers. All parts of the plant are poisonous when ingested.

grasses in wildflower meadows and other informal gardens. Use them in cutting gardens or on dry, sunny banks to control erosion.

CULTIVARS: 'Gold Plate' is taller than the species with 6-inch (15 cm) deep yellow flower heads on 6-foot (1.8 m) stems. 'Parker's Variety' grows 3–4 feet (90–120 cm) tall, with golden yellow flowers on self-supporting stems.

OTHER SPECIES:

A. x 'Coronation Gold' grows 3 feet (90 cm) tall with stout self-supporting stems, gray-green leaves, and 5-inch (12.5 cm) wide clusters of mustard yellow flowers.

A. millefolium, common yarrow, grows 1–2½ feet (30–75 cm) tall. White, pink, or red flowers are produced on stout stems for several months in summer. Plants may spread rapidly and become invasive. Choose a named selection such as 'New White', 'Cerise Queen', or 'Fire King'. The closely related Galaxy series of new yarrows arose from hybrids with *A. taygetea*. Plants resemble common yarrow with 2–3-inch (5–7.5 cm) flower heads on sturdy stems. Colors range from creamy yellow to salmon-rose and brick red. Flowers fade with age, giving the plants a multicolored appearance.

A. x 'Moonshine' is a popular hybrid. It grows 1–2 feet (30–60 cm) tall, with soft blue-gray foliage and sulfur yellow flowers.

FLOWER COLOR: Deep blue hooded flowers in dense spikes.

FLOWERING TIME: Late summer and fall.

HEIGHT AND SPREAD: 2–3 feet (60–90 cm) tall; 2 feet (60 cm) wide. Open and somewhat vase-shaped, especially in shade.

TEMPERATURE REQUIREMENTS: Zones 3–7. Prefers climates with cool summer nights and warm days with low humidity.

POSITION: Fertile, humus-rich, moist but well-drained soil. Full sun to light shade; afternoon shade in warmer zones.

CULTIVATION: Dislikes disturbance once established. Space 2–3 feet (60–90 cm) apart with the crowns just below the surface. Take care not to damage the brittle roots. Divide if plants become overcrowded.

PROPAGATION: Divide crowns in fall or early spring. Replant strong, healthy divisions into soil that has been enriched with organic matter.

PEST AND DISEASE PREVENTION: Crowns will rot if soil is wet and temperatures are hot. Site plants properly to avoid problems.

LANDSCAPE USE: Plant azure monkshood near the middle or rear of borders with other fall-blooming perennials and ornamental grasses or in groups with fruiting shrubs like the *Viburnum* species.

CULTIVARS: 'Barker's Variety' has large deep blue flowers.

| *Ajuga reptans* | Labiatae | *Alcea rosea* | Malvaceae |

COMMON BUGLEWEED

HOLLYHOCK

Common bugleweed is a low, rosette-forming groundcover that spreads by creeping, aboveground stems to form broad, dense mats. The spoon-shaped leaves are evergreen in mild climates.

FLOWER COLOR: Tiered whorls of small, intense blue flowers on stalks 6–10 inches (15–25 cm) long.

FLOWERING TIME: Late spring and early summer.

HEIGHT AND SPREAD: 4–10 inches (10–25 cm) tall; 8–10 inches (20–25 cm) wide. Clumps may spread to several feet across from a single plant.

TEMPERATURE REQUIREMENTS: Zones 3–9. Tolerates heat, humidity, and cold.

POSITION: Average to humus-rich, moist but well-drained soil. Will not tolerate extended drought or excessive moisture. Full sun to light shade.

CULTIVATION: Plant in spring or fall. Spreads rapidly to form a dense weed-proof groundcover and may be somewhat invasive, especially in lawns.

PROPAGATION: Propagate by division anytime during the growing season or from seed sown in spring.

PEST AND DISEASE PREVENTION: Provide good drainage and air circulation to prevent crown rot, which causes patches to wither and die out.

LANDSCAPE USE: Use as a groundcover under trees and shrubs or for edging beds.

CULTIVARS: 'Atropurpurea' has bronze-purple leaves. 'Burgundy Glow' has white, pink, and green foliage. 'Catlin's Giant' has large bronze leaves. 'Silver Beauty' has gray-green leaves with white edges.

Hollyhocks are tall, coarse biennials or short-lived perennials with rounded or lobed foliage. The saucer-shaped flowers bloom along the upper half of the stem.

FLOWER COLOR: Ranges from white and pale yellow to pink, rose, and deep red.

FLOWERING TIME: Summer and early fall. May bloom for 2 months.

HEIGHT AND SPREAD: 2–8 feet (60–240 cm) tall; 2–3 feet (60–90 cm) wide.

TEMPERATURE REQUIREMENTS: Zones 2–8. Prefers cool nights and low humidity.

POSITION: Average to humus-rich, well-drained soil. Full sun to partial shade.

CULTIVATION: Hollyhocks are short-lived and benefit from annual division. Lift plants after blooming and remove basal offsets from old flowering stalks. Replant healthy divisions into prepared soil.

PROPAGATION: Sow seed indoors in winter for bloom in the summer or outdoors in summer for bloom the following summer.

PEST AND DISEASE PREVENTION: Rust infection results in yellow blotches on the surface of leaves and raised yellow spots underneath. Dust infected foliage with sulfur. Deter spider mites by spraying infested plants with insecticidal soap.

LANDSCAPE USE: Plant at the back of borders where their foliage is obscured by bushy perennials. Perfect by a garden shed or along a fence or garage wall.

CULTIVARS: 'Chater's Double' has fully double flowers in a range of mixed or single colors. 'Farmyard Strain' has large single flowers in mixed colors.

Alchemilla mollis	Rosaceae

LADY'S-MANTLE

Lady's-mantles form mounded clumps of pleated foliage. The 4–6 inch (10–15 cm) pale green leaves are covered in soft hair that collects beads of water like jewels on velvet.

FLOWER COLOR: Foamy clusters of small greenish yellow flowers.

FLOWERING TIME: Spring and early summer.

HEIGHT AND SPREAD: 6–8 inches (15–20 cm) tall; 12–24 inches (30–60 cm) wide.

TEMPERATURE REQUIREMENTS: Zones 4–8. Excessive heat and humidity can damage the foliage.

POSITION: Humus-rich, evenly moist soil. Full sun; provide afternoon shade where summer heat and humidity are excessive.

CULTIVATION: Set the stout crowns at the soil surface. Cut tattered foliage to the ground; fresh leaves will quickly appear.

PROPAGATION: Divide crowns in spring or fall. Sow fresh seed outdoors in summer. Plants often self-sow.

PEST AND DISEASE PREVENTION: No serious pests or diseases. Mulch with organic matter to keep the soil evenly moist.

LANDSCAPE USE: Choose lady's-mantle for the front of formal and informal beds and borders or for edging walks. The greenish yellow flowers add light to the garden in evening. Combine with other plants that enjoy moist soil like Siberian iris (*Iris sibirica*), astilbe, and hosta.

CULTIVARS: 'Auslese' has erect flower stems.

Allium christophii	Liliaceae

STAR OF PERSIA

Star of Persia produces 1½-foot (45 cm) strap-like blue-green leaves that arch outward from the bulbs. Starry flowers radiate from stout 1–1½-foot (30–45 cm) stalks.

FLOWER COLOR: Metallic, lilac-pink flowers are carried in 10-inch (25 cm) globose heads.

FLOWERING TIME: Early to midsummer.

HEIGHT AND SPREAD: 1–1½ feet (30–45 cm) tall; 1 foot (30 cm) wide.

TEMPERATURE REQUIREMENTS: Zones 4–8.

POSITION: Humus-rich, well-drained soil. Full sun.

CULTIVATION: New bulbs planted in fall multiply slowly to form spectacular flowering clumps. Plants go dormant after flowering.

PROPAGATION: Divide in mid- to late summer as plants go dormant. Sow ripe seed outdoors in summer or fall.

PEST AND DISEASE PREVENTION: No serious pests or diseases. Mulch with organic matter to keep the soil evenly moist.

LANDSCAPE USE: Plant bulbs at the front of borders where their stalks will explode into bloom above mounding plants like cranesbills (*Geranium* spp.). Combine with shrubs and overplant with a groundcover.

OTHER SPECIES:

A. giganteum, giant onion, grows 3–5 feet (90–150 cm) tall, with 5-inch (12.5 cm) rounded heads of deep purple flowers.

A. sphaerocephalum, drumstick chives, has slender 1½–3-foot (45–90 cm) stems crowned by tight heads of small, red-violet flowers. Zones 4–9.

| *Alstroemeria aurantiaca* | Amaryllidaceae | *Amsonia tabernaemontana* | Apocynaceae |

PERUVIAN LILY

WILLOW BLUE STAR

Peruvian lilies have tall, leafy stems crowned by open clusters of flaring, saucer-shaped flowers. The gray-green leaves are narrow and pointed. Plants grow from thick, fibrous roots.

FLOWER COLOR: Showy orange or yellow flowers with brownish purple flares on the upper petals.

FLOWERING TIME: Throughout summer.

HEIGHT AND SPREAD: 2–3 feet (60–90 cm) tall; 2 feet (60 cm) wide.

TEMPERATURE REQUIREMENTS: Zones 7–10.

POSITION: Evenly moist but well-drained, humus-rich soil. Full sun to partial shade; protect from strong winds.

CULTIVATION: Plant dormant roots in early spring or fall. Growth begins early in the season, and plants may be damaged by late frost. Mulch with organic matter in fall to avoid frost heaving. Achieves best performance after the third year.

PROPAGATION: Divide clumps in early spring or fall. Take care not to damage the brittle roots. Sow fresh seed indoors after 4–6 weeks of cold (35°–40°F/ 4°–5°C), moist stratification. To stratify, mix seed with damp peat moss or seed-starting medium in a plastic bag and close with a twist-tie. Place the bag in the refrigerator for the appropriate time period, then sow the mixture as you would other seed.

PEST AND DISEASE PREVENTION: No serious pests or diseases.

LANDSCAPE USE: Plant Peruvian lilies in beds and borders with perennials, in partial shade with ferns, or in containers. Excellent for cutting.

Willow blue star is a tough, shrubby plant with lance-shaped leaves, stout stems, and terminal clusters of tiny blue flowers. Plants grow from a woody, fibrous-rooted crown.

FLOWER COLOR: Steel blue, ½-inch (12 mm), five-petaled starry flowers.

FLOWERING TIME: Spring, with some secondary shoots blooming in early summer.

HEIGHT AND SPREAD: 1–3 feet (30–90 cm) tall; 3 feet (90 cm) wide.

TEMPERATURE REQUIREMENTS: Zones 3–9. Heat- and cold-tolerant.

POSITION: Average to humus-rich, moist but well-drained soil. Full sun to partial shade.

CULTIVATION: A single plant will reach shrub-like proportions with age. Plants in shade may be floppy. If necessary, prune stems back to 6–8 inches (15–20 cm) after flowering. New shoots will form an attractive, compact mound. Leaves turn bright orange to golden yellow in fall.

PROPAGATION: Divide plants in early spring or fall. Take 4–6-inch (10–15 cm) stem cuttings in early summer. Sow ripe seed outdoors in fall or indoors after soaking in hot water for several hours before planting.

PEST AND DISEASE PREVENTION: No serious pests or diseases. Mulch with organic matter to keep the soil evenly moist.

LANDSCAPE USE: Use the shrubby clumps to add structure to the garden, either alone as a mass planting or combined with other perennials.

OTHER COMMON NAMES: Willow amsonia.

Anchusa azurea	Boraginaceae	*Anemone* x *hybrida*	Ranunculaceae

ITALIAN BUGLOSS

JAPANESE ANEMONE

Italian bugloss has lush oblong leaves covered in stiff hair. Long branches bear terminal clusters of flowers. This fibrous-rooted plant may reach 5 feet (1.5 m) in height.

FLOWER COLOR: Brilliant blue ¾-inch (18 mm), five-petaled flowers.

FLOWERING TIME: Late spring.

HEIGHT AND SPREAD: 2–5 feet (60–150 cm) tall; 2 feet (60 cm) wide.

TEMPERATURE REQUIREMENTS: Zones 3–8.

POSITION: Humus-rich, well-drained soil. Full sun to light shade.

CULTIVATION: Since seed-grown plants may be short-lived, choose a named cultivar for better performance and longevity. Cut plants back after blooming to encourage more flowers. Divide every 2–3 years to keep plants vigorous.

PROPAGATION: Divide clumps after flowering. Replant strong, healthy divisions into soil that has been enriched with organic matter. Take root cuttings in early spring. Plants freely self-sow.

PEST AND DISEASE PREVENTION: No serious pests or diseases.

LANDSCAPE USE: Plant among bright flowers such as shasta daisies (*Chrysanthemum* x *superbum*) and yarrows or use in mass plantings with flowering shrubs.

CULTIVARS: 'Dropmore' is a compact, 4-foot (1.2 m) selection with deep blue flowers. 'Loddon Royalist' is 3 feet (90 cm) tall with gentian blue flowers.

Japanese anemone produces clouds of flowers on slender stems. The deeply divided, hairy leaves are mostly basal. Stem leaves have fewer dissections. Plants grow from thick, tuberous roots.

FLOWER COLOR: Ranges from white to pink and rose; single or double blooms.

FLOWERING TIME: Late summer and fall.

HEIGHT AND SPREAD: 3–5 feet (90–150 cm) tall; 2–3 feet (60–90 cm) wide.

TEMPERATURE REQUIREMENTS: Zones 5–8.

POSITION: Humus-rich, evenly moist soil. Full sun to light shade. Protect from hot afternoon sun in warmer zones.

CULTIVATION: Spreads by creeping underground stems to form broad clumps once established. Thin overgrown clumps in spring if bloom wanes. Replant into soil that has been enriched with organic matter. Mulch plants in colder zones.

PROPAGATION: Take root cuttings after plants go dormant in fall. Sow fresh seed outdoors in summer or fall. Divide in early spring.

PEST AND DISEASE PREVENTION: No serious pests or diseases.

LANDSCAPE USE: Group with other late-season perennials and ornamental grasses. Combine with shrubs or ferns in moist, open shade.

CULTIVARS: 'Honorine Jobert' bears pure white single blooms on stems 3–4 feet (90–120 cm) tall. 'Margarete' has deep pink semidouble flowers on 3-foot (90 cm) stems. 'Max Vogel' has large pink single flowers on 4-foot (1.2 m) stems. 'Whirlwind' has white semidouble flowers.

HYBRID COLUMBINE

Hybrid columbines are graceful plants with curious nodding flowers. Each flower has five spurred petals surrounded by five petal-like sepals. Plants grow from a thick taproot.

FLOWER COLOR: Single- or bi-colored variable flowers. Yellow, red, blue, purple, pink, and white are common. The spurs may be ½–4 inches (12–100 mm) long.

FLOWERING TIME: Spring and early summer.

HEIGHT AND SPREAD: 2–3 feet (60–90 cm) tall; 1–2 feet (30–60 cm) wide.

TEMPERATURE REQUIREMENTS: Zones 3–9. Tolerate heat and cold.

POSITION: Light, average to humus-rich, well-drained soil. Full sun to partial shade.

CULTIVATION: Hybrid columbines may be short-lived even under the best garden conditions. They generally live 2–4 years, rewarding the gardener with a month or more of bloom. Plants self-sow prolifically and new plants are always developing.

PROPAGATION: Sow seed outdoors in spring or summer. Sow indoors in winter after dry storing them in a refrigerator for 4–6 weeks. Plants develop quickly.

PEST AND DISEASE PREVENTION: Leafminers create pale tunnels and blotches in the leaves. Remove and destroy damaged foliage. In severe cases spray weekly with insecticidal soap. Borers also attack columbines, causing the plant to collapse dramatically. Remove and destroy all portions of affected plants.

Hybrid columbines often reseed themselves, popping up in the most unexpected places. Seedlings from hybrid plants are usually quite variable in form and color.

LANDSCAPE USE: Hybrid columbines look best in groups or drifts. Plant with spring and early-summer perennials, tulips, and daffodils. Combine with wildflowers, ferns, and hostas in light shade or try them along stone walls or in rock gardens.

CULTIVARS: 'Biedermeier' hybrids come in mixed colors. Plants are only 12 inches (30 cm) tall. 'Crimson Star' grows 2½ feet (75 cm) tall with crimson-and-white flowers. 'Dragonfly' hybrids are 10–12 inches (25–30 cm) tall and come in mixed colors. 'McKana' is a strain of large-flowered hybrids in mixed colors. 'Nora Barlow' has double flowers in red, white, and green combination.

OTHER SPECIES:

A. caerulea, Rocky Mountain columbine, has graceful, upfacing blue-and-white flowers with long spurs. 'Blue Star' is a heat-resistant selection with deep blue and white flowers. Zones 3–8.

A. canadensis, wild columbine, is a beloved wildflower with nodding red-and-yellow flowers that are eagerly visited by hummingbirds. 'Corbett' has pale yellow flowers. Zones 3–8.

A. chrysantha, golden columbine, has huge 2–3-inch (5–7.5 cm) yellow flowers with 4-inch (10 cm) spurs. Zones 3–9.

A. flabellata, fan columbine, is a compact grower with showy blue-green foliage and short-spurred deep blue or white flowers. Zones 3–9.

| *Arabis caucasica* | Cruciferae | *Arenaria montana* | Caryophyllaceae |

WALL ROCK CRESS

MOUNTAIN SANDWORT

Wall rock cress is an attractive evergreen groundcover only 4–6 inches (10–15 cm) high. The 1-inch (2.5 cm) leaves are clothed in soft hair and are often obscured by the spring flowers.

Mountain sandwort is a dense, mat-forming groundcover with tiny needle-like leaves and flat, white five-petaled flowers. Plants grow from thin, fibrous roots.

FLOWER COLOR: White or pink.

FLOWERING TIME: Late winter and early spring.

HEIGHT AND SPREAD: 6–10 inches (15–25 cm) tall; 12–18 inches (30–45 cm) wide.

TEMPERATURE REQUIREMENTS: Zones 3–7. Plants languish in warmer zones.

POSITION: Average, well-drained soil. Full sun to light shade. Tolerates a wide range of soil moisture and fertility.

CULTIVATION: Spreads quickly to form loose mats of foliage. Cut plants back after flowering to encourage new shoots and to keep them neat. Divide every 2–4 years to keep plants healthy.

PROPAGATION: Take cuttings in spring. Layer by burying 6 inches (15 cm) of a low-growing stem and leaving the leafy tip exposed. Divide in spring or fall.

PEST AND DISEASE PREVENTION: No serious pests or diseases.

LANDSCAPE USE: Rock cress looks great tumbling over a stone wall or creeping through a rock garden. Interplant with spring bulbs and early perennials along borders.

CULTIVARS: 'Rosabella' has rose pink flowers. 'Snow Cap' is a robust plant with profuse white flowers.

VARIETIES: *A. caucasica* var. *flore-plena* has double flowers that are mostly sterile and last for several weeks.

FLOWER COLOR: White.

FLOWERING TIME: Spring and early summer.

HEIGHT AND SPREAD: 2–4 inches (5–10 cm) tall; 12 inches (30 cm) tall in flower; 10–12 inches (25–30 cm) wide; larger with age.

TEMPERATURE REQUIREMENTS: Zones 4–8.

POSITION: Average sandy or loamy, well-drained soil. Full sun. Plants dislike acid soil.

CULTIVATION: Spreads slowly to form low, moss-like mats of foliage. Shallow-rooted; keep moist during dry spells.

PROPAGATION: Divide in spring or fall. Sow seed outdoors in fall or inside in early spring.

PEST AND DISEASE PREVENTION: No serious pests or diseases.

LANDSCAPE USE: Plant between pavers in walkways or among rocks in loosely constructed walls. Excellent in rock gardens and perfect for pot or trough culture.

Arisaema triphyllum Araceae	*Armeria maritima* Plumbaginaceae
# JACK-IN-THE-PULPIT	# THRIFT

Jack-in-the-pulpits are spring wildflowers. The unusual flower hides beneath single or paired leaves, each with three broad leaflets. Plants grow from a button-like tuber.

FLOWER COLOR: Green flowers striped with yellow or purple. Glossy red berries ripen in late summer.

FLOWERING TIME: Spring.

HEIGHT AND SPREAD: 1–3 feet (30–90 cm) tall; 1–1½ feet (30–45 cm) wide.

TEMPERATURE REQUIREMENTS: Zones 3–9.

POSITION: Evenly moist, humus-rich soil. Partial to full shade. Tolerates wet soil.

CULTIVATION: Easy to grow and long-lived. Clumps grow slowly from offsets or seed.

PROPAGATION: Remove the pulp from ripe berries and sow the seed outdoors in spring or fall. Seedlings develop slowly and may take several years to bloom. Propagate from natural offsets in spring.

PEST AND DISEASE PREVENTION: No serious pests or diseases.

LANDSCAPE USE: Plant among low wildflowers for an eye-catching vertical accent. Combine with fringed bleeding heart (*Dicentra eximia*), bloodroot (*Sanguinaria canadensis*), hostas, and ferns. Plant under shrubs or flowering trees.

Thrift forms dense tufts of grass-like, gray-green evergreen leaves. The taller bloom stalks arise from the centers of the tightly packed rosettes.

FLOWER COLOR: Small pink flowers crowded into rounded 1-inch (2.5 cm) heads.

FLOWERING TIME: Late spring and summer.

HEIGHT AND SPREAD: 10–14 inches (25–35 cm) tall; 8–10 inches (20–25 cm) wide.

TEMPERATURE REQUIREMENTS: Zones 4–8.

POSITION: Average to humus-rich, moist but well-drained soil. Full sun. Prefers cool nights and low humidity.

CULTIVATION: Drought-tolerant once established; will grow in rock crevices where water is scarce. Tolerates air- and soilborne salt; perfect for seaside gardens.

PROPAGATION: Divide clumps in early spring or fall. Sow seed indoors in winter on a warm (70°F/21°C) seedbed.

PEST AND DISEASE PREVENTION: No serious pests or diseases.

LANDSCAPE USE: Plant in rock and wall gardens or along paths.

OTHER COMMON NAMES: Sea pink.

CULTIVARS: 'Alba' has white flowers on 5-inch (12.5 cm) stems. 'Dusseldorf Pride' has wine red flowers on 6–8-inch (15–20 cm) stems. 'Robusta' has 3-inch (7.5 cm) pink flower heads on 12–15-inch (30–37.5 cm) stems. 'Vindictive' is only 6 inches (15 cm) tall with bright rose pink flowers.

Artemisia absinthium   Compositae

COMMON WORMWOOD

Common wormwood is a stout, shrubby perennial with stems that become woody with age. Soft hair on the deeply lobed, aromatic foliage gives the plant a muted gray-green tone.

FLOWER COLOR: Inconspicuous yellow flowers borne in terminal clusters.

FLOWERING TIME: Late summer and fall.

HEIGHT AND SPREAD: 2–3 feet (60–90 cm) tall; 2 feet (60 cm) wide.

TEMPERATURE REQUIREMENTS: Zones 3–9.

POSITION: Average sandy or loamy, well-drained soil. Full sun.

CULTIVATION: Thrives in all but the most inhospitable garden spots. Overly rich soils result in weak growth. Encourage compact growth by pruning back untidy plants by at least half.

PROPAGATION: Grow from stem cuttings taken in late summer or spring. Dust the cut surfaces with a rooting hormone to speed production of new roots.

PEST AND DISEASE PREVENTION: No serious pests or diseases.

LANDSCAPE USE: Combine with yarrows and other drought-tolerant perennials. The soft foliage is lovely with ornamental grasses.

CULTIVARS: 'Lambrook Silver' has beautiful deeply cut silver gray foliage.

Aruncus dioicus   Rosaceae

GOAT'S BEARD

Goat's beards are showy shrub-like perennials with large three-lobed leaves and airy plumes of flowers. Male and female flowers are borne on separate plants.

FLOWER COLOR: Creamy white flowers with small petals.

FLOWERING TIME: Late spring and early summer.

HEIGHT AND SPREAD: 3–6 feet (90–180 cm) tall; 3–5 feet (90–150 cm) wide.

TEMPERATURE REQUIREMENTS: Zones 3–7; avoid areas with hot nights.

POSITION: Moist, humus-rich soil. Full sun (in cooler zones) to partial shade.

CULTIVATION: Plant 4–5 feet (1.2–1.5 m) apart to allow for the plants' impressive mature size. The tough rootstocks are difficult to move once established. Divide plants only if necessary to revitalize the clumps. Lift in early spring and replant strong, healthy divisions into soil that has been enriched with organic matter.

PROPAGATION: Sow seed in summer outdoors or inside on a warm (70°F/21°C) seedbed.

PEST AND DISEASE PREVENTION: No serious pests or diseases.

LANDSCAPE USE: Use with ferns, wildflowers, and hostas in a lightly shaded woodland garden or as an accent with flowering shrubs. Combines well with other perennials in beds and borders.

CULTIVARS: 'Child of Two Worlds' is a compact grower only 3–4 feet (90–120 cm) tall. 'Kneiffii' grows 3 feet (90 cm) tall and has deeply cut ruffled foliage.

Asarum europaeum　　　　Aristolochiaceae

EUROPEAN WILD GINGER

European wild ginger is a slow-creeping evergreen groundcover. The glossy kidney-shaped leaves are mottled along the veins. The aromatic rhizomes creep at or just below the soil surface.

FLOWER COLOR: Jug-like dull brown flowers usually hidden under the foliage.

FLOWERING TIME: Spring.

HEIGHT AND SPREAD: 6–12 inches (15–30 cm) tall; 12 inches (30 cm) wide. Forms broad clumps with age.

TEMPERATURE REQUIREMENTS: Zones 4–8.

POSITION: Moist, humus-rich soil. Partial to full shade. Drought-tolerant once established but best when moisture is adequate.

CULTIVATION: An exceptional groundcover. Clumps spread steadily to form tight mats of weed-proof foliage. Divide crowded plants in early spring or fall.

PROPAGATION: Divide in spring. Sow fresh seed outdoors in summer.

PEST AND DISEASE PREVENTION: No serious pests or diseases.

LANDSCAPE USE: Plant along a garden path with ferns and wildflowers or in a shaded rock garden.

OTHER SPECIES:

　　A. canadense, Canada wild ginger, is a deciduous groundcover with heart-shaped leaves that is hardier and faster spreading. Zones 3–8.

Aster x *frikartii*　　　　Compositae

FRIKART'S ASTER

Frikart's aster produces open clusters of flowers on loosely branched stems. Plants grow from short, slow-creeping rhizomes with fibrous roots.

FLOWER COLOR: Lavender-blue 2½-inch (6 cm) flowers with bright yellow centers.

FLOWERING TIME: Midsummer through fall.

HEIGHT AND SPREAD: 2–3 feet (60–90 cm) tall; 2–3 feet (60–90 cm) wide. Stems often lean on other plants for support.

TEMPERATURE REQUIREMENTS: Zones 5–8; Zone 4 with mulch protection or consistent winter snow.

POSITION: Moist but well-drained soil. Full sun to light shade. Plants will rot in sodden soil, especially in winter.

CULTIVATION: Frikart's aster may be short-lived. Clumps spread slowly. Divide plants as necessary in spring or fall.

PROPAGATION: Take stem cuttings in spring. Divide in early spring or fall.

PEST AND DISEASE PREVENTION: Plant in a well-drained position to deter root rot.

LANDSCAPE USE: Combine Frikart's aster with late-summer and fall perennials like garden phlox (*Phlox paniculata*), coneflowers (*Rudbeckia* spp.), and ornamental grasses. They grow well in containers in Zones 6–8.

CULTIVARS: 'Monch' has erect stems and deep lavender-blue flowers. 'Wonder of Staffa' is more open in habit with paler flowers.

| *Aster novae-angliae* | Compositae | *Astilbe* x *arendsii* | Saxifragaceae |

NEW ENGLAND ASTER

New England aster is a tall, stately plant with hairy stems and clasping, lance-shaped leaves. Most selections are best planted at the back of the perennial border.

FLOWER COLOR: Lavender to purple 1½–2-inch (3.5–5 cm) flowers with bright yellow centers. Flowers may vary in color from white to pink and rose.

FLOWERING TIME: Late summer through fall.

HEIGHT AND SPREAD: 3–6 feet (90–180 cm) tall; 3 feet (90 cm) wide. Matures into broad clumps.

TEMPERATURE REQUIREMENTS: Zones 3–8.

POSITION: Moist, humus-rich soil. Full sun to light shade.

CULTIVATION: Clumps become quite large with age. Divide every 3–4 years in spring. Plants may need staking.

PROPAGATION: Take 4–6-inch (10–15 cm) stem cuttings in late spring or early summer. Divide in early spring or fall.

PEST AND DISEASE PREVENTION: Powdery mildew turns leaves dull gray. Thin stems to promote air circulation. Dust affected plants with sulfur.

LANDSCAPE USE: Plant with fall perennials like sunflowers (*Helianthus* spp.), Japanese anemone (*Anemone* x *hybrida*), and ornamental grasses.

CULTIVARS: 'Alma Potschke' has dark salmon-pink flowers on 2–4-foot (60–120 cm) plants. 'Purple Dome' is a dwarf selection with royal purple flowers on 2-foot (60 cm) late-flowering clumps.

OTHER SPECIES:
A. *novi-belgii,* New York aster, has single or double flowers in a rainbow of colors.

ASTILBE

Astilbes have showy flower clusters and ferny, dissected leaves with shiny broad leaflets. The emerging spring shoots are often tinged with red.

FLOWER COLOR: Upright, often-plumed flower clusters bear tightly packed, fuzzy blooms in shades of red, pink, rose, lilac, cream, and white.

FLOWERING TIME: Spring and early summer.

HEIGHT AND SPREAD: 2–4 feet (60–120 cm) tall; 2–3 feet (60–90 cm) wide. Leafy clumps spread steadily outward. Each clump maintains a distinct crown.

TEMPERATURE REQUIREMENTS: Zones 3–9.

POSITION: Moist, slightly acid, humus-rich soil. Full to partial shade; tolerates more sun in cool-summer areas. Dry soil will result in shriveled foliage.

CULTIVATION: Astilbes are heavy feeders and benefit from an annual application of balanced organic fertilizer. Top-dress with compost or lift and replant the clumps if crowns rise above the soil. Divide clumps every 3–4 years and replant into soil that has been enriched with organic matter. Keep plants well watered.

PROPAGATION: Propagate the true species by sowing fresh seed outdoors in summer or early fall. Propagate cultivars by spring or fall division only.

PEST AND DISEASE PREVENTION: Spider mites may be a problem in warm areas. Spray with insecticidal soap as necessary. Control root rot with good drainage and good air circulation.

LANDSCAPE USE: Plant at stream- or pondside where their plumes are reflected in the water. In borders

ASTILBE—CONTINUED

MASTERWORT

Astilbes are perfect for planting in a moist shade garden or along a stream or pond. Evenly moist soil is the key to keeping these plants looking good all season long.

combine them with lungworts (*Pulmonaria* spp.), hostas, and wildflowers.

OTHER COMMON NAMES: False spirea.

CULTIVARS: 'Amethyst' is an early bloomer with lilac purple flowers on 1½–2-foot (45–60 cm) stems. 'Bridal Veil' has open, drooping clusters of creamy white flowers. 'Fanal' has deep red flowers on compact 1–1½-foot (30–45 cm) plants. 'Cattleya' is a midseason bloomer with lilac-pink flowers on 3-foot (90 cm) stems. 'Glut' is a late-flowering red with 1½–2-foot (45–60 cm) stems.

OTHER SPECIES:

A. chinensis, Chinese astilbe, is a creeping plant with rose pink late-summer flowers. The variety *pumila* is a low-growing groundcover.

A. japonica, Japanese astilbe, is an early-blooming species with glossy leaves. 'Deutschland' has white flowers on 1½-foot (45 cm) stems. 'Europa' has light pink flowers on 2–2½-foot (60–75 cm) stems.

A. simplicifolia, star astilbe, is a dwarf species with glossy, deeply lobed leaves and open, drooping flower clusters. 'Bronze Elegans' has pink flowers and red-tinted foliage. 'Sprite' has creamy pink flowers and dark green leaves.

A. taquetti, fall astilbe, is similar to *A. chinensis* but is 3–4 feet (90–120 cm) tall. 'Superba' is a midsummer bloomer with upright plumes of lavender-rose flowers.

Masterwort is a showy perennial with bold, deeply lobed palmate leaves on a stout, fibrous-rooted crown. Leafy branched flower stalks rise from the center of the foliage clumps.

FLOWER COLOR: Creamy white button-like flower heads surrounded by a whorl of starry pointed bracts. The stiff bracts remain after the flowers fade, prolonging the display.

FLOWERING TIME: Early to late summer. Reblooms frequently if deadheaded.

HEIGHT AND SPREAD: 2–3 feet (60–90 cm) tall; 1–2 feet (30–60 cm) wide. Clumps become quite large with age.

TEMPERATURE REQUIREMENTS: Zones 4–7. Intolerant of high temperatures, especially at night.

POSITION: Evenly moist, humus-rich soil. Full sun to partial shade. Tolerates wet soil.

CULTIVATION: Clumps increase by creeping underground stems and may outgrow their position. Divide to control their size and spread.

PROPAGATION: Divide plants in fall or early spring or remove runners from the main clump. Sow fresh seed outdoors in late summer.

PEST AND DISEASE PREVENTION: No serious pests or diseases.

LANDSCAPE USE: Plant along borders where masterwort's bold foliage and unusual flowers will complement airy meadow rues (*Thalictrum* spp.), ornamental grasses, and spiky mulleins (*Verbascum* spp.). Or plant at pondside with irises and ferns.

CULTIVARS: 'Rosea' has pink flowers and bracts.

| *Aubrieta deltoidea* | Cruciferae | *Aurinia saxatilis* | Cruciferae |

ROCK CRESS

BASKET-OF-GOLD

Rock cress is a low, mounding, spring-blooming plant with weak stems clothed in sparsely toothed evergreen leaves. Plants spread by thin rhizomes to form broad clumps.

FLOWER COLOR: Four-petaled ¾-inch (18 mm) flowers may be white, rose, or purple.

FLOWERING TIME: Early spring.

HEIGHT AND SPREAD: 6–8 inches (15–20 cm) tall; 8–12 inches (20–30 cm) wide. Forms tight mounds of foliage smothered in flowers.

TEMPERATURE REQUIREMENTS: Zones 4–8. Grows best where summer humidity and temperatures are not excessive.

POSITION: Average, well-drained, sandy or loamy, neutral soil. Full sun to light shade.

CULTIVATION: Plants tend to flop after flowering. Shear clumps to promote compact growth and to encourage repeat bloom.

PROPAGATION: Divide in fall. Take stem cuttings after flowering. Sow seed indoors or outdoors from spring to fall.

PEST AND DISEASE PREVENTION: Plant in well-drained soil to avoid root rot, especially where nighttime temperatures are high.

LANDSCAPE USE: Rock cress is at home in cracks and crevices of walls and rock gardens. Plant at the edge of walks or at the front of beds and borders.

CULTIVARS: 'Aurea Variegata' has yellow-variegated leaves and blue-violet flowers. 'Carnival' produces a profusion of violet flowers. 'Purple Gem' has royal purple flowers. 'Royal Blue' has dark blue flowers.

Basket-of-gold produces mounds of 6-inch (15 cm) oblong gray-green leaves from a thick crown. Hairy leaves and deep roots help the plant endure dry soil and warm temperatures.

FLOWER COLOR: Brilliant yellow flowers have four rounded petals and are carried in upright, branched clusters.

FLOWERING TIME: Early spring.

HEIGHT AND SPREAD: 10–12 inches (25–30 cm) tall; 12 inches (30 cm) wide.

TEMPERATURE REQUIREMENTS: Zones 3–7. Tolerates hot, dry conditions.

POSITION: Average, well-drained, loamy or sandy soil. Full sun. Avoid excessively hot and humid climates.

CULTIVATION: Clumps spread by creeping stems and may flop after flowering. Cut stems back by two thirds after flowering to encourage compact growth.

PROPAGATION: Divide in fall. Take stem cuttings in spring or fall. Sow seed in fall.

PEST AND DISEASE PREVENTION: Heavy moist soils and high humidity will encourage root rot. Plant in well-drained soils only.

LANDSCAPE USE: Basket-of-gold lends color to rock walls, rock gardens, and walkways. Combine with rock cresses (*Aubrieta* spp.) and pinks (*Dianthus* spp.).

CULTIVARS: 'Citrinum' has clear lemon yellow flowers. 'Compactum' forms tight clumps only 8 inches (20 cm) tall. 'Sunny Border Apricot' has peach-colored flowers.

Baptisia australis Leguminosae	*Belamcanda chinensis* Iridaceae

BLUE FALSE INDIGO
BLACKBERRY LILY

Blue false indigo is a spectacular perennial that reaches shrub-like proportions. Mature plants form dense, rounded mounds of three-lobed blue-green leaves.

FLOWER COLOR: Deep blue 1-inch (2.5 cm) flowers are carried in narrow, open clusters and resemble lupines. The dried gray pods are showy in fall and winter.

FLOWERING TIME: Late spring and early summer.

HEIGHT AND SPREAD: 2–4 feet (60–120 cm) tall; 3–4 feet (90–120 cm) wide.

TEMPERATURE REQUIREMENTS: Zones 3–9. Tolerant of heat and cold.

POSITION: Average to humus-rich, moist but well-drained soil. Full sun to partial shade.

CULTIVATION: Grows slowly until its taproot establishes. Mature plants have massive, tough root systems that resent disturbance. Space young plants 3–4 feet (90–120 cm) apart. Division is seldom necessary.

PROPAGATION: Take cuttings after flowering or sow fresh seed outdoors in fall. Treat stored seed by pouring near-boiling water over it and soaking for 12–24 hours before sowing. Divide clumps in fall, late winter, or early spring using a sharp knife.

PEST AND DISEASE PREVENTION: No serious pests or diseases.

LANDSCAPE USE: Plant toward the rear of the border with Siberian iris (*Iris sibirica*), peonies, and other bold-textured plants. Use them in meadow and prairie plantings with ornamental grasses.

OTHER COMMON NAMES: Baptisia.

Blackberry lilies produce showy, curved fans of foliage that resemble irises. Branched clumps grow from creeping rhizomes and may produce dozens of orange flowers.

FLOWER COLOR: Six-petaled 2-inch (5 cm) orange flowers are speckled with red. Inflated seed capsules split in fall to expose the berry-like clusters of black seeds that give the plant its common name.

FLOWERING TIME: Mid- to late summer.

HEIGHT AND SPREAD: 2–4 feet (60–120 cm) tall; 1–2 feet (30–60 cm) wide.

TEMPERATURE REQUIREMENTS: Zones 4–10. May need winter protection in colder areas of Zone 4.

POSITION: Average to humus-rich, well-drained soil. Full sun to light shade. Afternoon shade may prolong the life of individual flowers.

CULTIVATION: Plants spread by creeping rhizomes to form dense clumps. Divide as necessary to control spread. Self-sown seedlings often appear.

PROPAGATION: Divide in late summer or sow fresh seed outdoors in spring.

PEST AND DISEASE PREVENTION: No serious pests or diseases.

LANDSCAPE USE: Plant with garden phlox (*Phlox paniculata*), daylilies, and other plants with large flowers that contrast with blackberry lily's small starry flowers.

OTHER SPECIES:
The closely related *Belamcanda flabellata* grows 1–2 feet (30–60 cm) tall and has yellow flowers.

Bergenia cordifolia   Saxifragaceae

HEART-LEAVED BERGENIA

Heart-leaved bergenias are handsome plants with broad, oval, leathery evergreen foliage. The 10–12-inch (25–30 cm) leaves emerge in a whorl from a stout, creeping rhizome.

FLOWER COLOR: Nodding pink or rose flowers are carried above the foliage on thick, branched stems.

FLOWERING TIME: Late winter and early spring.

HEIGHT AND SPREAD: 12–14 inches (30–35 cm) tall; 12 inches (30 cm) wide.

TEMPERATURE REQUIREMENTS: Zones 3–9. Foliage benefits from winter protection where snowfall is not consistent.

POSITION: Moist, humus-rich soil. Full sun to partial shade. Provide afternoon shade in warmer zones to protect leaves from burning.

CULTIVATION: These long-lived perennials creep slowly from branching rhizomes. As clumps age, they become bare in the center. Lift plants in spring and remove old portions of the rhizome with a sharp knife. Replant into soil that has been enriched with organic matter. Protect with a winter mulch of evergreen boughs or marsh hay.

PROPAGATION: Divide in spring. Sow ripe seed indoors on a warm (70°F/21°C) seedbed. Leave seed uncovered. Young plants develop slowly.

PEST AND DISEASE PREVENTION: Exclude slugs with barrier strips of diatomaceous earth, wood ashes, or sand; or bait them with shallow pans of beer set flush with the soil surface

LANDSCAPE USE: Use as accents at the base of rock walls or along a garden path. Plant under shrubs for a glossy, deep green groundcover.

Boltonia asteroides   Compositae

BOLTONIA

Boltonias are tall, late-season perennials with masses of flowers smothering the gray-green willow-like foliage. The mounded plants are lovely in foliage; the flowers are a bonus.

FLOWER COLOR: A profusion of 1-inch (2.5 cm) white daisies with bright yellow centers is carried in open clusters.

FLOWERING TIME: Late summer through fall.

HEIGHT AND SPREAD: 4–6 feet (1.2–1.8 m) tall; 4 feet (1.2 m) wide.

TEMPERATURE REQUIREMENTS: Zones 3–9.

POSITION: Moist, humus-rich soil. Full sun to light shade. Dry soil produces smaller plants.

CULTIVATION: These easy-to-grow plants form sturdy, dense stems that seldom need staking.

PROPAGATION: Divide oversized clumps in spring. Take cuttings in early summer. Seed collected from cultivars will produce seedlings unlike the parent plants and in most cases inferior to them.

PEST AND DISEASE PREVENTION: No serious pests or diseases.

LANDSCAPE USE: Combine with fall-blooming perennials like asters, Japanese anemones (*Anemone* x *hybrida*), goldenrods (*Solidago* spp.), Joe-Pye weeds (*Eupatorium* spp.), and ornamental grasses.

CULTIVARS: 'Pink Beauty' sports soft-pink flowers in open clusters. Cool summers produce brighter colors. 'Snowbank' is a compact selection with bright white flowers borne throughout fall.

Brunnera macrophylla   Boraginaceae

SIBERIAN BUGLOSS

Siberian bugloss is grown for both its flowers and its foliage. The bold, 8-inch (20 cm) heart-shaped leaves rise in a tight mound from a short, fibrous-rooted rhizome.

FLOWER COLOR: Sprays of ¼-inch (6 mm) forget-me-not blue flowers cover the plants before the leaves emerge.

FLOWERING TIME: Early spring. Flowering often continues for 3–4 weeks.

HEIGHT AND SPREAD: 1–1½-feet (30–45 cm) tall; 2 feet (60 cm) wide. Foliage reaches mature size in summer.

TEMPERATURE REQUIREMENTS: Zone 3–8.

POSITION: Evenly moist, humus-rich soil. Partial to full shade; full sun in cooler zones. Tolerates short dry spells once established.

CULTIVATION: Plants are tough, increase slowly, and seldom need division. Self-sown seedlings appear regularly around the parent clumps. Keep soil moist; plants will go dormant in persistent drought.

PROPAGATION: Divide clumps in early spring or fall. Take 3–4-inch (7.5–10 cm) root cuttings in fall or early winter. Transplant self-sown seedlings to desired position.

PEST AND DISEASE PREVENTION: No serious pests or diseases.

LANDSCAPE USE: Plant as a groundcover under trees or shrubs with spring bulbs, wildflowers, and ferns.

CULTIVARS: 'Hadspen Cream' has leaves with creamy white borders. 'Langtrees' has regularly spaced silver blotches near the leaf margins.

Caltha palustris   Ranunculaceae

MARSH MARIGOLD

Marsh marigolds grow in moist soil and shallow wetlands. They produce yellow spring flowers over mounds of rounded leaves from a thick crown with fleshy white roots.

FLOWER COLOR: Butter yellow 1½-inch (3.5 cm) flowers have five shiny petals and are carried in open clusters.

FLOWERING TIME: Early to midspring.

HEIGHT AND SPREAD: 1–2 feet (30–60 cm) tall; up to 2 feet (60 cm) wide.

TEMPERATURE REQUIREMENTS: Zones 2–8.

POSITION: Wet, humus-rich or loamy soil. Full sun to partial shade. Grows even when covered with 1–4 inches (2.5–10 cm) of water. Once flowering is complete, moisture is less critical.

CULTIVATION: Divide overgrown plants a month after flowering when dormant.

PROPAGATION: Divide in summer. Sow fresh seed outdoors immediately upon ripening; plants will not germinate until the following spring.

PEST AND DISEASE PREVENTION: No serious pests or diseases.

LANDSCAPE USE: Perfect for water gardens or along the low banks of streams. Plant with primroses, irises, and ferns in bog gardens.

OTHER COMMON NAMES: Cowslip.

CULTIVARS: 'Flore Pleno' ('Multiplex') has fully double flowers that last for a week or more.

Campanula glomerata　　　　Campanulaceae

CLUSTERED BELLFLOWER

Clustered bellflower is a robust plant with erect, leafy, flowering stems and hairy 5-inch (12.5 cm) oval leaves. Plants grow from slow-creeping rhizomes with fibrous roots.

FLOWER COLOR: Purple to blue-violet flowers are carried in tiered clusters at the nodes of the flowering stem.

FLOWERING TIME: Late spring or early summer.

HEIGHT AND SPREAD: 1–3 feet (30–90 cm) tall; 1 foot (30 cm) wide.

TEMPERATURE REQUIREMENTS: Zones 3–8.

POSITION: Evenly moist, humus-rich soil. Full sun to partial shade. Tolerates alkaline soil.

CULTIVATION: Cut back flowering stems after blossoms fade. The summer foliage makes an attractive groundcover. Divide overgrown clumps to keep plants vigorous.

PROPAGATION: Divide in fall or early spring. Sow seed indoors; leave seed uncovered as light promotes germination. Self-sown seedlings will appear. Take cuttings after flowering.

PEST AND DISEASE PREVENTION: Exclude slugs with barrier strips of diatomaceous earth, wood ashes, or sand; bait them with shallow pans of beer set flush with the soil surface.

LANDSCAPE USE: Plant in borders with Siberian iris (*Iris sibirica*) and leopard's bane (*Doronicum* spp.) or in shaded gardens with ferns.

CULTIVARS: 'Crown of Snow' has large clusters of white flowers. 'Joan Elliot' is a delicate, floriferous selection with deep blue-violet flowers. 'Superba' grows 2½ feet (75 cm) tall with violet flowers.

Campanula persicifolia　　　　Campanulaceae

PEACH-LEAVED BELLFLOWER

Peach-leaved bellflower produces mounds of narrow 8-inch (20 cm) evergreen leaves from a fibrous-rooted crown. The summer blooms make long-lasting cut flowers.

FLOWER COLOR: Open bell-shaped lavender-blue flowers are carried on tall, narrow stalks.

FLOWERING TIME: Summer.

HEIGHT AND SPREAD: 1–3 feet (30–90 cm) tall; 2 feet (60 cm) wide.

TEMPERATURE REQUIREMENTS: Zones 3–8. Prefers cooler summer temperatures.

POSITION: Moist but well-drained, humus-rich soil. Full sun to partial shade; protect from hot afternoon sun in warmer zones.

CULTIVATION: Peach-leaved bellflower is a tough, easy-care plant that spreads slowly by sideshoots from the central crown. Division is seldom necessary. Plants may be short-lived in warmer zones.

PROPAGATION: Take tip cuttings in early summer. Divide clumps in early spring.

PEST AND DISEASE PREVENTION: Exclude slugs with barrier strips of diatomaceous earth, wood ashes, or sand; bait them with shallow pans of beer set flush with the soil surface.

LANDSCAPE USE: Plant toward the middle or rear of borders. The showy flowers combine well with yarrows, Russian sage (*Perovskia atriplicifolia*), and other fine-textured plants. Use them in drifts as an accent along a stone wall or garden fence.

CULTIVARS: 'Alba' has pure white flowers. 'Grandiflora' has 2-inch (5 cm) blue flowers. 'Telham Beauty' has pale blue flowers on 3-foot (90 cm) stems.

Catananche caerulea   Compositae

CUPID'S DART

Cupid's dart produces tufts of narrow, wooly leaves from a fibrous rootstock. The straw-like flowers look great in the summer garden and dry easily for flower arrangements.

FLOWER COLOR: Blue 2-inch (5 cm) flowers resemble asters but lack the bold yellow center. Carried singly on wiry stems.

FLOWERING TIME: Summer.

HEIGHT AND SPREAD: 18–24 inches (45–60 cm) tall; 10–12 inches (25–30 cm) wide.

TEMPERATURE REQUIREMENTS: Zones 4–9. Heat-tolerant.

POSITION: Light, well-drained, humus-rich soil. Full sun. Good drainage is imperative for healthy growth.

CULTIVATION: Plants may be short-lived, especially in heavy soil. Divide plants every year to promote longevity.

PROPAGATION: Divide in fall. Take 2–3-inch (5–7.5 cm) root cuttings in fall or winter. Sow seed indoors in early spring. Plants will bloom the first year.

PEST AND DISEASE PREVENTION: No serious pests or diseases.

LANDSCAPE USE: Use in mass plantings in rock gardens or at the front of a dry, sunny perennial garden. Combine with yarrows and sundrops (*Oenothera* spp.).

CULTIVARS: 'Blue Giant' is a stout cultivar with dark blue flowers. 'Major' has lavender-blue flowers on 3-foot (90 cm) stems.

Centaurea dealbata   Compositae

KNAPWEED

Knapweeds have lobed leaves with 8–10 wooly divisions. The leaves clothe thick, weakly upright stems over fibrous-rooted crowns. Use the blooms as fresh cut flowers or for drying.

FLOWER COLOR: Fringed pink flowers have broad white centers. They resemble bachelor's buttons and are borne one to a stem.

FLOWERING TIME: Late spring and early summer.

HEIGHT AND SPREAD: 1½–2½ feet (45–75 cm) tall; 1½ feet (45 cm) wide.

TEMPERATURE REQUIREMENTS: Zones 3–7.

POSITION: Moist but well-drained, humus-rich soil. Full sun.

CULTIVATION: Remove flower heads as they fade to promote rebloom. Cut plants back to remove floppy stems when flower production wanes. Divide clumps every 2–3 years to keep plants vigorous.

PROPAGATION: Divide in spring or fall. Sow seed outdoors in fall or indoors in late winter.

PEST AND DISEASE PREVENTION: No serious pests or diseases.

LANDSCAPE USE: Combine knapweeds with ornamental grasses, coneflowers (*Rudbeckia* spp.), and yarrows in informal gardens and meadow plantings.

OTHER COMMON NAMES: Persian cornflower.

CULTIVARS: 'Steenbergii' is a long-flowering, compact selection with rose pink flowers. 'John Coutts', a selection of the related *C. hypoleuca,* has rosy purple flowers on 2-foot (60 cm) stems.

| *Centranthus ruber* | Valerianaceae | *Cerastium tomentosum* | Caryophyllaceae |

RED VALERIAN

Red valerian is an upright perennial with opposite, gray-green oval leaves and white, pink, or red flowers on branching stems. Plants grow from a fibrous-rooted crown.

FLOWER COLOR: Small flowers are carried in domed, branched clusters. Colors range from white to pink, rose, or coral red.

FLOWERING TIME: Spring and summer.

HEIGHT AND SPREAD: 1–3 feet (30–90 cm) tall; 2 feet (60 cm) wide.

TEMPERATURE REQUIREMENTS: Zones 4–8. Plants perform best in cool-summer areas.

POSITION: Average, sandy or loamy, neutral or alkaline soil. Full sun. Grows readily in rock crevices where soil is limited.

CULTIVATION: Plants may become floppy after blooming. Shear them back to promote compact growth and reblooming.

PROPAGATION: Sow seed outdoors in summer. Plants often self-sow prolifically. To reproduce plants of a specific color, remove basal shoots and treat them like cuttings.

PEST AND DISEASE PREVENTION: No serious pests or diseases.

LANDSCAPE USE: Perfect for wall and rock gardens. The striking coral red flowers combine well with the neutral colors of stone or with creamy yellow flowers.

OTHER COMMON NAMES: Jupiter's beard.

VARIETIES: *C. ruber* var. *albus* has white flowers; var. *coccineus* has deep red flowers; var. *roseus* has deep rose flowers.

SNOW-IN-SUMMER

Snow-in-summer is a low-mounding plant with small, wooly leaves and clusters of white flowers on wiry stems. Plants grow from a dense tangle of fibrous roots.

FLOWER COLOR: Snow white 1-inch (2.5 cm) flowers have five deeply notched petals that give the impression of a ten-petaled flower. Borne in open clusters held well above the foliage.

FLOWERING TIME: Late spring and early summer.

HEIGHT AND SPREAD: 6–10 inches (15–25 cm) tall; 12 inches (30 cm) wide.

TEMPERATURE REQUIREMENTS: Zones 2–7; extremely cold-tolerant.

POSITION: Average, sandy or loamy, well-drained soil. Full sun.

CULTIVATION: Shear plants to the ground after flowering to promote fresh, compact growth. Clumps spread easily and may overgrow their position.

PROPAGATION: Divide in spring or fall and replant vigorous portions. Take tip cuttings in early summer.

PEST AND DISEASE PREVENTION: Relatively pest-free. May suffer from fungal rots that blacken the leaves and stems. Remove and destroy infected foliage. Well-drained soil and cool summer temperatures are the best preventive.

LANDSCAPE USE: Choose snow-in-summer for cascading over a wall, planting in a rock garden, or for edging a path. The profusion of flowers is a bright addition to the spring garden with late bulbs and Johnny jump-ups (*Viola tricolor*).

CULTIVARS: 'Silver Carpet' is a compact selection.

| *Ceratostigma plumbaginoides* | Plumbaginaceae | *Chelone lyonii* | Scrophulariaceae |

PLUMBAGO

PINK TURTLEHEAD

Plumbago is a creeping, semiwoody perennial with russet stems and sparse wedge-shaped leaves. Plants die back to the ground each year; prune out winter-damaged stems by late spring.

FLOWER COLOR: Deep gentian blue flowers are carried in clusters at the tips of the stems.

FLOWERING TIME: Mid- to late summer, often into fall.

HEIGHT AND SPREAD: 6–12 inches (15–30 cm) tall; 12–18 inches (30–45 cm) wide; wider with age.

TEMPERATURE REQUIREMENTS: Zones 5–9; quite heat-tolerant.

POSITION: Average to humus-rich, moist but well-drained soil. Full sun to partial shade. Plants will survive on dry, sunny banks or under shrubs, but not in the dense, dry shade of large trees.

CULTIVATION: Prune stems back to the ground in fall or spring. New growth emerges in late spring. Foliage often turns orange in fall.

PROPAGATION: Divide in early spring. Take tip cuttings in early summer.

PEST AND DISEASE PREVENTION: No serious pests or diseases.

LANDSCAPE USE: Plant as a groundcover under flowering shrubs, along walks, in rock walls, or at the front of the perennial garden. Interplant the creeping stems with spring- and fall-flowering bulbs like crocuses, miniature daffodils, spider lilies (*Lycoris* spp.), and fall crocuses (*Colchicum* spp.). The creeping stems hide the declining bulb foliage.

OTHER COMMON NAMES: Leadwort.

Pink turtleheads are bushy perennials with tall, leafy stems from a stout, fibrous-rooted crown. The 4–7-inch (10–17.5 cm) leaves are broadly ovate with toothed margins.

FLOWER COLOR: Rose pink inflated, tubular flowers resemble the head of a turtle with jaws open.

FLOWERING TIME: Late summer into fall.

HEIGHT AND SPREAD: 1–3 feet (30–90 cm) tall; 1–2 feet (30–60 cm) wide.

TEMPERATURE REQUIREMENTS: Zones 3–8; intolerant of excessive heat.

POSITION: Evenly moist, humus-rich soil. Full sun to partial shade. Tolerates drier soil once established.

CULTIVATION: Divide the crowns to reduce large clumps in aged plants.

PROPAGATION: Divide in spring or after flowering. Take stem cuttings in early summer; remove any flower buds. Sow seed outdoors in fall or indoors in late winter after stratification. To stratify, mix seed with moist peat moss or seed-starting medium in a plastic bag. Close the bag with a twist-tie and refrigerate for 4–6 weeks. Then sow the mixture as you would normal seed.

PEST AND DISEASE PREVENTION: No serious pests or diseases.

LANDSCAPE USE: Combine with asters, phlox, and goldenrods (*Solidago* spp.) for late summer color.

OTHER SPECIES:
C. glabra, white turtlehead, has narrow leaves and white flowers. Zones 3–8.
C. obliqua, rose turtlehead, is similar to *C. lyonii* but flowers later and is less cold hardy. Zones 5–9.

Chrysanthemum x *morifolium*   Compositae

GARDEN MUM

Hardy garden mums have stout stems clothed in lobed leaves. They grow from creeping stems with tangled fibrous roots. Most garden mums bloom in late summer and fall.

FLOWER COLOR: Garden mums bloom in a wide variety of colors from white to pale pink, rose, burgundy, red, golden brown, gold, yellow, and cream. Flower shapes range from button-like heads to pom-poms (double ball-shaped flowers), cushions (flat, fully double flowers), and decoratives (large double to semidouble heads). There are even novelty hybrids with spider-like heads and those with spoon-shaped petals. Flower sizes range from 1–6 inches (2.5–15 cm).

FLOWERING TIME: Late summer through fall.

HEIGHT AND SPREAD: 1½–5 feet (45–150 cm) tall; 1–3 feet (30–90 cm) wide.

TEMPERATURE REQUIREMENTS: Garden mums vary in their hardiness. Greenhouse crops are less hardy than those selected for extreme cold tolerance by the University of Minnesota and the Morden Arboretum in Canada. Zones 3–9.

POSITION: Light, humus-rich, well-drained soil. Full sun to light shade.

CULTIVATION: Many garden mums tend to sprawl in summer. Pinch the stems once or twice in May or June to promote compact growth. Stop pinching altogether by July 1 or you will sacrifice bloom. To encourage larger flowers, remove axillary buds, (those surrounding the largest main bud). This process, called disbudding, allows the stem to direct its energy into producing one large flower.

To promote the largest number of flowers on your mums, pinch the stems back once or twice during the summer. Stop pinching by July to allow buds to form for fall.

Garden mums spread outward from the center by creeping stems. Divide the fast-growing clumps every 1–2 years to keep them vigorous. Replant vigorous shoots into soil that has been enriched with organic matter.

PROPAGATION: Divide in spring. Tip cuttings taken in late spring or early summer root quickly and often bloom in the first season.

PEST AND DISEASE PREVENTION: Aphids may attack the young shoots and will deform growth and decrease vigor if not controlled. Spider mites may cause stippling and leaf curl. Spray with insecticidal soap or a botanical insecticide such as pyrethrin.

LANDSCAPE USE: The bright colors of garden mums are a familiar sight in late summer. Use them to breathe new life into tired annual displays or combine them with asters, goldenrods (*Solidago* spp.), and anemones for a showy fall display.

OTHER COMMON NAMES: Florist's chrysanthemum, hardy chrysanthemum, hardy mum, mum. Also known as *Dendranthema* x *grandiflorum*.

CULTIVARS: The array of garden mums available is astounding. Since they vary in hardiness and bloom time, consult your local garden center for the selections that are recommended for your area.

OTHER SPECIES: *C.* x 'Mei-kyo' (*Dendranthema* x 'Mei-kyo') is an old-fashioned hybrid with double rose

GARDEN MUM—Continued

SHASTA DAISY

Plant chrysanthemums in containers for a seasonal display of color, or use them in beds and borders to replace worn-out annuals at the end of the season.

pink flowers with yellow centers. Zones 6–9.

C. pacificum (*Ajania pacifica*), gold-and-silver chrysanthemum. This lovely foliage plant forms low mats of scalloped silver-edged leaves. The button-like yellow flowers open in October. Zones 5–9.

C. zawadskii var. *latilobum* (*Dendranthema zawadskii*) hardy garden chrysanthemum. Also sold as *C.* x *rubellum.* These early-blooming, hardy mums have deeply lobed leaves and 2-inch (5 cm) single flowers in August and September. 'Clara Curtis' has deep pink flowers. 'Duchess of Edinburgh' has semidouble wine red flowers. 'Mary Stoker' has straw yellow flowers tinged with apricot. Zones 4–9.

Shasta daisies are showy, summer-blooming plants with dense clusters of shiny 10-inch (25 cm), deep green, toothed leaves and short, creeping, fibrous-rooted stems.

FLOWER COLOR: Bright white 3-inch (7.5 cm) daisies with large, bright yellow centers are carried on stout, leafy stems.

FLOWERING TIME: Throughout summer.

HEIGHT AND SPREAD: 1–3 feet (30–90 cm) tall; 2 feet (60 cm) wide.

TEMPERATURE REQUIREMENTS: Zones 3–10. Extremely cold- and heat-tolerant. Exact zones vary by cultivar.

POSITION: Average to rich, well-drained soil. Full sun. Tolerates seaside conditions but not waterlogged soil.

CULTIVATION: Shasta daisies are easy-care perennials. Deadhead plants to promote continued bloom. Plants grow quickly but may be short-lived especially in warmer zones. Divide and replant clumps in organically enriched soil every 3–4 years to keep them vigorous.

PROPAGATION: Remove offsets from the main clump or divide in spring.

PEST AND DISEASE PREVENTION: No serious pests or diseases.

LANDSCAPE USE: Combine with summer-blooming perennials like daylilies, irises, and poppies. In a seaside garden, plant them with blanket flowers (*Gaillardia* spp.) and coreopsis.

OTHER NAMES: *Leucanthemum* x *superbum.*

CULTIVARS: 'Alaska' is an old-fashioned cultivar with

BLACK SNAKEROOT

The cheerful flowers of shasta daisies combine well with other colors in the summer garden. Try compact cultivars as edgings; use taller ones mid-border.

The wand-like spires of black snakeroot wave above an open cluster of large compound leaves with toothed leaflets. Plants grow from a stout, fibrous-rooted crown.

3-inch (7.5 cm) single white flowers on 2–3-foot (60–90 cm) stems. 'Little Miss Muffet' is a dwarf 8–12-inch (20–30 cm) tall selection with single, creamy white flowers. 'Polaris' is a stately 3-foot (90 cm) selection with huge, 5-inch (12.5 cm) single flowers. 'T. E. Killen' is a 3-foot (90 cm) tall, sturdy, single-flowered selection that blooms in mid- to late summer.

OTHER SPECIES:

C. coccineum (Tanacetum coccineum), painted daisy, pyrethrin. A robust plant with finely divided leaves and 3-inch (7.5 cm) pink, rose, or red single flowers in summer. Extracts from this plant are used to produce an insecticide that controls aphids, flies, and mosquitoes. Zones 3–7.

C. frutescens (Argyranthemum frutescens), marguerite. Marguerites are bushy plants with deeply lobed, dissected leaves and 2-inch (5 cm) white or yellow flowers on thin stems above the foliage. Zones 9–11. Often grown as an annual in colder zones.

C. leucanthemum (Leucanthemum vulgare), oxeye daisy. This popular roadside plant has 2-inch (5 cm) pure white flowers with bright yellow centers. 'May Queen' is a long-blooming selection. Zones 2–10.

C. parthenium (Tanacetum parthenium), feverfew. Small, tightly packed heads of foamy white flowers nearly obscure the lobed foliage of this fast-growing plant. Zones 4–8.

FLOWER COLOR: The small, ½-inch (12 mm) creamy white flowers have a dense whorl of fuzzy stamens (male reproductive structures) and no petals. They are carried on tall, sparsely branched spikes.

FLOWERING TIME: Early to midsummer.

HEIGHT AND SPREAD: 4–7 feet (1.2–2.1 cm) tall; 3–4 feet (90–120 cm) wide.

TEMPERATURE REQUIREMENTS: Zones 3–8.

POSITION: Moist, humus-rich soil. Full sun to partial shade. Protect from afternoon sun in warmer zones. Dense shade may produce sparse flowers. Somewhat drought-tolerant once established.

CULTIVATION: Black snakeroot is an extremely long-lived perennial. Young plants take several years to reach flowering size. Clumps increase gradually each year and may have 10–15 bloom stalks at maturity.

PROPAGATION: Divide clumps with a sharp knife in fall or spring. Leave at least one bud per division. Sow fresh seed outdoors in fall. It may take two seasons to germinate.

PEST AND DISEASE PREVENTION: No serious pests or diseases.

LANDSCAPE USE: Place at the rear of borders with bold flowers like phlox and daylilies. In the woodland garden, combine with ferns, hostas, and wildflowers.

OTHER COMMON NAMES: Black cohosh, bugbane.

Coreopsis verticillata   Compositae

THREAD-LEAVED COREOPSIS

Thread-leaved coreopsis is an airy, rounded plant with thread-like, three-lobed leaves and bright yellow summer flowers. Plants grow from a fibrous-rooted crown.

FLOWER COLOR: The 1–2-inch (2.5–5 cm) starry flowers are butter to golden yellow.

FLOWERING TIME: Throughout summer.

HEIGHT AND SPREAD: 1–3 feet (30–90 cm) tall; 2–3 feet (60–90 cm) wide.

TEMPERATURE REQUIREMENTS: Zones 3–9.

POSITION: Average to rich, moist but well-drained soil. Full sun or light shade; drought-tolerant once established.

CULTIVATION: Thread-leaved coreopsis is an easy-care perennial that demands little attention once established. Plants eventually die out at the center. Divide old clumps and replant in enriched soil.

PROPAGATION: Divide in spring or fall. Take stem cuttings in early summer.

PEST AND DISEASE PREVENTION: No serious pests or diseases.

LANDSCAPE USE: Perfect for the front of the border with cranesbills (*Geranium* spp.), yarrows, daylilies, and coneflowers (*Rudbeckia* and *Echinacea* spp.). Combine them with ornamental grasses or use a mass planting with shrubs.

CULTIVARS: 'Golden Showers' grows 2 feet (60 cm) tall with golden yellow flowers. 'Moonbeam' is a spreading plant from 1–2 feet (30–60 cm) wide with pale yellow flowers from early summer through fall. 'Zagreb' is a compact, 8–18-inch (20–45 cm) selection similar to 'Golden Showers'.

Crocosmia x *crocosmiiflora*   Iridaceae

CROCOSMIA

Crocosmia is a brightly colored perennial with vivid red or orange summer flowers and fans of sword-like leaves resembling gladiolus. They grow from button-like corms.

FLOWER COLOR: Tubular orange or red flowers are carried on erect, sparsely branched, zigzag stems.

FLOWERING TIME: Summer and early fall; varies with individual cultivars.

HEIGHT AND SPREAD: 2–3 feet (60–90 cm) tall; 1–2 feet (30–60 cm) wide.

TEMPERATURE REQUIREMENTS: Zones 6–9. In colder zones, lift corms in fall and store in a cool, dry place.

POSITION: Moist, humus-rich soil. Full sun.

CULTIVATION: Crocosmias spread to form broad clumps of tightly packed foliage fans. Remove the spent stalks after flowering. Divide overgrown clumps in spring. If you store corms over winter, replant them when temperatures moderate.

PROPAGATION: Remove corms from the outside of the clump in spring.

PEST AND DISEASE PREVENTION: Spider mites and thrips cause white or brown stippling or streaks on the leaves. Spray with insecticidal soap or with a botanical insecticide such as pyrethrin. Cut badly damaged plants to the ground and destroy the infested portions.

LANDSCAPE USE: Plant with summer perennials like phlox, daylilies, and poppies. Use large clumps as accents along walls or with shrubs.

CULTIVARS: 'Citronella' has orange-yellow flowers. 'Solfatare' has golden yellow flowers.

Delphinium x *elatum* hybrids   Ranunculaceae

HYBRID DELPHINIUM

Hybrid delphiniums are stately border plants with dense flower clusters atop tall stems with deeply cut, palmately lobed leaves. Plants grow from stout crowns with thick, fleshy roots.

Delphiniums are showstoppers in the summer garden. Plant them at the back of the border as a vertical accent to mounded plants like peonies.

FLOWER COLOR: Showy flowers ranging in color from white through all shades of true blue to lavender and purple. Five petal-like sepals surround two to four small, true petals that are often called the "bee." The top sepal has a long spur.

FLOWERING TIME: Late spring through summer, depending on the hybrid group. Plants may rebloom in fall.

HEIGHT AND SPREAD: 4½–6 feet (1.35–1.8 cm) tall; 2–3 feet (60–90 cm) wide.

TEMPERATURE REQUIREMENTS: Zones 4–7. Many hybrids are hardy to Zone 3.

POSITION: Evenly moist but well-drained, fertile, humus-rich soil. Full sun. A neutral to slightly acid soil is best. Add ground limestone to raise the pH if necessary.

CULTIVATION: Often short-lived in warm climates. Hybrid delphiniums are particularly sensitive to high night temperatures. The wild species are often longer-lived than the hybrids. Delphiniums are heavy feeders and benefit from an annual spring topdressing of a balanced organic fertilizer or well-rotted manure. Set out new plants in spring, taking care not to damage the thick roots. Mature plants produce many stems. Thin the clumps to three to five stems as they emerge to promote strong growth and to reduce the chance of disease. To encourage plants to rebloom, cut off old flowering stems above the foliage below the flower spike. New shoots often emerge from the crown. When they develop, cut the old shoots to the ground to enable the new ones to flower by fall. Divide overgrown plants and replant into soil that has been enriched with organic matter.

PROPAGATION: Divide in spring. Sow fresh seed in summer or fall. Take cuttings in spring from the new shoots; use the stems removed from thinning the clumps for propagation.

PEST AND DISEASE PREVENTION: Exclude (slugs which attack the leaves and stems) with a ring of diatomaceous earth, wood ashes, or sand around the clumps, or lure them to their demise in a shallow pan of beer set flush with the soil surface. Powdery mildew may cause white blotches on the leaves. Dust affected parts with sulfur. Plant resistant cultivars and thin the stems to avoid the problem.

LANDSCAPE USE: Plant at the rear of borders where their showy spires will tower over other summer-blooming perennials like phlox, lilies, lupines, and bellflowers (*Campanula* spp.). Flowers show off to best advantage when displayed in front of a wall or lush hedge.

HYBRIDS: Hundreds of hybrid delphiniums are available, many of which have *D. elatum* in their parentage. A few of the popular selections are listed here.

HYBRID DELPHINIUM—CONTINUED

COTTAGE PINKS

The ruffled flowers of delphiniums are a natural choice for a cottage garden. Combine them with lilies, irises, and poppies for a charming, informal effect.

Cottage pinks are popular, sweet-scented plants for the garden or for cutting. The broad, mounded plants produce dense clusters of 3-inch (7.5 cm), blue-green, grass-like leaves.

Blackmore and Langdon hybrids are a seed-grown strain of mixed colors. Mid-Century hybrids are mildew-resistant selections in mixed colors. 'Ivory Towers' has white flowers. 'Moody Blues' is light blue. 'Ultra Violet' is dark blue. The Pacific Hybrids have 1½–2-inch (3.5–5 cm) single or semi-double flowers. 'Astolat' is lavender with a dark center. 'Black Knight' has purple flowers. 'Galahad' has white flowers in midsummer. 'Summer Skies' is light blue with a darker center.

OTHER SPECIES:

D. x *belladonna* hybrids are hardy, heat-resistant, compact plants. 'Bellamosum' has deep blue flowers on 4-foot (1.2 m) stalks. 'Casa Blanca' has pure white flowers. 'Clivedon Beauty' grows 3 feet (90 cm) tall and has sky blue flowers. All are hardy to Zone 3.

FLOWER COLOR: Fragrant white or pink flowers are borne in open clusters on wiry stems.

FLOWERING TIME: Early to midsummer.

HEIGHT AND SPREAD: 1½–2 feet (45–60 cm) tall; 1 foot (30 cm) wide.

TEMPERATURE REQUIREMENTS: Zones 3–9. Tolerates extreme heat and cold.

POSITION: Average, well-drained, sandy or loamy soil. Full sun. The soil should be neutral or only slightly acid for best growth. Plants tolerate alkaline soil.

CULTIVATION: Plants may be short-lived, especially in warmer zones. Divide clumps every 2–3 years to keep them vigorous. Remove flowers as they fade to promote continued bloom.

PROPAGATION: Layer or take stem cuttings from the foliage rosettes in summer. Strip leaves from the lower third of a 2–3-inch (5–7.5 cm) cutting. Place cutting in a medium of one part vermiculite and two parts sand or perlite to allow excellent drainage and air circulation.

PEST AND DISEASE PREVENTION: Rust causes yellow blotches on the upper surface of the leaves and raised orange spots on the lower surface. To discourage rust, thin clumps for better air circulation and dust with sulfur.

LANDSCAPE USE: Plant at the front of borders or use them as an edging along paths. They grow well in sunny rock gardens or cascading over rock walls.

COMMON BLEEDING HEART

The brightly colored flowers of maiden pinks cover the low-growing foliage in summer. Maiden pinks are well suited to a rock garden or rock wall.

Common bleeding hearts are beloved, old-fashioned perennials with strings of hearts held above deeply divided blue-green foliage. Plants grow from thick, fleshy roots.

CULTIVARS: 'Essex Witch' has rose pink flowers. 'Helen' has double salmon-pink flowers. 'Mrs. Sinkins' has fragrant, double white flowers. 'Spring Beauty' is a seed-grown strain of clove-scented semidouble to double flowers in white, pink, rose, and red.

OTHER SPECIES:

D. alpinus, alpine pinks. These clump-forming perennials have bright green leaves and 1½-inch (3.5 cm) single pink flowers. Zones 3–7.

D. barbatus, sweet William. This biennial or short-lived perennial forms tufts of deep green, lance-shaped leaves and dense, rounded clusters of 1-inch (2.5 cm) bicolored pink, rose, or white flowers. Zones 3–9.

D. deltoides, maiden pinks. A mat-forming pink with green leaves and a mass of single rose-colored flowers borne one to a stem. Zones 3–9.

D. gratianopolitanus, cheddar pinks. This spring-blooming pink has 1-inch (2.5 cm), fragrant rose pink flowers borne singly or in pairs. Many varieties and cultivars are available. 'Bath's Pink' has fringed soft-pink flowers. 'Splendens' has deep red flowers. 'Tiny Rubies' has deep pink double flowers. *D. gratianopolitanus* var. *grandiflorus* has 1½-inch (3.5 cm) rose pink flowers. Zones 3–9.

D. superbus, lilac pinks. This stunning pink has deeply fringed pink, lavender, or white flowers borne in open clusters on wiry stems. Zones 4–8.

FLOWER COLOR: Bright pink heart-shaped flowers consist of two reflexed lobes with a central column that resembles a dangling drop of blood.

FLOWERING TIME: Early spring to early summer.

HEIGHT AND SPREAD: 1–2½ feet (30–75 cm) tall; 2–3 feet (60–90 cm) wide.

TEMPERATURE REQUIREMENTS: Zones 2–9. Extremely tolerant of heat and cold. Mulch in winter in colder zones.

POSITION: Evenly moist, humus-rich soil. Partial shade; tolerates full sun in cooler zones.

CULTIVATION: Common bleeding hearts will bloom for 4–6 weeks in spring. In warm climates or if soil is dry, plants will go dormant after blooming. Top-dress with well-rotted manure in early spring to maintain soil fertility. If plants lose vigor, lift and divide clumps and replant into soil that has been enriched with organic matter.

PROPAGATION: Divide clumps in fall or as they go dormant. Sow fresh seed outdoors in summer. Take root cuttings in late summer.

PEST AND DISEASE PREVENTION: No serious pests or diseases.

LANDSCAPE USE: Plant common bleeding hearts with spring bulbs, primroses, and wildflowers for a striking spring display. In warm zones combine them with hostas or groundcovers that will fill the void left by the declining foliage.

Dictamnus albus	Rutaceae	*Digitalis* x *mertonensis*	Scrophulariaceae

GAS PLANT

STRAWBERRY FOXGLOVE

Gas plant forms shrub-like clumps of stout stems with deep green, pinnately lobed leaves and erect flower spikes. Plants grow from thick, woody crowns with fibrous roots.

FLOWER COLOR: The 1-inch (2.5 cm), showy white flowers have five starry petals and ten long, curled stamens (male reproductive structures) that protrude from the flower. The starry seed capsules are attractive throughout summer.

FLOWERING TIME: Late spring or early summer.

HEIGHT AND SPREAD: 1–4 feet (30–120 cm) tall; 1–3 feet (30–90 cm) wide.

TEMPERATURE REQUIREMENTS: Zones 3–8.

POSITION: Well-drained, average to humus-rich soil. Full sun to light shade.

CULTIVATION: Gas plants are long-lived perennials that are slow to establish and resent disturbance once planted. Established plants are trouble-free.

PROPAGATION: Sow fresh seed outdoors in late summer. Seedlings appear the next season but grow slowly. Transplant young plants to their permanent position after 3 years of growth.

PEST AND DISEASE PREVENTION: No serious pests. Avoid soggy soils, which will encourage root rot. Dispose of infected plants.

LANDSCAPE USE: Combine gas plants with other perennials that need good drainage, such as oriental poppy (*Papaver orientale*), yarrows, and sundrops (*Oenothera* spp.).

OTHER COMMON NAMES: Dittany.

CULTIVARS: 'Purpureus' has dark-veined violet purple flowers. 'Ruber' has pale red-violet flowers.

The popular strawberry foxglove has fuzzy, broad, lance-shaped leaves. Rosettes of foliage form at the base of the flowering stems and persist over winter.

FLOWER COLOR: The 2–3-inch (5–7.5 cm) tubular flowers are flushed with pink, rose, or purple on the outside and heavily spotted with dark purple or brown on the inside. Some selections are pure white.

FLOWERING TIME: Plants flower throughout summer and often rebloom.

HEIGHT AND SPREAD: 3–4 feet (90–120 cm) tall; 1 foot (30 cm) wide.

TEMPERATURE REQUIREMENTS: Zones 3–8.

POSITION: Moist but well-drained, humus-rich soil. Full sun to partial shade.

CULTIVATION: Strawberry foxgloves are easy-care perennials that bloom tirelessly with little care. Divide overgrown clumps and replant into soil that has been enriched with organic matter. Remove spent bloom stalks to promote rebloom. Leave one stalk to self-sow.

PROPAGATION: Divide in spring or fall. Sow fresh seed outdoors in fall. Seedlings emerge the next spring and will bloom the second year.

PEST AND DISEASE PREVENTION: No serious pests or diseases.

LANDSCAPE USE: Plant at the middle or rear of perennial gardens. In informal gardens combine them with ferns and ornamental grasses. Use mass plantings along a wall or fence or in combination with flowering shrubs.

LEOPARD'S BANE

The graceful flower spikes of common foxgloves are a traditional favorite for the cottage garden. Plants usually self-sow if you allow them to set seed.

OTHER SPECIES:

   D. ferruginea, rusty foxglove, grows 4–5 feet (1.2–1.5 m) tall, with narrow spikes of 1-inch (2.5 cm) rusty brown-and-white flowers. Zones 4–7.

   D. grandiflora, yellow foxglove, has 2-inch (5 cm) soft-yellow flowers on 1–3-foot (30–90 cm) stalks. The lush foliage is also attractive. Zones 3–8.

   D. lutea has small creamy yellow flowers in narrow 2–3-foot (60–90 cm) spikes. Zones 4–8.

   D. purpurea, common foxglove, is a biennial or short-lived perennial with 2–5-foot (60–150 cm) spikes of purple, rose, pink, or white flowers. Set out new plants in spring for bloom the same season or in fall for bloom the following year. To promote rebloom, divide the plants after flowering. Remove the new rosettes from the bloom stalk and replant into soil that has been enriched with organic matter. 'Alba' has white flowers. 'Excelsior' hybrids have dense spikes in a variety of colors.

Leopard's bane (also listed as D. caucasicum*) is a brightly colored spring daisy with deep green, triangular leaves in open clusters from a fibrous-rooted crown.*

FLOWER COLOR: Dozens of 1–2-inch (2.5–5 cm) bright yellow single daisies are borne on slender, leafless stems.

FLOWERING TIME: Spring and early summer.

HEIGHT AND SPREAD: 1–2 feet (30–60 cm) tall; 1 foot (30 cm) wide.

TEMPERATURE REQUIREMENTS: Zones 3–8.

POSITION: Moist, humus-rich soil. Full sun to shade. Soil must not dry out while plant is actively growing.

CULTIVATION: Leopard's banes emerge early in spring and may be damaged by late frosts. Plants go dormant after flowering in warmer zones. In colder zones, the foliage remains all season, so moist soil is imperative. Mulch will help keep the soil cool. Divide clumps every 2–3 years to keep them vigorous.

PROPAGATION: Divide in spring or fall. Sow seed indoors in late winter or early spring.

PEST AND DISEASE PREVENTION: No serious pests or diseases.

LANDSCAPE USE: Combine with clustered bellflower (*Campanula glomerata*), Virginia bluebells (*Mertensia virginica*), spring bulbs, and wildflowers. Plant foliage plants such as hostas to fill the voids when plants go dormant.

CULTIVARS: 'Magnificum' has showy 2-inch (5 cm) flowers.

| *Echinacea purpurea* | Compositae | *Echinops ritro* | Compositae |

PURPLE CONEFLOWER

Purple coneflowers are showy summer daisies with sparse, 6-inch (15 cm) oval or broadly lance-shaped leaves on stout, hairy stems. Plants grow from thick, deep taproots.

FLOWER COLOR: Red-violet to rose pink flowers have broad, drooping rays (petal-like structures) surrounding raised, bristly cones.

FLOWERING TIME: Mid- to late summer.

HEIGHT AND SPREAD: 2–4 feet (60–120 cm) tall; 1–2 feet (30–60 cm) wide.

TEMPERATURE REQUIREMENTS: Zones 3–8. Extremely heat-tolerant.

POSITION: Average to humus-rich, moist but well-drained soil. Full sun. Drought-tolerant once established.

CULTIVATION: Plants increase from basal buds to form broad, long-lived clumps. Division is seldom necessary and is not recommended.

PROPAGATION: Sow seed outdoors in fall or indoors after stratification. To stratify, mix seed with moist peat moss or seed-starting medium in a plastic bag. Close the bag with a twist-tie and place it in the refrigerator for 4–6 weeks. Sow the mixture as you would normal seed. Take root cuttings in fall.

PEST AND DISEASE PREVENTION: No serious pests or diseases.

LANDSCAPE USE: Plant in formal perennial gardens or meadow and prairie gardens. The flowers combine well with most perennials and ornamental grasses.

CULTIVARS: 'Alba' has creamy white flowers. 'Bright Star' has flat rose pink flowers. 'Magnus' has huge, flat rose-purple flowers.

GLOBE THISTLE

Globe thistles are stout, coarse perennials with spiky round flower heads, erect stems, and spiny, lobed leaves. They grow from thick, deep-branched taproots.

FLOWER COLOR: Small steel blue flowers are packed into 1–2-inch (2.5–5 cm) spherical heads.

FLOWERING TIME: Midsummer.

HEIGHT AND SPREAD: 2–4 feet (60–120 cm) tall; 2–3 feet (60–90 cm) wide.

TEMPERATURE REQUIREMENTS: Zones 3–8. Heat-tolerant.

POSITION: Average to humus-rich, well-drained soil. Full sun. Good drainage is essential, especially in winter.

CULTIVATION: Globe thistles are tough, long-lived perennials. They are drought-tolerant once established and thrive for many years without staking or division.

PROPAGATION: Remove sideshoots from the main clump without disturbing the crown in fall or late winter. Take root cuttings in spring or fall.

PEST AND DISEASE PREVENTION: No serious pests. Plant in well-drained soil to avoid root rot.

LANDSCAPE USE: Combine showy globe thistles with other drought-tolerant perennials like Russian sages (*Perovskia* spp.), sedums, catmints (*Nepeta* spp.), and oriental poppy (*Papaver orientale*). Position them near the middle or rear of borders. The flowers are perfect for cutting fresh or for drying.

CULTIVARS: 'Taplow Blue' has 2-inch (5 cm) blue heads. 'Veitch's Blue' is darker with sturdier stems.

Epimedium x *versicolor*   Berberidaceae

PERSIAN EPIMEDIUM

Persian epimedium is a woodland groundcover with semi-evergreen leaves divided into glossy heart-shaped leaflets. The wiry, trailing stems have matted, fibrous roots.

FLOWER COLOR: The unusual flowers have eight yellow petal-like sepals and four spurred petals that are tinged with red. They are held above the new leaves as they emerge.

FLOWERING TIME: Early to midspring.

HEIGHT AND SPREAD: 10–12 inches (25–30 cm) tall; 12 inches (30 cm) wide.

TEMPERATURE REQUIREMENTS: Zones 5–8.

POSITION: Moist, humus-rich soil. Partial to full shade. Avoid waterlogged soil, especially during winter.

CULTIVATION: Persian epimediums thrive for years with little attention. They perform well under adverse conditions, even in the dry shade of mature trees. Mulch plants in winter. Cut foliage to the ground to allow the flowers to emerge unobscured.

PROPAGATION: Divide overgrown clumps in late summer or spring.

PEST AND DISEASE PREVENTION: No serious pests or diseases.

LANDSCAPE USE: Plant in woodland gardens with hostas, wildflowers, and ferns. Combine them with spring bulbs, hellebores (*Helleborus* spp.), and primroses.

OTHER COMMON NAMES: Bicolor barrenwort.

CULTIVARS: 'Neosulphureum' has yellow flowers with short spurs. 'Sulphureum' has yellow flowers and leafy flowering stems. 'Versicolor' has two-toned yellow flowers.

Eremurus stenophyllus   Liliaceae

FOXTAIL LILY

Foxtail lilies are robust, stately perennials with tall flower spikes and clumps of strap-like foliage. Plants grow from a thickened crown with brittle, spreading roots.

FLOWER COLOR: Starry, 1-inch (2.5 cm) six-petaled flowers are crowded on tall, pointed spikes.

FLOWERING TIME: Spring and summer.

HEIGHT AND SPREAD: 2–3 feet (60–90 cm) tall; 2 feet (60 cm) wide.

TEMPERATURE REQUIREMENTS: Zones 5–9.

POSITION: Moist but well-drained, humus-rich soil. Full sun to light shade. Soggy soil, especially in winter, promotes root rot.

CULTIVATION: Plant crowns 4–6 inches (10–15 cm) deep. Do not allow them to dry out. Mulch to protect emerging leaves from late frosts. Divide clumps if they become crowded or if bloom wanes.

PROPAGATION: Divide in fall. Sow fresh seed outdoors in fall or indoors after stratification. To stratify, mix seed with moist peat moss or seed-starting medium in a plastic bag. Close the bag with a twist-tie and place it in the refrigerator for 4–6 weeks. Then sow the mixture as you would normal seed.

PEST AND DISEASE PREVENTION: No serious pests or diseases.

LANDSCAPE USE: Plant among perennials or against a wall or hedge. Surround with bold poppies (*Papaver* spp.), daylilies (*Hemerocallis* spp.), and irises.

CULTIVARS: 'Shelford Hybrids' are a hybrid group with 5–6-foot (1.5–1.8 cm) spikes of white, yellow, or pink flowers.

| _Erigeron speciosus_ | Compositae | _Eryngium amethystinum_ | Umbelliferae |

DAISY FLEABANE

AMETHYST SEA HOLLY

Daisy fleabane forms leafy clumps of hairy, 6-inch (15 cm) lance-shaped leaves that spring from fibrous-rooted crowns. The colorful flowers bloom in summer.

FLOWER COLOR: The 1½-inch (3.5 cm) aster-like flowers have white, pink, rose, or purple rays surrounding bright yellow centers.

FLOWERING TIME: Early to midsummer; occasional rebloom.

HEIGHT AND SPREAD: 1½–2½ feet (45–75 cm) tall; 1–2 feet (30–60 cm) wide.

TEMPERATURE REQUIREMENTS: Zones 2–9. Tolerant of heat and cold.

POSITION: Moist but well-drained, average to humus-rich soil. Full sun to light shade.

CULTIVATION: Fleabanes are long-lived perennials that benefit from division every 2–3 years.

PROPAGATION: Divide in fall. Take cuttings in spring before the flower buds form. Sow seed outdoors in fall or indoors in spring.

PEST AND DISEASE PREVENTION: No serious pests or diseases.

LANDSCAPE USE: Plant at the front of beds and borders with summer-blooming perennials like cranesbills (_Geranium_ spp.), cinquefoils (_Potentilla_ spp.), evening primroses (_Oenothera_ spp.), and phlox. Daisy fleabanes make long-lasting cut flowers.

HYBRIDS: Many hybrid cultivars originate from crosses with _E. speciosus_. 'Azure Fairy' has semidouble lavender-blue flowers. 'Darkest of All' has violet-blue flowers. 'Foerster's Darling' has reddish pink flowers. 'Prosperity' has pale lilac flowers.

Amethyst sea holly is an architectural plant with stiff flowering stems and mostly basal, pinnately divided leaves. Plants grow from thick taproots.

FLOWER COLOR: Small, steel blue globose flower heads are surrounded by thin, spiny bracts.

FLOWERING TIME: Summer.

HEIGHT AND SPREAD: 1–1½ feet (30–45 cm) tall; 1–2 feet (30–60 cm) wide.

TEMPERATURE REQUIREMENTS: Zone 2–8. Heat- and cold-tolerant.

POSITION: Average, well-drained soil. Full sun. Extremely drought-tolerant once established.

CULTIVATION: Set plants out in their permanent location while they are young. Older plants resent disturbance. Division is seldom necessary.

PROPAGATION: Sow fresh seed outdoors in fall or indoors after stratification. To stratify, mix seed with moist peat moss or seed-starting medium in a plastic bag. Close the bag with a twist-tie and place it in the refrigerator for 4–6 weeks. Then sow the mixture as you would normal seed.

PEST AND DISEASE PREVENTION: No serious pests or diseases.

LANDSCAPE USE: Plant in the middle of borders with goldenrods (_Solidago_ spp.), asters, phlox, and ornamental grasses.

OTHER SPECIES:

E. alpinum, alpine sea holly, is similar but has larger, showier flowers and lobed leaves. Zones 3–8.

_E._ x _zabelii_, zabel eryngo, is a showy hybrid with large blue-violet flowers. Zones 4–8.

Euphorbia myrsinites   Euphorbiaceae

MYRTLE EUPHORBIA

Myrtle euphorbia is a creeping plant with thick stems and succulent, blue-gray wedge-shaped leaves. It grows from fleshy, fibrous roots. The showy yellow flower heads appear in spring.

FLOWER COLOR: Unusual flower heads consist of tiny yellow flowers surrounded by showy funnel-shaped yellow bracts (modified leaves).

FLOWERING TIME: Spring.

HEIGHT AND SPREAD: 6–10 inches (15–25 cm) tall; 12–24 inches (30–60 cm) wide.

TEMPERATURE REQUIREMENTS: Zones 5–9.

POSITION: Average to humus-rich, well-drained soil. Full sun to light shade. Plants will grow in poor, gravelly soils.

CULTIVATION: Myrtle euphorbias are long-lived, easy-care garden residents. They thrive on neglect. Divide the clumps if they overgrow their position.

PROPAGATION: Take stem cuttings after flowering in spring. Place them in a well-drained medium before the cut end dries out. Divide in spring or fall. Sow seed outdoors in fall or spring or indoors in early spring.

PEST AND DISEASE PREVENTION: No serious pests or diseases.

LANDSCAPE USE: Plant in a sunny rock garden, in a rock wall, or at the front of borders. Combine them with early-blooming perennials like rock cresses (*Arabis* spp. and *Aubrietia* spp.), phlox, and bulbs.

OTHER SPECIES:
  E. epithymoides, cushion spurge, is a mounding plant with showy vibrant yellow flower heads in spring. Zones 3–8.

Filipendula rubra   Rosaceae

QUEEN-OF-THE-PRAIRIE

Queen-of-the-prairie is a towering perennial with huge flower heads on stout, leafy stalks. The showy 1-foot (30 cm) leaves are deeply lobed and star-like. Plants grow from creeping stems.

FLOWER COLOR: Small five-petaled pink flowers are crowded into large heads that resemble cotton candy.

FLOWERING TIME: Late spring and early summer.

HEIGHT AND SPREAD: 4–6 feet (1.2–1.8 cm) tall; 2–4 feet (60–120 cm) wide.

TEMPERATURE REQUIREMENTS: Zones 3–9.

POSITION: Evenly moist, humus-rich soil. Full sun to light shade. Plants will not tolerate prolonged dryness.

CULTIVATION: Established clumps make an arresting display when in bloom. If leaves become tattered after bloom, cut plants to the ground; new leaves will emerge. Plants spread quickly in moist soil. Divide every 3–4 years to keep them from overtaking their neighbors.

PROPAGATION: Division is the best method. Lift clumps in spring or fall, or dig crowns from the edge of the clump. Sow seed indoors in spring.

PEST AND DISEASE PREVENTION: No serious pests or diseases.

LANDSCAPE USE: Plant queen-of-the-prairie at the rear of borders with shrub roses, irises, daylilies, and phlox. Use them at pondside with ferns and ornamental grasses.

CULTIVARS: 'Venusta' has deep rose pink flowers, but many plants sold as the cultivar are seed-grown and vary in color.

| *Gaillardia* x *grandiflora* | Compositae | *Gaura lindheimeri* | Onagraceae |

BLANKET FLOWER

WHITE GAURA

The showy hybrid blanket flower blooms throughout the summer on loose stems with hairy, lobed leaves. Plants grow from fibrous-rooted crowns and may be short-lived.

FLOWER COLOR: Ragged yellow-and-orange daisy-like flowers have single or double rows of toothed petal-like rays surrounding a raised yellow center.

FLOWERING TIME: Throughout summer.

HEIGHT AND SPREAD: 2–3 feet (60–90 cm) tall; 2 feet (60 cm) wide.

TEMPERATURE REQUIREMENTS: Zones 4–9.

POSITION: Average to poor, well-drained soil. Full sun. Rich, moist soil causes plants to overgrow and flop.

CULTIVATION: Blanket flowers are drought-tolerant and thrive in seaside conditions. Divide every 2–3 years to keep them vigorous.

PROPAGATION: Divide in early spring. Sow seed outdoors in fall or indoors in spring after stratification. To stratify, mix seed with moist peat moss or seed-starting medium in a plastic bag. Close the bag with a twist-tie and place it in the refrigerator for 4–6 weeks. Then sow the mixture as you would normal seed. Seedlings often bloom the first year.

PEST AND DISEASE PREVENTION: No serious pests or diseases.

LANDSCAPE USE: Choose blanket flowers for rock gardens, borders, or seaside gardens.

CULTIVARS: 'Baby Cole' is a dwarf 8-inch (20 cm) selection with orange-centered yellow flowers. 'Bremen' has copper red flowers tipped in yellow. 'Burgundy' has deep red flowers. 'Goblin' is 1 foot (30 cm) tall with red-and-yellow flowers.

White gaura is a shrubby perennial with airy flower clusters on wiry stems and small, hairy leaves. This dependable, long-blooming plant grows from a thick, deep taproot.

FLOWER COLOR: Unusual white flowers are tinged with pink. They have four triangular petals, long curled stamens (male reproductive structures), and dance in slender spikes above the foliage.

FLOWERING TIME: Throughout summer.

HEIGHT AND SPREAD: 3–4 feet (90–120 cm) tall; 3 feet (90 cm) wide.

TEMPERATURE REQUIREMENTS: Zones 5–9. Extremely heat-tolerant.

POSITION: Moist, well-drained, average to rich soil. Full sun.

CULTIVATION: White gaura is an easy-care perennial that thrives for years with little attention. Plants bloom nonstop all summer despite high heat and humidity. Remove old bloom stalks to make way for the new ones.

PROPAGATION: Sow seed outdoors in spring or fall. Self-sown seedlings are likely to appear.

PEST AND DISEASE PREVENTION: No serious pests or diseases.

LANDSCAPE USE: White gaura is a lovely addition to formal and informal gardens alike. The flower clusters look like a swirl of dancing butterflies. Combine them with low-mounding perennials like verbenas (*Verbena* spp.), cranesbills (*Geranium* spp.), and sedums. In late summer they are beautiful with tawny ornamental grasses.

| *Gentiana asclepidea* | Gentianaceae | *Geranium endressii* | Geraniaceae |

WILLOW GENTIAN

ENDRES CRANESBILL

Willow gentian is a late-blooming perennial with leafy arching stems that grow from a crown with thick, fleshy roots. The lance-shaped, opposite leaves have prominent veins.

FLOWER COLOR: Deep blue flowers are carried in pairs along the arching stems. Each flower is tubular, with five flaring, starry lobes.

FLOWERING TIME: Late summer and fall.

HEIGHT AND SPREAD: 1½–2 feet (45–60 cm) tall; 2–3 feet (60–90 cm) wide.

TEMPERATURE REQUIREMENTS: Zones 5–7.

POSITION: Evenly moist, humus-rich soil. Full sun to partial shade. Provide shade from hot afternoon sun to avoid leaf browning, especially in warmer zones.

CULTIVATION: Gentians are long-lived perennials that thrive with little care. Plants seldom need division and dislike root disturbance.

PROPAGATION: Divide carefully in spring. Sow fresh seed outside in late fall or indoors in late winter after stratification. To stratify, mix seed with moist peat moss or seed-starting medium in a plastic bag. Close the bag with a twist-tie and place it in the refrigerator for 4–6 weeks. Then sow the mixture as you would normal seed.

PEST AND DISEASE PREVENTION: No serious pests or diseases.

LANDSCAPE USE: Plant in borders or use with ferns and wildflowers in the wild garden. Combine them with asters, goldenrods (*Solidago* spp.), and other fall-blooming plants.

Endres cranesbill is a mounding plant with deeply cut, five-lobed leaves arising from a slow-creeping, fibrous-rooted crown. Pink flowers appear from early to midsummer.

FLOWER COLOR: Soft-pink saucer-shaped, five-petaled flowers are carried above foliage in sparse clusters.

FLOWERING TIME: Early to midsummer bloom.

HEIGHT AND SPREAD: 15–18 inches (37.5–45 cm) tall; 18 inches (45 cm) wide.

TEMPERATURE REQUIREMENTS: Zones 4–8.

POSITION: Evenly moist, humus-rich soil. Full sun to partial shade. Protect from hot afternoon sun in warmer zones.

CULTIVATION: Heat slows blooming. In cooler zones plants may bloom all summer. Divide crowded plants and replant into soil that has been enriched with organic matter.

PROPAGATION: Divide in spring or fall. Sow seed outdoors in fall or indoors in spring on a warm (70°F/21°C) seedbed. Take stem cuttings in summer.

PEST AND DISEASE PREVENTION: No serious pests or diseases.

LANDSCAPE USE: Plant at the front of borders to tie plantings together or as an edging along walks. Combine with sundrops (*Oenothera* spp.), catmints (*Nepeta* spp.), bellflowers (*Campanula* spp.), phlox, and irises.

OTHER COMMON NAMES: Pyrenean cranesbill.

CULTIVARS: 'A. T. Johnson' has dozens of silvery pink flowers. 'Claridge Druce', a hybrid with *G. versicolor,* has lilac-pink flowers with violet veins. 'Wargrave Pink' has pure pink flowers.

'Johnson's Blue' is a floriferous hybrid with cup-shaped blue flowers. The plant starts blooming in early summer and often continues through early fall.

Bigroot cranesbill produces mounds of large, fragrant green leaves that turn reddish orange in fall. It makes a great flowering groundcover for a shady spot.

OTHER SPECIES:

G. cinereum, gray-leaved cranesbill, is a low, spreading plant with small, deeply incised leaves and saucer-shaped pink flowers veined with violet. They are best suited to the rock garden. 'Ballerina' is a hybrid with large lilac-pink flowers that have striking veins and purple eyes. 'Guiseppii' has dark-eyed magenta flowers. 'Splendens' has bright pink flowers with dark eyes. Zones 4 (with protection) or 5–8.

G. clarkei, Clark's geranium, is a floriferous species with white, pink, or lilac dark-veined flowers. The rounded leaves are deeply divided into seven lobes. This plant was recently separated from *G. pratense.* 'Kashmir Purple' has purple-blue flowers. 'Kashmir White' has white flowers with violet veins. Zones 4–8.

G. dalmaticum, Dalmatian cranesbill, is a low, rounded plant with small, curly, lobed leaves and 1-inch (2.5 cm) mauve flowers. Plants spread rapidly by creeping stems. The variety *album* has white flowers. 'Biokovo' is a hybrid with pale pink flowers. Zones 4–8.

G. himalayense, lilac cranesbill, is an open, mounding plant with deeply incised leaves and 2-inch (5 cm) violet-blue flowers. 'Birch Double' has double lavender flowers. 'Gravetye' is a compact grower with violet-centered blue flowers. Zones 4–8.

G. ibiricum, Caucasus cranesbill, is a robust plant with large seven- to nine-lobed leaves and 2-inch (5 cm) purple-blue flowers on stout stems. Zones 3–8.

G. macrorrhizum, bigroot cranesbill, is a fast-spreading plant with fragrant, seven-lobed leaves and bright pink flowers. 'Album' has white flowers with pink sepals. 'Ingwersen's Variety' has light pink flowers and glossy leaves. 'Spessart' has white flowers with pale pink sepals. Zones 3–8.

G. maculatum, wild cranesbill, is a woodland plant with five-lobed leaves and tall, sparsely flowering stalks of clear-pink or white flowers. Zones 4–8.

G. pratense, meadow cranesbill, has deeply incised leaves and 1½-inch (3.5 cm) purple flowers with red veins. 'Mrs. Kendall Clarke' has lilac-blue flowers. Zones 3–8.

G. sanguineum, blood red cranesbill, is a low, wide-spreading plant with deeply cut starry leaves and flat magenta flowers held just above the foliage. 'Album' is more rambling than the species and has white saucer-shaped flowers. 'Shepherd's Warning' is low growing with deep rose pink flowers. The variety *striatum* (also sold as *lancastriense*) is prostrate with pale pink rose-veined flowers. Zones 3–8.

G. sylvaticum, wood cranesbill, is an early-spring bloomer with lobed leaves and pink or white flowers. Zones 3–8.

Gypsophila paniculata Caryophyllaceae	*Helenium autumnale* Compositae

BABY'S-BREATH

COMMON SNEEZEWEED

Baby's-breath is an old-fashioned perennial with airy flower clusters and sparse, smooth blue-green foliage. The stems and basal leaves grow from a thick, deep taproot.

FLOWER COLOR: Small, single or double white flowers are carried in large domed clusters.

FLOWERING TIME: Summer.

HEIGHT AND SPREAD: 3–4 feet (90–120 cm) tall; 2–3 feet (60–90 cm) wide.

TEMPERATURE REQUIREMENTS: Zones 3–9. Heat- and cold-tolerant.

POSITION: Near neutral to alkaline, moist, humus-rich soil. Full sun to light shade.

CULTIVATION: Set out in spring and do not disturb the crowns once plants are established. Good drainage is essential for longevity. Some double-flowered cultivars are grafted onto seed-grown, single root-stocks. Plant them with the crowns below the surface to encourage the stems to form their own roots. Tall cultivars may need staking.

PROPAGATION: Take cuttings in summer. Sow seed outdoors in spring or fall or indoors in spring.

PEST AND DISEASE PREVENTION: No serious pests or diseases.

LANDSCAPE USE: Use the airy sprays to hide the yellowing foliage of bulbs and perennials such as oriental poppy (*Papaver orientale*) that go dormant in summer. Combine them with bold and spiky perennials for dramatic effect.

CULTIVARS: 'Bristol Fairy' has double flowers on compact 2-foot (60 cm) plants. 'Perfecta' has large double flowers. 'Pink Fairy' has double pink flowers.

Common sneezeweed is a showy, late-season perennial with tall, leafy stems that spring from a fibrous-rooted crown. The hairy, lance-shaped leaves are edged with a few large teeth.

FLOWER COLOR: The 2-inch (5 cm), yellow daisy-like flowers have broad, petal-like rays.

FLOWERING TIME: Late summer and fall.

HEIGHT AND SPREAD: 3–5 feet (90–150 cm) tall; 2–3 feet (60–90 cm) wide.

TEMPERATURE REQUIREMENTS: Zones 3–8.

POSITION: Evenly moist, humus-rich soil. Full sun or light shade. Plants tolerate wet soil.

CULTIVATION: Either stake it or pinch the stem tips in early summer to promote compact growth. Divide the clumps every 3–4 years to keep them vigorous.

PROPAGATION: Divide in spring or fall. Take stem cuttings in early summer. Sow seed of the species outdoors in spring or fall.

PEST AND DISEASE PREVENTION: No serious pests or diseases.

LANDSCAPE USE: Common sneezeweeds offer late-season color. Combine them with asters, goldenrods (*Solidago* spp.), and garden phlox (*Phlox paniculata*).

OTHER COMMON NAMES: Helen's flower.

CULTIVARS: 'Butterpat' has bright yellow flowers on 3–4-foot (90–120 cm) stems. 'Crimson Beauty' has mahogany flowers. 'Riverton Beauty' has golden yellow flowers with bronze-red centers.

HYBRIDS: 'Baudirektor Linne' is a late-bloomer with mahogany-red flowers. 'Kugelsonne' has bright yellow flowers on self-supporting stems. 'Zimbelstern' is an early bloomer with gold rays and brown centers.

Helianthus decapetalus   Compositae

THIN-LEAVED SUNFLOWER

Thin-leaved sunflowers are showy summer flowers with stout stems clothed in wide, 8-inch (20 cm), wedge-shaped leaves. Plants grow from stout, fibrous-rooted crowns.

FLOWER COLOR: The 2–3-inch (5–7.5 cm) daisy-like flowers have bright yellow petal-like rays and yellow centers.

FLOWERING TIME: Mid- to late summer.

HEIGHT AND SPREAD: 4–5 feet (1.2–1.5 cm) tall; 2–3 feet (60–90 cm) wide.

TEMPERATURE REQUIREMENTS: Zones 4–8.

POSITION: Moist, average to humus-rich soil. Full sun. Plants will tolerate wet soil.

CULTIVATION: Thin-leaved sunflowers are easy to grow but need room to spread. Divide every 3–4 years. The stems are usually self-supporting, except when plants are grown in partial shade.

PROPAGATION: Divide in fall. Take stem cuttings in early summer or sow seed outdoors in fall.

PEST AND DISEASE PREVENTION: No serious pests or diseases.

LANDSCAPE USE: Sunflowers add bold splashes of color to the summer garden. Combine them with garden phlox (*Phlox paniculata*), asters, goldenrods (*Solidago* spp.), sedums, and ornamental grasses.

OTHER SPECIES:

H. x *multiflorus*, perennial sunflower, is a hybrid from crosses between *H. decapetalus* and the annual *H. annuus*. The plants are similar to thin-leaved sunflowers but more robust. 'Flore-Plena' has double flowers. 'Loddon Gold' has large golden yellow flowers on sturdy 5–6-foot (1.5–1.8 m) stems.

Heliopsis helianthoides   Compositae

SUNFLOWER HELIOPSIS

Sunflower heliopsis is a bright summer daisy with 5-inch (12.5 cm) triangular leaves covering a tall-growing, bushy plant. It grows from a fibrous-rooted crown.

FLOWER COLOR: The bright golden yellow 2–3-inch (5–7.5 cm) flowers have broad petal-like rays and yellow centers that turn brown with age.

FLOWERING TIME: Early to midsummer.

HEIGHT AND SPREAD: 3–6 feet (90–180 cm) tall; 2–4 feet (60–120 cm) wide.

TEMPERATURE REQUIREMENTS: Zones 3–9.

POSITION: Average to humus-rich, moist but well-drained soil. Full sun to light shade.

CULTIVATION: In rich soils plants spread quickly. Divide every 2–3 years to promote longevity. May require staking. The cultivars are longer-lived and have more self-supporting stems.

PROPAGATION: Divide in spring or fall. Take stem cuttings in late spring or early summer. Sow seed outdoors in fall or spring. Plants often self-sow.

PEST AND DISEASE PREVENTION: No serious pests or diseases.

LANDSCAPE USE: Combine sunflower heliopsis with summer-blooming perennials and ornamental grasses in formal borders, meadows, and prairies. Plant with garden phlox (*Phlox paniculata*), gayfeathers (*Liatris* spp.), and asters.

CULTIVARS: 'Golden Plume' has double flowers on compact 3–3½-foot (90–105 cm) plants. 'Karat' has 3-inch (7.5 cm) single flowers on 4-foot (1.2 m) stems. 'Summer Sun' has 4-inch (10 cm) bright yellow flowers on 2–3-foot (60–90 cm) plants.

| *Helleborus niger* | Ranunculaceae | *Hemerocallis* hybrids | Liliaceae |

CHRISTMAS ROSE

DAYLILY

Christmas roses are winter or early-spring perennials with deeply lobed, leathery leaves growing from a stout crown with fleshy roots. The flowers open white and turn pink with age.

FLOWER COLOR: White flowers have five petal-like sepals surrounded by green leafy bracts.

FLOWERING TIME: Early winter through spring.

HEIGHT AND SPREAD: 1–1½ feet (30–45 cm) tall; 1–2 feet (30–60 cm) wide.

TEMPERATURE REQUIREMENTS: Zones 3–8.

POSITION: Evenly moist, humus-rich soil. Light to partial shade. Established plants tolerate dry soil and deep shade.

CULTIVATION: In spring remove any damaged leaves. Plants take 2–3 years to become established and resent disturbance. Divide only to propagate.

PROPAGATION: Lift clumps after flowering in spring and separate the crowns. Replant the divisions immediately. Self-sown seedlings often appear. Sow seed outdoors in spring or early summer.

PEST AND DISEASE PREVENTION: No serious pests or diseases.

LANDSCAPE USE: Combine with early spring bulbs, wildflowers, and ferns. The lovely foliage is attractive all season.

OTHER SPECIES:

H. argutifolius, Corsican hellebore, has three-lobed leaves and green flowers. Zones 6 (with winter protection)–8.

H. orientalis, lenten rose, is similar to *H. niger* but has broader leaflets and pink, red, or white flowers borne in loose clusters. Zones 4–9.

Daylily hybrids are among the most popular perennials. Although each flower only lasts one day, a profusion of new buds keeps the plants in bloom for a month or more.

FLOWER COLOR: Daylily flowers vary in color and form. The majority of the wild species are orange or yellow with wide petals and narrow, petal-like sepals. Modern hybrids come in many colors.

FLOWERING TIME: Late spring through summer.

HEIGHT AND SPREAD: 1–5 feet (30–150 cm) tall; 2–3 feet (60–90 cm) wide. There are miniature and standard sizes as well as extremely tall kinds.

TEMPERATURE REQUIREMENTS: Zones 3–9 for most hybrids.

POSITION: Evenly moist, average to humus-rich soil. Full sun to light shade. Most modern hybrids need at least 8 hours of direct sun to flower well. Some of the older selections and the species will bloom in partial shade.

CULTIVATION: Daylilies are long-lived, easy-care perennials. Plant container-grown or bareroot plants in spring or fall. Place the crowns just below the soil surface. Plants take a year to become established and then spread quickly to form dense clumps. Most hybrids and species can remain in place for many years without disturbance. Some hybrids have so many bloom stalks that the flowers crowd together and lose their beauty. Divide these plants every 3 years. Lift the clumps and pull or cut the tangled crowns apart. Deadhead the plants regularly to keep them looking their best. The foliage of most daylilies remains nice all season. If

Daylily—Continued

Hybrid coral bells

Daylily flowers come in a range of forms and a rainbow of colors with the exception of blues and true white. Many have blazes, eyes, or blotches on the petals.

Hybrid coral bells are attractive in foliage and in flower. The evergreen leaves may be deep green, gray-green, or mottled with silver. Plants grow from woody, fibrous-rooted crowns.

leaves are yellow, grasp them firmly and give them a quick tug to remove them from the base.

PROPAGATION: Hybrids must be propagated by division only in fall or spring. Seed-grown plants will be variable and are often inferior to the parent plant.

PEST AND DISEASE PREVENTION: Although daylilies are usually pest-free, aphids and thrips may attack the foliage and flower buds. Wash off aphids with a stream of water or spray them with insecticidal soap. Thrips make small white lines in the foliage and may deform flower buds if damage is severe. Spray with insecticidal soap or a botanical insecticide such as pyrethrin. Deter slugs and snails from new growth with shallow pans of beer set flush with the soil surface.

LANDSCAPE USE: Perfect for mass plantings. In beds and borders combine them with summer-blooming perennials and ornamental grasses.

CULTIVARS: Hundreds of cultivars are available in a full range of colors. It's best to buy plants after you see them to make sure they are the size and color you want. A few old favorites are listed below. 'Catherine Woodbery' is shell pink with a yellow throat. 'Chicago Royal' is purple with a green throat. 'Hyperion' has fragrant yellow flowers. 'Ice Carnival' is nearly white. 'Mary Todd' has fluffy yellow flowers. 'Stella d'Oro' is a repeat-blooming 1-foot (30 cm) plant with creamy gold flowers.

FLOWER COLOR: Small, fringed flowers are carried in slender, branching clusters. Colors vary from white through shades of pink and red.

FLOWERING TIME: Late spring through summer. Variable by cultivar.

HEIGHT AND SPREAD: 1–2½ feet (30–45 cm) tall; 1–2 feet (30–60 cm) wide.

TEMPERATURE REQUIREMENTS: Zones 3–8. More heat-tolerant than other coral bells.

POSITION: Moist but well-drained, humus-rich soil. Full sun to partial shade. In warmer zones provide shade from hot afternoon sun.

CULTIVATION: Coral bells are long-lived perennials. Remove old bloom stalks to promote reblooming. As plants grow, they rise above the soil on woody crowns. Lift plants every 3–4 years and replant the crowns into soil enriched with organic matter.

PROPAGATION: Propagate by division only in spring or early fall.

PEST AND DISEASE PREVENTION: No serious pests or diseases.

LANDSCAPE USE: Plant at the front of borders, along walkways, or in a lightly shaded rock garden. Combine them with cranesbills (*Geranium* spp.), catmints (*Nepeta* spp.), and columbines (*Aquilegia* spp.).

CULTIVARS: 'Chatterbox' has large rose pink flowers. 'Coral Cloud' is coral pink. 'June Bride' has large white flowers. 'Mt. St. Helens' is brick red.

| *Hibiscus moscheutos* | Malvaceae | *Hosta* hybrids | Liliaceae |

COMMON ROSE MALLOW

HOSTA

The showy flowers of common rose mallow are borne in profusion on a shrub like plant that grows from a thick, woody crown. The broad, oval leaves have three to five shallow lobes.

FLOWER COLOR: The 6–8-inch (15–20 cm) flowers have five pleated white petals that surround a central, fuzzy column bearing the male and female reproductive structures. The flowers have bright red centers.

FLOWERING TIME: Throughout summer.

HEIGHT AND SPREAD: 4–8 feet (1.2–2.4 m) tall; 3–5 feet (90–150 cm) wide.

TEMPERATURE REQUIREMENTS: Zones 5–10.

POSITION: Evenly moist, humus-rich soil. Full sun to light shade. Tolerates some dryness once established; quite tolerant of wet soil.

CULTIVATION: Space young plants 3–4 feet (90–120 cm) apart to accommodate their eventual spread. Once established, clumps dislike disturbance and are difficult to move.

PROPAGATION: Take cuttings in summer. Remove the flower buds and cut the leaves back by one-half to reduce water loss. Seeds gathered from the parent plant are variable and often inferior. Sow fresh seed of the true species outdoors in fall.

PEST AND DISEASE PREVENTION: Japanese beetles may skeletonize the leaves. Pick them off and drop them in a pail of soapy water.

LANDSCAPE USE: Plant mallows wherever you need a bold dash of color. They make great accent plants and are lovely in borders with ornamental grasses and airy summer perennials.

Hostas are indispensable foliage plants for shaded gardens. Their thick, pleated or puckered leaves grow from stout crowns with thick fleshy roots.

FLOWER COLOR: Lavender, purple, or white flowers are carried in slender spikes. Individual flowers have three petals and three petal-like sepals.

FLOWERING TIME: Summer or fall depending on hybrid and origin.

HEIGHT AND SPREAD: 6 inches–3 feet (15–90 cm) tall; 6 inches–5 feet (15–150 cm) wide.

TEMPERATURE REQUIREMENTS: Zones 3–8. Some selections are probably hardy to Zone 2.

POSITION: Evenly moist, humus-rich soil. Light to full shade. Adaptable to both dry and wet soil conditions. Filtered sun encourages the best leaf color in the gold- and blue-leaved forms. All hostas need protection from hot afternoon sun, especially in warm zones. Variegated and yellow-leaved cultivars are particularly susceptible to burning.

CULTIVATION: Hostas take several years to reach mature form and size, especially the large-leaved cultivars. Allow ample room when planting to accommodate their ultimate size. New shoots are slow to emerge in spring, so take care not to damage them during spring cleanup. Plant small bulbs such as snowdrops (*Galanthus* spp.) and squills (*Scilla* spp.) around the clumps to mark their location.

PROPAGATION: Divide in late summer.

PEST AND DISEASE PREVENTION: Set shallow pans of beer flush with the soil surface to drown slugs and

Iberis sempervirens — Cruciferae

PERENNIAL CANDYTUFT

Hostas come in a range of leaf colors, from deep green to greenish yellow, golden yellow, and shades of gray and blue. Yellow and white variegations are common.

snails, or exclude them with a barrier of diatomaceous earth, wood ashes, or sand around each plant.

LANDSCAPE USE: Use the smaller cultivars to edge beds or as groundcover under shrubs and trees. Choose giants for creating drama in a mixed planting or alone as an accent. Plant hostas with wildflowers, ferns, sedges (*Carex* spp.), and shade perennials.

CULTIVARS: Hundreds of cultivars are available; a few are listed below. 'Antioch' is a medium to large plant with creamy edged green leaves. 'August Moon' has large golden yellow leaves. 'Francee' is medium sized with white-edged, deep green leaves. 'Golden Tiara' is a small to medium hosta with gold-edged green leaves. 'Honeybells' has fragrant white flowers tinged with violet and large, glossy green leaves. 'Kabitan' has narrow yellow leaves with green edges. 'Royal Standard' has medium-sized, glossy green leaves and fragrant white flowers. 'Sum and Substance' has huge golden yellow leaves.

Perennial candytuft is a floriferous, semiwoody subshrub with persistent stems tightly clothed in 1½-inch (3.5 cm), narrow deep green leaves. Plants grow from fibrous-rooted crowns.

FLOWER COLOR: The tight, rounded clusters consist of many ¼-inch (6 mm), four-petaled flowers.

FLOWERING TIME: Early spring.

HEIGHT AND SPREAD: 6–12 inches (15–30 cm) tall; 12–24 inches (30–60 cm) wide.

TEMPERATURE REQUIREMENTS: Zones 3–9.

POSITION: Average to humus-rich, well-drained soil. Full sun to light shade.

CULTIVATION: Space plants 1–1½ feet (30–45 cm) apart in informal plantings or 6 inches (15 cm) apart if edging a planting. Shear after flowering to promote compact growth. Mulch plants in Zones 3 and 4 to protect stems from winter damage.

PROPAGATION: Layer or take cuttings in early summer. Sow seed outdoors in spring or fall.

PEST AND DISEASE PREVENTION: No serious pests or diseases.

LANDSCAPE USE: Use perennial candytuft to edge formal plantings, walks, or walls. Plant it in rock gardens or in combination with spring bulbs and early-blooming perennials. Try them with bleeding hearts (*Dicentra* spp.), basket-of-gold (*Aurinia saxatilis*), rock cresses (*Arabis* spp. and *Aubrieta* spp.), and columbines (*Aquilegia* spp.).

CULTIVARS: 'Autumn Snow' has large white flowers and reblooms in fall. 'Pygmaea' is a low-spreading selection. 'Snowflake' has large flower clusters on 8–10-inch (20–25 cm) stems.

| *Incarvillea delavayi* | Bignoniaceae | *Iris sibirica* | Iridiceae |

HARDY GLOXINIA

SIBERIAN IRIS

Hardy gloxinias are showy plants with 1-foot (30 cm) pinnately divided leaves. They are slow to emerge in spring; mark their location to avoid damaging the crowns.

Siberian irises produce graceful early-summer flowers in a wide range of colors. Plants form tight fans of narrow sword-like leaves from slow-creeping rhizomes.

FLOWER COLOR: The 2–3-inch (5–7.5 cm) tubular rose pink flowers have flat five-petaled faces. They are borne in clusters 1–2 feet (30–60 cm) above the foliage.

FLOWERING TIME: Spring and early summer.

HEIGHT AND SPREAD: 1½–2 feet (45–60 cm) tall; 1½ feet (45 cm) wide.

TEMPERATURE REQUIREMENTS: Zones 5–8. Intolerant of high temperatures.

POSITION: Average to humus-rich, well-drained soil. Full sun to partial shade. Protect plants from hot afternoon sun in warm zones.

CULTIVATION: Plants are easy to grow. Good drainage is important to success. Mulch plants to protect them from winter cold.

PROPAGATION: Sow seed in spring or fall on a warm (70°F/21°C) seedbed. Keep soil moist and cover with clear plastic wrap to encourage humidity. Seedlings develop in 10–20 days. Divide large plants in spring or fall.

PEST AND DISEASE PREVENTION: No serious pests or diseases.

LANDSCAPE USE: Combine with groundcover plants like rock cresses (*Arabis* spp.), candytufts (*Iberis* spp.), and sedums for a colorful spring show. In partial shade plant them with wild ginger (*Asarum* spp.) and other foliage plants.

FLOWER COLOR: Flowers range in color from pure white, cream, and yellow to all shades of blue, violet, and purple. Some cultivars come close to true red. The flowers are uniquely constructed. Three segments, called falls, ring the outside of the flowers. They are usually reflexed downward and bear a central white or yellow blaze. The center of the flower boasts three slender segments called standards. They are often upright but also may be flat or reflexed. A triad of flat columns bearing the reproductive structures declines over the falls.

FLOWERING TIME: Early summer; some cultivars rebloom.

HEIGHT AND SPREAD: 1–3 feet (30–90 cm) tall; 1–2 feet (30–60 cm) wide.

TEMPERATURE REQUIREMENTS: Zones 3–9. Heat- and cold-tolerant.

POSITION: Evenly moist, humus-rich soil. Full sun to partial shade. Plant bareroot iris in fall and container-grown plants in spring, summer, and fall.

CULTIVATION: Siberian irises are easy-care perennials. They thrive for many years without division. If bloom begins to wane or plants outgrow their position, divide and replant into soil that has been enriched with organic matter.

PROPAGATION: Divide plants in late summer. Seed collected from cultivars will be variable and often inferior to the parent plant. Sow fresh seed of the

To keep bearded irises looking their best, you should divide plants every 3–5 years. Discard the old parts of the rhizomes and replant the vigorous sections.

Hybrid bearded irises are classics for the June garden. They combine well with other summer-blooming perennials like peonies, poppies, and cranesbills (Geranium *spp.*).

species outdoors in summer or fall.

PEST AND DISEASE PREVENTION: Susceptible to iris borer. The moths lay their eggs in the leaves and the young larvae tunnel down the leaves to hollow out the rhizome. Borers also spread bacterial rot, which kills the iris from the ground up. Good culture is the best preventive. Remove dead foliage in spring and fall. Smash the grubs between your fingers while they are in the leaves. Dig up affected plants and cut off affected portions of the rhizome.

LANDSCAPE USE: Plant in formal or informal gardens with perennials, ornamental grasses, and ferns. Their strap-like foliage and lovely flowers combine with rounded perennials like peonies, baptisia (*Baptisia* spp.), and cranesbills (*Geranium* spp.). At pondside, ferns, hostas, primroses, and astilbes are suitable companions.

CULTIVARS: 'Caesar' has blue-purple flowers on 3-foot (90 cm) stems. 'Dewful' has blue flowers on 3½-foot (1.05 m) stems. 'Ego' has rich blue ruffled flowers on 2½-foot (75 cm) stems. 'My Love' is a soft medium blue rebloomer with 2½-foot (75 cm) stems. 'Orville Fay' is medium blue with 3-foot (90 cm) stems. 'Sky Wings' is a pale blue bitone with 3-foot (90 cm) stems.

HYBRIDS: Hybrid bearded irises are as popular as Siberian irises. They have showy, fragrant flowers with wide, bearded falls and wide, upright stands.

Plants range in size from less than 15 inches (37.5 cm) to over 28 inches (70 cm) tall. They grow well in the same conditions as Siberian irises but good drainage is critical. Hundreds of cultivars are available. Some of the best include 'Beverly Sills', with ruffled coral pink flowers; 'Lacy Snowflake', with pure white fringed blooms; and 'Titan's Glory', with deep purple-blue flowers. Zones 3–8.

OTHER SPECIES:

I. cristata, crested iris, is an 8-inch (20 cm) spring-blooming woodland iris with sky blue flowers. Zones 3–9. Prefers semishade.

I. ensata, Japanese iris, is a wet-soil iris with lovely blue or purple flowers. Many stunning cultivars are available with flattened flowers up to 8 inches (20 cm) across. Zones 4–9. Prefers partial shade in hot, sunny climates.

I. pseudacorus, yellow flag, is a stout 3–4 foot (90–120 cm) iris with bright yellow flowers. Zones 4–9. Grows well in full sun to partial shade. Thrives in a water garden.

I. tectorum, roof iris, is a short, stout 1–1½-foot (30–45 cm) iris with delicate, flattened, spotted lilac-blue flowers. Zones 4–9. Prefers sheltered partial shade with protection from hot afternoon sun.

I. versicolor, blue flag iris, is a tall 1½–3-foot (30–45 cm) iris with purple-blue flowers. Zones 2–8. Thrives in moist soil or shallow water.

Kniphofia uvaria Liliaceae	*Lavandula angustifolia* Labiatae

COMMON TORCH LILY

LAVENDER

Common torch lily is a commanding perennial with tufts of narrow evergreen leaves from a fleshy rooted crown. The flower spikes add a dramatic accent to summer gardens.

FLOWER COLOR: Long slender spikes consist of tightly packed, tubular flowers. The lowest on the spike are yellow-white; the upper ones are red.

FLOWERING TIME: Late spring and summer.

HEIGHT AND SPREAD: 3–5 feet (90–150 cm) tall; 2–4 feet (60–120 cm) wide.

TEMPERATURE REQUIREMENTS: Zones 5–9.

POSITION: Average to humus-rich, well-drained soil. Full sun. Established plants are quite drought-tolerant.

CULTIVATION: Set out young plants 2–2½-feet (60–75 cm) apart. Leave established plants undisturbed. Plants increase to form broad, floriferous clumps.

PROPAGATION: Remove a few crowns from the edges of clumps in fall. Sow seed indoors in winter after stratification. To stratify, mix seed with moist peat moss or seed-starting medium in a plastic bag. Close the bag with a twist-tie and place it in the refrigerator for 4–6 weeks. Then sow the mixture as you would normal seed.

PEST AND DISEASE PREVENTION: Provide excellent drainage to avoid crown rot.

LANDSCAPE USE: The bold, vertical form of common torch lilies adds excitement to perennial borders and rock gardens. Combine with ornamental grasses, wormwoods (*Artemisia* spp.), sundrops (*Oenothera* spp.), and other summer perennials.

OTHER COMMON NAMES: Red-hot poker.

Lavender is a small, rounded shrub beloved for its herbal and ornamental qualities. The fragrant gray-green leaves clothe soft hairy stems topped with spikes of purple-blue flowers.

FLOWER COLOR: The ½-inch (1 cm) purple-blue flowers are carried in tight, narrow clusters.

FLOWERING TIME: Early to late summer.

HEIGHT AND SPREAD: 2–3 feet (60–90 cm) tall; 2–3 feet (60–90 cm) wide.

TEMPERATURE REQUIREMENTS: Zones 5–8.

POSITION: Average to humus-rich, well-drained soil. Full sun to light shade. Neutral or slightly alkaline soil is best. Extremely drought-tolerant.

CULTIVATION: Shoots may be partially killed in winter. Prune out any dead wood and reshape the shrubs in spring. Shear plants every few years to encourage fresh new growth and to promote bloom.

PROPAGATION: Layer or take tip cuttings in summer. Place cuttings in a well-drained medium; transplant them as soon as they root to avoid rot.

PEST AND DISEASE PREVENTION: No serious pests or diseases.

LANDSCAPE USE: Plant lavender in ornamental and herb gardens. Use as an edging plant or to configure knot gardens. In borders combine them with other plants that need excellent drainage such as yarrows and sundrops (*Oenothera* spp.).

CULTIVARS: 'Dwarf Blue' has dark blue flowers on 1-foot (30 cm) plants. 'Hidcote' grows 1½ feet (45 cm) tall with purple-blue flowers. 'Jean Davis' has pale pink flowers. 'Munstead' has lavender-blue flowers on 1½-foot (45 cm) plants.

Liatris spicata   Compositae

SPIKE GAYFEATHER

Spike gayfeather is a tall perennial with slender flower spikes. The erect stems arise from basal tufts of grass-like, medium green foliage. Plants grow from a fat corm.

FLOWER COLOR: Rose-purple flowers are carried in small heads that are crowded together into dense spikes. The spikes open from the top down.

FLOWERING TIME: Midsummer.

HEIGHT AND SPREAD: 2–3 feet (60–90 cm) tall; 1–2 feet (30–60 cm) wide.

TEMPERATURE REQUIREMENTS: Zones 3–9.

POSITION: Average to humus-rich, moist soil. Full sun. Plants tend to flop in partial shade.

CULTIVATION: Spike gayfeathers are long-lived perennials that offer lots of flowers for little effort. Clumps increase slowly and seldom need division.

PROPAGATION: Divide plants in spring or early fall. Sow seed outdoors in fall or indoors in late winter after stratification. To stratify, mix seed with moist peat moss or seed-starting medium in a plastic bag. Close the bag with a twist-tie and place it in the refrigerator for 4–6 weeks. Then sow the mixture as you would normal seed.

PEST AND DISEASE PREVENTION: No serious pests or diseases.

LANDSCAPE USE: Lovely in perennial gardens, meadows, and prairie plantings. Combine them with purple coneflowers (*Echinacea* spp.), coreopsis (*Coreopsis* spp.), and ornamental grasses.

OTHER COMMON NAMES: Blazing star.

CULTIVARS: 'Kobold' is a popular cultivar with red-violet flowers on 1½–2½-foot (45–75 cm) stems.

Ligularia dentata   Compositae

BIG-LEAVED LIGULARIA

Big-leaved ligularia has bright, daisy-like flowers and 1–2-foot (30–60 cm) round or kidney-shaped leaves on long stalks. Plants grow from stout crowns with thick, fleshy roots.

FLOWER COLOR: The 5-inch (12.5 cm) bright orange-yellow flowers are like spidery daisies. They are carried in open clusters.

FLOWERING TIME: Late summer.

HEIGHT AND SPREAD: 3–4 feet (90–120 cm) tall; 3–4 feet (90–120 cm) wide.

TEMPERATURE REQUIREMENTS: Zones 3–8.

POSITION: Consistently moist, humus-rich soil. Light to partial shade. Plants do not tolerate dry soil.

CULTIVATION: The huge leaves lose water rapidly. In hot sun plants go into dramatic collapse, but they will recover as temperatures moderate in the evening. Plants form big clumps but do not need frequent division.

PROPAGATION: Lift clumps in early spring or fall and cut the crowns apart with a sharp knife. Replant into soil that has been enriched with organic matter.

PEST AND DISEASE PREVENTION: Trap slugs with shallow pans of beer set flush with the soil surface, or exclude them with a ring of diatomaceous earth, wood ashes, or sand.

LANDSCAPE USE: Big-leaved ligularias are bold accent plants. Use at pondside or in gardens with ferns, hostas, irises, and grasses.

CULTIVARS: 'Desdemona' has purple leaves in spring that fade to green with purple undersides. 'Othello' is similar but has smaller leaves.

Limonium latifolium	Plumbaginaceae	*Lobelia cardinalis*	Campanulaceae

SEA LAVENDER

CARDINAL FLOWER

Sea lavender has airy clusters of pink flowers above showy rosettes of spatula-shaped to narrowly oval shiny green leaves. Plants grow from stout, woody crowns.

FLOWER COLOR: Tiny pink flowers are carried in broad, domed clusters.

FLOWERING TIME: Summer.

HEIGHT AND SPREAD: 2–2½ feet (60–75 cm) tall; 2–2½ feet (60–75 cm) wide.

TEMPERATURE REQUIREMENTS: Zones 3–9.

POSITION: Average to humus-rich, moist but well-drained soil. Full sun. Extremely drought-tolerant. Grows in alkaline or saline soil.

CULTIVATION: Slow to establish and should not be disturbed after planting.

PROPAGATION: Remove small crowns from the main clump in fall. Sow seed outdoors in fall. Seedlings are slow-growing.

PEST AND DISEASE PREVENTION: Plant on a well-drained site; subject to crown rot in wet soil.

LANDSCAPE USE: Plant in borders or seaside gardens. Combine the airy flowers with irises, phlox, yarrows, asters, and ornamental grasses.

OTHER COMMON NAMES: Statice.

CULTIVARS: 'Violetta' has dark purple-blue flowers.

Cardinal flowers have fiery colored flower spikes on leafy stems and grow from a fibrous-rooted crown. The lance-shaped leaves may be fresh green or red-bronze.

FLOWER COLOR: Brilliant scarlet tubular flowers have three lower and two upper petals that look like delicate birds in flight.

FLOWERING TIME: Late summer to fall.

HEIGHT AND SPREAD: 2–4 feet (60–120 cm) tall; 1–2 feet (30–60 cm) wide.

TEMPERATURE REQUIREMENTS: Zones 2–9.

POSITION: Evenly moist, humus-rich soil. Full sun to partial shade.

CULTIVATION: Cardinal flowers are shallow-rooted and subject to frost heaving. Where winters are cold, mulch plants to protect the crowns. In warmer zones winter mulch may rot the crowns. Replant in spring if frost has lifted them. Plants may be short-lived, but self-sown seedlings are numerous.

PROPAGATION: Divide in late fall or spring. Sow seed uncovered outdoors in fall or spring or indoors in late winter. Seedlings grow quickly and will bloom the first year from seed.

PEST AND DISEASE PREVENTION: No serious pests or diseases.

LANDSCAPE USE: Cardinal flowers need even moisture so they are commonly used around pools, along streams, or in informal plantings. Combine them with irises, hostas, ligularias (*Ligularia* spp.), and ferns.

CULTIVARS: 'Royal Robe' has ruby red flowers.

Lupinus polyphyllus	Leguminosae	*Lychnis chalcedonica*	Caryophyllaceae

WASHINGTON LUPINE

MALTESE CROSS

Washington lupine has conical flower spikes on stout stems with large palmately divided leaves. Plants grow from thick roots. Lupines add a dramatic vertical accent to borders.

FLOWER COLOR: The ¾-inch (18 mm), blue-purple or yellow pea-like flowers are crowded into 1–2-foot (30–60 cm) spikes.

FLOWERING TIME: Spring and summer.

HEIGHT AND SPREAD: 3–5 feet (90–150 cm) tall; 2–3 feet (60–90 cm) wide.

TEMPERATURE REQUIREMENTS: Zones 3–7. Sensitive to high summer temperatures.

POSITION: Moist but well-drained, acid, humus-rich soil. Full sun to light shade.

CULTIVATION: Washington lupines are heavy feeders. Top-dress in spring with a balanced organic fertilizer. Protect plants from hot, dry winds. They may be short-lived, especially in warmer zones.

PROPAGATION: Remove sideshoots from around the clump in fall. Sow seed outdoors in fall or inside in winter. Before sowing indoors, soak seed overnight and then stratify. To stratify, mix seed with moist peat moss or seed-starting medium in a plastic bag. Close the bag with a twist-tie and place it in the refrigerator for 4–6 weeks. Then sow the mixture as you would normal seed.

PEST AND DISEASE PREVENTION: No serious pests or diseases.

LANDSCAPE USE: Plant strong vertical Washington lupines with border perennials like columbines (*Aquilegia* spp.), cranesbills (*Geranium* spp.), bellflowers (*Campanula* spp.), irises, and peonies.

Maltese cross is an old-fashioned perennial with brilliant flower clusters atop tall stems with opposite, oval leaves. Plants grow from fibrous-rooted crowns.

FLOWER COLOR: Brilliant scarlet flowers are held in compact, domed, terminal clusters.

FLOWERING TIME: Midsummer.

HEIGHT AND SPREAD: 2–3 feet (60–90 cm) tall; 1–1½ feet (30–45 cm) wide.

TEMPERATURE REQUIREMENTS: Zones 4–8.

POSITION: Average to humus-rich, moist but well-drained soil. Full sun to light shade.

CULTIVATION: Maltese cross spreads quickly to form tight clumps. Divide every 2–3 years to keep it strong and healthy.

PROPAGATION: Divide in spring or fall. Sow seed outdoors in fall.

PEST AND DISEASE PREVENTION: No serious pests or diseases.

LANDSCAPE USE: Use the strong-colored flowers of Maltese cross to create excitement in a subdued scheme of blues and pale yellows. Perfect for hot color combinations with coneflowers (*Rudbeckia* spp.), blanket flowers (*Gaillardia* spp.), and sundrops (*Oenothera* spp.).

OTHER SPECIES:

L. x *arkwrightii,* Arkwright's campion, is a hybrid with showy, 1½-inch (3.5 cm) orange-red flowers and bronze foliage. Zones 3–8.

L. coronaria, rose campion, has magenta flowers in open clusters above basal rosettes of silver gray leaves. 'Alba' has white flowers. Zones 4–8.

Macleaya cordata   Papaveraceae

PLUME POPPY

The imposing plume poppy is tree-like in stature, with 10-inch (25 cm) lobed leaves clothing erect stems. Plants grow from stout, creeping roots that can quickly become invasive.

FLOWER COLOR: The 12-inch (30 cm) plumes consist of small cream-colored flowers that give way to showy, flat rose-colored seed pods.

FLOWERING TIME: Summer.

HEIGHT AND SPREAD: 6–10 feet (1.8–3 m) tall; 4–8 feet (1.2–2.4 m) wide.

TEMPERATURE REQUIREMENTS: Zones 3–8.

POSITION: Moist, average to humus-rich soil. Full sun to partial shade. Stems are not as sturdy on shade-grown plants.

CULTIVATION: Established clumps of plume poppy can double in size each season. Control is inevitably necessary to avert a total takeover. Chop off the creeping roots with a spade as soon as you see new stems emerging.

PROPAGATION: Remove new offsets in spring or fall or take root cuttings in winter.

PEST AND DISEASE PREVENTION: No serious pests or diseases.

LANDSCAPE USE: Place plume poppies at the rear of borders where there is ample room for them to grow. A mature clump is a lovely site. Plant them as accents along stairs or fences or use them like shrubs as a focal point.

Mertensia virginica   Boraginaceae

VIRGINIA BLUEBELLS

Virginia bluebells are lovely spring wildflowers with graceful flowers on arching stems clothed with thin blue-green leaves. Plants grow from thick roots and go dormant after flowering.

FLOWER COLOR: Nodding sky blue bells open from pink buds.

FLOWERING TIME: Spring.

HEIGHT AND SPREAD: 1–2 feet (30–60 cm) tall; 1–2 feet (30–60 cm) wide.

TEMPERATURE REQUIREMENTS: Zones 3–9.

POSITION: Consistently moist, well-drained, humus-rich soil. Full sun to shade.

CULTIVATION: Virginia bluebells emerge early in spring and go dormant soon after flowering. Sun is essential to bloom but plants are shade-tolerant once dormant. Place where you will not dig into them by accident.

PROPAGATION: Divide large clumps after flowering or in fall; leave at least one bud per division. Self-sown seedlings are usually abundant. They will bloom the second or third year.

PEST AND DISEASE PREVENTION: No serious pests or diseases.

LANDSCAPE USE: Plant along a woodland path with spring bulbs like daffodils and squills (*Scilla* spp.), as well as wildflowers like spring beauty (*Claytonia virginica*), and bloodroot (*Sanguinaria canadensis*). Interplant clumps with foliage plants such as ferns and hostas to fill the gaps left by dormant plants.

| *Monarda didyma* | Labiatae | *Nepeta* x *faassenii* | Labiatae |

BEE BALM

CATMINT

Bee balm is a lovely perennial with bright flowers on sturdy stems that grow from fast-creeping runners. The pointed oval leaves give Earl Grey tea its distinctive aroma and flavor.

Catmint produces terminal flower clusters in spring and early summer. The wiry stems are clothed in soft, hairy, gray-green oval leaves and grow from fibrous-rooted crowns.

FLOWER COLOR: Tight heads of tubular red flowers are surrounded by a whorl of colored leafy bracts (modified leaves).

FLOWERING TIME: Summer.

HEIGHT AND SPREAD: 2–4 feet (60–120 cm) tall; 2–3 feet (60–90 cm) wide.

TEMPERATURE REQUIREMENTS: Zones 4–8.

POSITION: Evenly moist, humus-rich soil. Full sun to partial shade. If plants dry out, the lower foliage will be shed.

CULTIVATION: Plants spread quickly; divide every 2–3 years to keep them within bounds.

PROPAGATION: Divide in spring or fall. Sow seed indoors or outdoors in spring.

PEST AND DISEASE PREVENTION: Powdery mildew causes white blotches on the foliage and may cover the entire plant. Thin the stems to allow good air circulation. Cut affected plants to the ground.

LANDSCAPE USE: Plant in formal or informal gardens. Bee balm's lovely flowers add brilliant color to the summer garden and are favored by hummingbirds.

OTHER COMMON NAMES: Bergamot, oswego tea.

CULTIVARS: 'Blue Stocking' has violet flowers. 'Cambridge Scarlet' has brilliant scarlet flowers. 'Croftway Pink' is soft pink. 'Mahogany' has ruby red flowers. 'Marshall's Delight' is a mildew-resistant pink. 'Prairie Night' has red-violet flowers. 'Snow Queen' is creamy white.

FLOWER COLOR: Violet-blue flowers are carried in whorls on slender spikes.

FLOWERING TIME: Spring through midsummer.

HEIGHT AND SPREAD: 1½–3 feet (45–90 cm) tall; 2–3 feet (60–90 cm) wide.

TEMPERATURE REQUIREMENTS: Zones 3–8.

POSITION: Average to humus-rich, moist but well-drained soil. Full sun to light shade. Plants tolerate poor, dry soil.

CULTIVATION: Clumps get quite rangy after bloom. Cut back finished flower stalks to encourage fresh growth and repeat bloom.

PROPAGATION: Divide plants in spring or fall. Take cuttings in early summer.

PEST AND DISEASE PREVENTION: No serious pests or diseases.

LANDSCAPE USE: Catmints are perfect for edging walks and beds or for planting along rock walls. In borders combine them with bellflowers (*Campanula* spp.), cranesbills (*Geranium* spp.), coreopsis, peonies, and ornamental grasses.

CULTIVARS: 'Six Hills Giant' has deep purple-blue flowers on 3-foot (90 cm) stems.

OTHER SPECIES:

N. mussinii, Persian nepeta, grows 1–1½ feet (30–45 cm) tall with a 2-foot (60 cm) spread. Lavender-blue flowers cover the plants for months. 'Blue Wonder' has deep blue flowers. Zones 3–8.

| *Oenothera macrocarpon* | Onagraceae | *Paeonia lactiflora* | Ranunculaceae |

OZARK SUNDROPS

COMMON GARDEN PEONY

Ozark sundrops are showy perennials with yellow flowers and narrow pale green leaves on sprawling stems. Plants grow from a deep taproot and spread by creeping stems.

Common garden peonies are shrub-like, with sturdy stalks clothed in compound, shiny green leaves. Plants grow from thick, fleshy roots and may live 100 years or more.

FLOWER COLOR: Bright lemon yellow flowers are saucer-shaped and 3–4 inches (7.5–10 cm) wide.

FLOWERING TIME: Late spring and early summer, sporadically throughout the season.

HEIGHT AND SPREAD: 6–12 inches (15–30 cm) tall; 12–36 inches (30–90 cm) wide.

TEMPERATURE REQUIREMENTS: Zones 4–8.

POSITION: Average to humus-rich, well-drained soil. Full sun. Established plants are extremely drought- and heat-tolerant.

CULTIVATION: Plants form large clumps with age so space at least 30 inches (75 cm) apart. Stems root as they spread.

PROPAGATION: Divide rosettes in early spring. Take stem cuttings in early summer. Sow seed outdoors in fall or indoors in early spring.

PEST AND DISEASE PREVENTION: No serious pests or diseases.

CULTIVARS: 'Greencourt Lemon' has 2-inch (5 cm) soft, sulfur yellow flowers.

LANDSCAPE USE: Use ozark sundrops at the front of borders with phlox, cranesbills (*Geranium* spp.), catmints (*Nepeta* spp.), yarrows, and other early-season perennials. Performs well in rock gardens and meadow plantings.

OTHER COMMON NAMES: Missouri primrose. Formerly known as *O. missouriensis.*

FLOWER COLOR: Ranges in color from white, cream, and yellow to pink, rose, burgundy, and scarlet. Flowers may be single, semidouble, or double.

FLOWERING TIME: Common garden peonies are classified by their bloom time; early May (April in the South) blooming; mid-May blooming; and late May (early June in the North) blooming.

HEIGHT AND SPREAD: 1½–3 feet (45–90 cm) tall; 3–4 feet (90–120 cm) wide.

TEMPERATURE REQUIREMENTS: Zones 2–8. Extremely cold-tolerant. Winter temperatures in the deep south are not cool enough to initiate flowering.

POSITION: Moist, humus-rich soil. Full sun to light shade. Good drainage is important to avoid root rot.

CULTIVATION: Plant container-grown peonies in spring or fall. Plant bareroot plants in September and October. Dig a hole 8–10 inches (20–25 cm) deep in well-prepared soil. Place the "eyes" (buds) 1–1½ inches (2.5–3 cm) below the soil surface. Space plants 3–4 feet (90–120 cm) apart to allow for spreading. Mulch new plants to protect from frost heaving. An annual winter mulch is advised where winter temperatures dip below 0°F (-18°C). Taller selections and those with double flowers may need staking to keep their faces out of the mud. Plants may grow undisturbed for years, but

COMMON GARDEN PEONY—CONTINUED   ## ORIENTAL POPPY

Peonies with single and semidouble flowers tend to be more resistant to wind and water damage. Stake plants with double flowers to keep them from flopping.

if roots become too crowded, flowering will drop off. Lift plants in fall, divide the roots leaving at least one eye (bud) per division, and replant into soil that has been enriched with organic matter.

PROPAGATION: Divide in fall.

PEST AND DISEASE PREVENTION: Spray or dust foliage with an organically acceptable fungicide such as sulfur or bordeaux mix to discourage the fungal disease Botrytis.

LANDSCAPE USE: Combine the deep red new shoots of common garden peony (*Galanthus* spp.) with early spring bulbs like snowdrops and squills (*Scilla* spp.). Spring and early-summer perennials such as irises, foxgloves (*Digitalis* spp.), and columbines (*Aquilegia* spp.) are excellent companions. The rich green foliage is a lovely foil to later-blooming perennials.

OTHER COMMON NAMES: Chinese peony.

CULTIVARS: Many cultivars are available in a range of colors and forms. 'Duchess de Nemours' is an early white double. 'Festiva Maxima' is an early white double flecked with red that is good for Southern gardens. 'Gay Paree' is a midseason cerise-and-white anemone. 'Nippon Beauty' is a garnet red Japanese. 'Sara Bernhart' is a fragrant midseason double. 'Sea Shell' is a tall, midseason pink single. 'White Swan' is a midseason white single.

Oriental poppies are prized for their colorful, crêpe-paper-like flowers. Plants produce rosettes of coarse, hairy, lobed foliage from a thick taproot. They often go dormant after flowering.

FLOWER COLOR: The 3–4-inch (7.5–10 cm) flowers have crinkled scarlet-red petals with black spots at their base. They surround a raised knob that becomes the seedpod.

FLOWERING TIME: Early summer.

HEIGHT AND SPREAD: 2–3 feet (60–90 cm) tall; 2–feet (60–90 cm) wide.

TEMPERATURE REQUIREMENTS: Zones 2–7.

POSITION: Average to rich, well-drained, humus-rich soil. Full sun to light shade. Established plants are tough and long-lived.

CULTIVATION: In warm zones plants go dormant after flowering, leaving a bare spot. In fall new foliage rosettes emerge. Divide overgrown plants at this time.

PROPAGATION: Divide in fall. Take root cuttings in late summer, fall, or winter.

PEST AND DISEASE PREVENTION: No serious pests or diseases.

LANDSCAPE USE: Plant showy oriental poppies with border perennials and ornamental grasses. Combine them with bushy plants like catmints (*Nepeta* spp.) or asters to fill the gap left by the declining foliage.

CULTIVARS: 'Bonfire' has brilliant red flowers. 'Helen Elizabeth' has pale salmon-pink flowers without spots. 'Snow Queen' is pure white with large black spots. 'Watermelon' is rosy pink.

COMMON BEARDTONGUE

Common beardtongue is a showy plant with erect flower spikes clothed in shiny, broadly lance-shaped leaves. Flowering stems and basal foliage rosettes grow from fibrous-rooted crowns.

FLOWER COLOR: The 1–1½-inch (2.5–3.5 cm) irregular tubular pink flowers have two upper and three lower lips.

FLOWERING TIME: Late spring to early summer.

HEIGHT AND SPREAD: 1½–3 feet (45–90 cm) tall; 1–2 feet (30–60 cm) wide.

TEMPERATURE REQUIREMENTS: Zones 3–8.

POSITION: Average to humus-rich, well-drained soil. Full sun to light shade. Good drainage is essential for success.

CULTIVATION: Plants form dense clumps with maturity and benefit from division every 4–6 years. More frequent division is required when plants are growing in rich soil.

PROPAGATION: Divide in spring. Sow seed outdoors in fall or indoors in winter after stratification. To stratify, mix seed with moist peat moss or seed-starting medium in a plastic bag. Close the bag with a twist-tie and place it in the refrigerator for 4–6 weeks. Then sow the mixture as you would normal seed. Seedlings may bloom the first year.

PEST AND DISEASE PREVENTION: No serious pests or diseases

LANDSCAPE USE: Plant beardtongues in formal borders, informal gardens, and rock gardens. Combine their spiky flowers, with rounded plants like cranesbills (*Geranium* spp.), yarrows, and coral bells (*Heuchera* spp.).

To grow penstemons successfully, you need to choose species that are adapted to your climate and growing conditions. Good drainage is critical for most species.

CULTIVARS: 'Bashful' has salmon-pink flowers on 12–14-inch (30–35 cm) stems. 'Elfin Pink' has bright pink flowers on 1-foot (30 cm) stems. 'Pink Beauty' has pink flowers on 2–2½-foot (60–75 cm) stems.

OTHER SPECIES:

P. australis, Southern penstemon, is a heat-tolerant species with soft, hairy leaves and pale pink flowers. Zones 5–9.

P. digitalis, foxglove penstemon, has 2½–5 foot (75–150 cm) tall stems with clusters of 1-inch (2.5 cm) white flowers and shiny deep green leaves. Plants thrive in moist soil. 'Husker Red' has deep ruby red leaves. Zones 4–8.

P. hirsutus, hairy beardtongue, is a fuzzy penstemon with purple flowers. 'Pygmaeus' is a dwarf selection only 8 inches (20 cm) high. Zones 4–8.

P. pinifolius is a shrubby plant with small scarlet flowers and stiff, needle-like leaves. Zones 6–8.

P. smallii, Small's beardtongue, has dense clusters of rose-purple flowers. Plants need poor soil and are often short-lived. Zones 6–8.

HYBRIDS: Hybrids of mixed origin are available. 'Firebird' has scarlet flowers. 'Mesa' has deep violet flowers. 'Prairie Dusk' has pendent purple flowers. 'Prairie Fire' has orange-red flowers.

Perovskia atriplicifolia   Labiatae

RUSSIAN SAGE

*Russian sage is a shrubby, branching summer-blooming peren-
nial with erect stems clothed in gray-green deeply lobed leaves.
Plants grow from fibrous-rooted crowns.*

FLOWER COLOR: Small, irregularly shaped blue flow-
    ers are carried in slender 12–15-inch (30–37.5 cm)
    sprays.
FLOWERING TIME: Mid- to late summer.
HEIGHT AND SPREAD: 3–5 feet (90–150 cm) tall; 3–
    5 feet (90–150 cm) wide.
TEMPERATURE REQUIREMENTS: Zones 4–9.
POSITION: Average to rich, well-drained soil. Full sun.
    Good drainage is essential for success.
CULTIVATION: The stems of Russian sage become
    woody with age. After hard frost, cut the stems
    back to 1 foot (30 cm). In cooler zones plants die
    back to the soil line but resprout from the roots.
    Division is seldom necessary.
PROPAGATION: Take stem cuttings in early summer.
PEST AND DISEASE PREVENTION: No serious pests or
    diseases.
LANDSCAPE USE: Plant toward the middle or back of
    borders where the airy gray flower buds and soft-
    blue flowers mix well with yellow, pink, deep
    blue, and purple flowers. Combine with yarrows,
    gayfeathers (*Liatris* spp.), balloon flower (*Platycodon
    grandiflorus*), sedum, phlox, and ornamental
    grasses.
CULTIVARS: 'Blue Spire' has violet-blue flowers on
    strong upright stems. 'Longin' has stout stems and
    grows 3–4 feet (90–120 cm) tall.

Phlox divaricata   Polemoniaceae

WILD BLUE PHLOX

*Wild blue phlox is a sweet-scented woodland species with blue
spring flowers and creeping stems clothed in evergreen oval
leaves. Plants have fibrous white roots.*

FLOWER COLOR: Soft blue to sky blue flowers borne in
    open, domed clusters on upright stems.
FLOWERING TIME: Spring.
HEIGHT AND SPREAD: 10–15 inches (25–37.5 cm)
    tall; 12–24 inches (30–60 cm) wide.
TEMPERATURE REQUIREMENTS: Zones 3–9.
POSITION: Evenly moist, humus-rich soil. Partial to
    full shade. Sun is necessary in spring, but protec-
    tion from summer sun is critical.
CULTIVATION: Plants spread to form clumps of lovely
    flowers. Divide as necessary to control spread.
PROPAGATION: Divide after flowering. Take cuttings
    in late spring or early summer from nonblooming
    stems. Sow seed in fall or spring. Self-sown seed-
    lings often appear.
PEST AND DISEASE PREVENTION: Powdery mildew
    may attack, causing white patches on leaves. Spray
    with sulfur to keep the disease from spreading.
LANDSCAPE USE: Plant in shade or wild gardens with
    spring bulbs, hellebores (*Helleborus* spp.), wild-
    flowers, and ferns. Grows well under flowering
    shrubs as a groundcover.
OTHER SPECIES:
    P. x 'Chattahoochee' has clusters of lavender blue
    flowers with violet eyes. Zones 3–9.
    P. stolonifera, creeping phlox, forms low mats of
    rounded foliage and upright spikes of blue or pink
    flowers similar to *P. divaricata*. Zones 2–8.

GARDEN PHLOX

Garden phlox is a popular summer-blooming perennial with domed clusters of fragrant, richly colored flowers atop stiff, leafy stems. Plants grow from fibrous-rooted crowns.

To keep garden phlox looking its best, cut off the spent flower clusters. Some cultivars, like this white-flowered 'Mt. Fujiyama', may rebloom in late summer.

FLOWER COLOR: Varies from magenta to pink and white. Hybrids have a wide color range, including purples, reds, and oranges. Bicolored and "eyed" forms are also popular.

FLOWERING TIME: Mid- to late summer.

HEIGHT AND SPREAD: 3–4 feet (90–120 cm) tall; 2–4 feet (60–120 cm) wide.

TEMPERATURE REQUIREMENTS: Zones 3–8. Cold hardiness varies with cultivars.

POSITION: Moist but well-drained, humus-rich soil. Full sun to light shade.

CULTIVATION: Divide clumps every 3–4 years to keep them vigorous.

PROPAGATION: Divide in spring. Take stem cuttings in late spring or early summer. Take root cuttings in the fall.

PEST AND DISEASE PREVENTION: Powdery mildew is the bane of phlox growers. It causes white patches on the leaves or, in bad cases, turns entire leaves white. To avoid problems, thin the stems before plants bloom to increase air circulation. Select resistant cultivars, especially hybrids with *P. maculata*.

LANDSCAPE USE: Garden phlox are beautiful and versatile garden perennials. Combine with summer daisies, bee balms (*Monarda* spp.), daylilies, asters, goldenrods (*Solidago* spp.), and ornamental grasses. Lovely in informal situations and on the edges of lightly shaded woodlands.

OTHER COMMON NAMES: Summer phlox.

CULTIVARS: Dozens of named selections are available. They vary in bloom time, mildew resistance, flower size, and cold hardiness. 'Bright Eyes' has pink flowers with crimson eyes and is mildew-resistant. 'Caroline van den Berg' has purple flowers. 'David' has large heads of white flowers and is mildew-resistant. 'Dodo Hanbury Forbes' has large clear pink flowers with rose eyes. 'Mt. Fujiyama' is a compact late-summer white. 'Sandra' is a compact plant with scarlet flowers. 'The King' has red-violet flowers.

OTHER SPECIES:

P. carolina, thick-leaved phlox, has glossy oval leaves and elongated clusters of lavender, pink, or white flowers in early summer. 'Miss Lingard' has white flowers with yellow eyes. 'Rosalinde' has bright pink flowers. Zones 4–9.

P. maculata, wild sweet William, is similar to *P. carolina* but the foliage is lance-shaped. 'Alpha' has rose pink flowers with a darker eye. 'Omega' has white flowers with lilac-pink eyes. Zones 3–9.

P. ovata, mountain phlox, is an upright but spreading species with shiny oval leaves and open clusters of pink to magenta flowers. 'Spring Delight' has deep rose pink flowers in late spring and early summer. Zones 4–8.

| *Physostegia virginiana* | Labiatae | *Platycodon grandiflorus* | Campanulaceae |

OBEDIENT PLANT

BALLOON FLOWER

Fast-spreading obedient plant is named for the tendency of its flowers to remain in any position when shifted in their four-ranked clusters. Plants grow from creeping stems.

FLOWER COLOR: The tubular, bilobed flowers are rose pink to lilac-pink.

FLOWERING TIME: Late summer.

HEIGHT AND SPREAD: 3–4 feet (90–120 cm) tall; 2–4 feet (60–120 cm) wide.

TEMPERATURE REQUIREMENTS: Zones 3–9.

POSITION: Moist, average to humus-rich soil. Full sun to light shade. Grows well in moist to wet soil.

CULTIVATION: Wild forms of obedient plant tend to flop in rich soil. Stake the plants or choose a compact cultivar. Divide every 2–4 years to control their spread.

PROPAGATION: Divide in spring. Take stem cuttings in early summer.

PEST AND DISEASE PREVENTION: No serious pests or diseases.

LANDSCAPE USE: Use cultivars of obedient plant in formal gardens with asters, goldenrods (*Solidago* spp.), garden phlox (*Phlox paniculata*), boltonia (*Boltonia asteroides*), and ornamental grasses. The wild form is lovely in informal plantings.

OTHER COMMON NAMES: False dragonhead.

CULTIVARS: 'Pink Bouquet' has bright pink flowers on 3–4-foot (90–120 cm) stems. 'Summer Snow' has white flowers on compact, 3-foot (90 cm) stems. 'Variegata' has leaves edged in creamy white and pale pink flowers. 'Vivid' has vibrant rose pink flowers.

Balloon flowers are showy summer-blooming plants with saucer-shaped flowers on succulent stems clothed in toothed, triangular leaves. Plants grow from thick, fleshy roots.

FLOWER COLOR: The rich blue flowers have five-pointed petals that open from inflated buds that resemble balloons.

FLOWERING TIME: Summer.

HEIGHT AND SPREAD: 2–3 feet (60–90 cm) tall; 1–2 feet (30-60 cm) wide.

TEMPERATURE REQUIREMENTS: Zones 3–8.

POSITION: Well-drained, average to humus-rich soil. Full sun to light shade. Established plants are drought-tolerant.

CULTIVATION: New shoots are slow to emerge in spring. Take care not to damage them by mistake. Remove spent flowers to encourage more bloom. Established clumps seldom need division.

PROPAGATION: Lift and divide clumps in spring or early fall; dig deeply to avoid root damage. Take basal cuttings of nonflowering shoots in summer, preferably with a piece of root attached. Sow seed outdoors in fall. Self-sown seedlings may appear.

PEST AND DISEASE PREVENTION: No serious pests or diseases.

LANDSCAPE USE: Plant balloon flower with summer perennials like yellow yarrows (*Achillea* spp.), sages (*Salvia* spp.), bee balms (*Monarda* spp.), and phlox.

CULTIVARS: 'Apoyama' has blue-violet flowers on 6-inch (15 cm) plants. 'Double Blue' has double flowers on 2-foot (60 cm) plants. 'Shell Pink' has pale pink flowers on 2-foot (60 cm) plants.

<table>
<tr><td>Polemonium caeruleum</td><td>Polemoniaceae</td></tr>
</table>

JACOB'S LADDER

Jacob's ladder has tall, leafy stems crowned with loose clusters of nodding flowers. The showy leaves are pinnately divided with many leaflets. Plants grow from fibrous-rooted crowns.

FLOWER COLOR: Saucer-shaped blue or white flowers with five overlapping petals.

FLOWERING TIME: Throughout summer.

HEIGHT AND SPREAD: 1½–2½ feet (45–75 cm) tall; 1–1½ feet (30–45 cm) wide.

TEMPERATURE REQUIREMENTS: Zones 3–7. Sensitive to high temperatures.

POSITION: Evenly moist, humus-rich soil. Full sun to partial shade.

CULTIVATION: Remove spent flowers to encourage reblooming. Plants are carefree and seldom need division.

PROPAGATION: Sow seed outdoors in fall. Self-sown seedlings may appear.

PEST AND DISEASE PREVENTION: No serious pests or diseases.

LANDSCAPE USE: Plant in formal gardens with goat's beard (*Aruncus dioicus*), Russian sage (*Perovskia atriplicifolia*), phlox, and ornamental grasses. Massed plantings are effective in informal gardens with ferns or under flowering trees.

VARIETIES: *P. caeruleum* var. *album* has white flowers.

OTHER SPECIES:

P. reptans, creeping Jacob's ladder, is a woodland plant with deep blue flowers on 8–16-inch (20–40 cm) stems. The foliage makes an elegant summer groundcover. Zones 2–8.

<table>
<tr><td>Polygonatum odoratum</td><td>Liliaceae</td></tr>
</table>

FRAGRANT SOLOMON'S SEAL

Fragrant Solomon's seal has graceful, arching stems with broad, oval blue-green leaves arranged like stairs up the stem. The cultivar 'Variegatum' has white-edged leaves.

FLOWER COLOR: Tubular, pale green, fragrant flowers are carried in clusters at the nodes. Showy blue-black fruit is produced in late summer.

FLOWERING TIME: Spring.

HEIGHT AND SPREAD: 1½–2½ feet (45–75 cm) tall; 2–4 feet (60–120 cm) wide.

TEMPERATURE REQUIREMENTS: Zones 3–9.

POSITION: Moist, humus-rich soil. Partial to full shade. Tolerates dry soil.

CULTIVATION: Spreads from thick, creeping rhizomes to form wide clumps. Divide to control its spread.

PROPAGATION: Divide clumps in spring or fall or sow fresh seed outdoors in fall. Seedlings may not appear for 2 years and take several years to bloom.

PEST AND DISEASE PREVENTION: No serious pests or diseases.

LANDSCAPE USE: Fragrant Solomon's seal provides grace and beauty to the shade garden. Combine it with hostas, lungworts (*Pulmonaria* spp.), irises, wildflowers, and ferns. Use massed plantings under shrubs or in the dry shade of mature trees.

CULTIVARS: 'Variegatum' is prized for its broad, oval leaves with creamy white margins.

OTHER COMMON NAMES: Japanese Solomon's seal.

OTHER SPECIES:

P. biflorum, Solomon's seal, grows 1–3 feet (30–90 cm) tall with narrow, oval leaves and flowers in pairs. Zones 3–9.

Polygonum bistorta Polygonaceae	*Primula* x *polyantha* Primulaceae

SNAKEWEED

POLYANTHUS PRIMROSE

Snakeweed is a vigorous perennial with upright flower spikes and pointed, broadly lance-shaped leaves with prominent central veins. The plants grow from creeping stems.

Polyanthus primroses are hybrids with large, showy flowers in a rainbow of colors. The broad, crinkled leaves rise directly from stout crowns with thick, fibrous roots.

FLOWER COLOR: Small pink flowers are tightly packed into erect spikes.

FLOWERING TIME: Early summer.

HEIGHT AND SPREAD: 1½–2½ feet (45–75 cm) tall; 1–3 feet (30–90 cm) wide.

TEMPERATURE REQUIREMENTS: Zones 3–8.

POSITION: Constantly moist, humus-rich soil. Full sun to partial shade. Plants tolerate wet soil.

CULTIVATION: Plants spread rapidly to form wide clumps. Frequent removal of some plants is necessary to keep them from taking over.

PROPAGATION: Divide in fall or spring. Sow seed outdoors in fall or spring or indoors in late winter.

PEST AND DISEASE PREVENTION: No serious pests or diseases.

LANDSCAPE USE: Snakeweed is a showy, fast-spreading groundcover. Combine it with irises, astilbes, hostas, ferns, and ornamental grasses.

OTHER COMMON NAMES: Bistort.

CULTIVARS: 'Superbum' has thick, showy flower spikes.

OTHER SPECIES:

P. affine, Himalayan fleeceflower, grows 6–10 inches (15–25 cm) tall. Plants grow from creeping roots to form wide patches of lance-shaped leaves. The narrow spikes of pink flowers open in summer. 'Border Jewel' has rose pink flowers. 'Dimity' has light pink flowers. Zones 3–7.

FLOWER COLOR: Flat, five-petaled flowers vary in color from white, cream, and yellow to pink, rose, red, and purple. Many bicolored and eyed forms are available.

FLOWERING TIME: Spring and early summer.

HEIGHT AND SPREAD: 8–12 inches (20–30 cm) tall; 12 inches (30 cm) wide.

TEMPERATURE REQUIREMENTS: Zones 3–8.

POSITION: Evenly moist, humus-rich soil. Light to partial shade. Plants can tolerate dryness in the summer if they go dormant.

CULTIVATION: In cooler zones mulch plants to avoid frost heaving and crown damage. Divide overgrown clumps after flowering and replant into soil that has been enriched with organic matter.

PROPAGATION: Divide in fall to increase your stock. Species are easy to grow from fresh seed sown outdoors or indoors in early spring.

PEST AND DISEASE PREVENTION: No serious pests or diseases.

LANDSCAPE USE: Plant drifts of primroses with spring bulbs like daffodils, tulips, and Spanish bluebells (*Hyacinthoides hispanicus*). Combine them with early-blooming perennials like hellebores (*Helleborus* spp.), lungworts (*Pulmonaria* spp.), forget-me-nots (*Myosotis* spp.), and cranesbills (*Geranium* spp.). Wildflowers, ferns, and sedges (*Carex* spp.) are excellent companions.

BETHLEHEM SAGE

The pale yellow blooms of English primroses are among the first flowers to appear in the spring. Plant them with violets and early bulbs for a welcome spot of color.

Bethlehem sage is a lovely spring-blooming foliage plant with wide, hairy leaves variously spotted and blotched with silver. Plants grow from crowns with thick, fibrous roots.

CULTIVARS: Many hybrids and seed-grown strains are available. 'Barnhaven Hybrids' are small plants with large flowers in mixed colors. 'Pacific Giant' is a seed strain with large mixed-colored flowers.

OTHER SPECIES:

P. auricula, auricula primrose, is a hardy species with thick, spoon-shaped evergreen leaves and showy clusters of white, pink, burgundy, rose, and bicolored flowers. Zones 2–8.

P. denticulata, drumstick primrose, bears round heads of small pink, lavender, or white flowers on tall stalks. Leafy clumps develop as flowers fade. Plants need constant moisture. Zones 3–8.

P. elatior, oxslip, has broad, puckered leaves and open clusters of nodding soft-yellow flowers. Zones 3 (with winter protection)–7.

P. japonica, Japanese primrose, has lush paddle-shaped foliage and pink, rose, or white flowers in tiered clusters on tall, naked stems.

P. sieboldii, Siebold's primrose, has fuzzy, heart-shaped, toothed leaves and open clusters of pink, rose, or white flowers with notched petals. Zones 4–8.

P. veris, cowslip primrose, has fragrant nodding yellow flowers and broad leaves. Zones 3–8.

P. vulgaris, English primrose, has wrinkled, tongue-like leaves and flat pale yellow flowers. Zones 3–8.

FLOWER COLOR: The nodding, five-petaled flowers vary from pink to medium blue. Some buds open pink and change to blue. They are held in tight clusters on shortlived stems.

FLOWERING TIME: Spring.

HEIGHT AND SPREAD: 9–18 inches (23–45 cm) tall; 12–24 inches (30–60 cm) wide.

TEMPERATURE REQUIREMENTS: Zones 3–8.

POSITION: Moist, humus-rich soil. Partial to full shade.

CULTIVATION: The foliage of Bethlehem sage remains attractive all season unless soil remains dry for an extended period. Plants seldom need division.

PROPAGATION: Divide in spring (after bloom) or fall.

PEST AND DISEASE PREVENTION: Trap slugs in shallow pans of beer set flush with the soil surface.

LANDSCAPE USE: Plant Bethlehem sage with spring bulbs, primroses, bleeding hearts (*Dicentra* spp.), foamflowers (*Tiarella* spp.), wildflowers, and ferns.

OTHER COMMON NAMES: Lungwort.

CULTIVARS: 'Janet Fisk' has densely spotted white leaves and lavender-pink flowers. 'Mrs. Moon' has spotted leaves and pink flowers. 'Sissinghurst White' is a hybrid with white flowers.

OTHER SPECIES:

P. angustifolia, blue lungwort, has narrow, deep green leaves and gentian blue flowers. Zones 2–8.

P. longifolia, long-leaved lungwort, has spotted leaves and electric blue flowers. Zones 3–8.

Pulsatilla vulgaris Ranunculaceae

PASQUE FLOWER

Pasque flowers are early-blooming perennials with cupped flowers over rosettes of deeply incised, lobed leaves clothed in soft hairs. Plants grow from deep, fibrous roots.

FLOWER COLOR: The purple flowers have five starry petals surrounding a central ring of fuzzy orange-yellow stamens (male reproductive structures). The flowers are followed by clusters of fuzzy seeds.

FLOWERING TIME: Early to midspring.

HEIGHT AND SPREAD: 6–12 inches (15–30 cm) tall; 10–12 inches (25–30 cm) wide.

TEMPERATURE REQUIREMENTS: Zones 3–8.

POSITION: Average to humus-rich, well-drained soil. Full sun to light shade. Does not tolerate soggy soil.

CULTIVATION: Pasque flowers begin blooming in spring and continue for several weeks. After seed is set, plants go dormant unless conditions are cool. Seldom needs division.

PROPAGATION: Divide clumps after flowering or in fall. Sow seed outdoors in fall or spring. Self-sown seedlings are plentiful.

PEST AND DISEASE PREVENTION: No serious pests or diseases.

LANDSCAPE USE: Perfect for rock gardens with bulbs, rock cresses (*Arabis* spp.), basket-of-gold (*Aurinia saxatilis*), perennial candytuft (*Iberis sempervirens*), and columbines (*Aquilegia* spp.).

OTHER SPECIES:
P. patens, prairie pasque flower, has white or pale blue flowers. Plant only in sandy well-drained soil. Goes dormant in hot weather. Zones 3–7.

Rodgersia pinnata Saxifragaceae

RODGERSIA

Rodgersias are bold perennials with pinkish red flowers and large, pinnately compound leaves. These moisture-loving plants grow from stout, fibrous-rooted crowns.

FLOWER COLOR: The small rose red flowers are carried in 1–2-foot (30–60 cm) plume-like clusters.

FLOWERING TIME: Late spring and early summer.

HEIGHT AND SPREAD: 3–4 feet (90–120 cm) tall; 4 feet (1.2 m) wide.

TEMPERATURE REQUIREMENTS: Zones 4–7.

POSITION: Constantly moist, humus-rich soil. Partial to full shade. Protect from hot afternoon sun in warm zones.

CULTIVATION: Rodgersias form huge clumps from large crowns that can remain in place for years. Be sure to provide at least 3–4 feet (90–120 cm) of room for each plant.

PROPAGATION: Divide plants in fall or spring. Sow seed outdoors in fall or indoors in spring.

PEST AND DISEASE PREVENTION: No serious pests or diseases.

LANDSCAPE USE: Plant rodgersias in bog and water gardens or along streams. Combine them with hostas, irises, astilbes, ferns, ligularias (*Ligularia* spp.), and primroses.

OTHER COMMON NAMES: Rodger's flower.

OTHER SPECIES:
R. aesculifolia, finger-leaved rodgersia, has palmately divided leaves and creamy white flowers. Zones 4–7.
R. sambucifolia, elder-leaved rodgersia, is similar to *R. pinnata* but with white flowers. Zones 4–7.

Rudbeckia fulgida Compositae	*Salvia* x *superba* Labiatae

ORANGE CONEFLOWER

VIOLET SAGE

Orange coneflowers are cheery summer daisies with oval to broadly lance-shaped, rough, hairy foliage on stiff stems. Plants grow from fibrous-rooted crowns.

Violet sage is covered with colorful flower spikes in summer. The bushy, well-branched plants have aromatic triangular leaves. They grow from a fibrous-rooted crown.

FLOWER COLOR: The daisy-like flowers have yellow-orange rays (petal-like structures) and raised dark brown centers.

FLOWERING TIME: Mid- to late summer.

HEIGHT AND SPREAD: 1½–3 feet (45–90 cm) tall; 2–4 feet (60–120 cm) wide.

TEMPERATURE REQUIREMENTS: Zones 3–9. Extremely heat-tolerant.

POSITION: Average, moist but well-drained soil. Full sun to light shade. Good drainage is important.

CULTIVATION: Orange coneflowers are tough, long-lived perennials. They spread outward to form large clumps. The edges of the clumps are the most vigorous. Divide every 2–4 years and replant into soil that has been enriched with organic matter.

PROPAGATION: Divide in spring or fall. Sow seed outdoors in fall or spring or indoors in late winter.

PEST AND DISEASE PREVENTION: No serious pests or diseases.

LANDSCAPE USE: Plant orange coneflowers with other daisies, sedums, phlox, bee balms (*Monarda* spp.), chrysanthemums, and ornamental grasses.

OTHER COMMON NAMES: Black-eyed Susan.

VARIETIES: *R. fulgida* var. *sullivantii* is a stout grower with wide leaves. 'Goldsturm' is a popular compact cultivar of this variety. The variety *speciosa* (also known as *R. neumanii*) has narrow leaves and smaller flowers.

FLOWER COLOR: The violet-blue flowers are carried in narrow spikes. Below each flower is a leaf-like bract.

FLOWERING TIME: Early to midsummer. Plants often rebloom.

HEIGHT AND SPREAD: 1½–3½ feet (45–105 cm) tall; 2–3 feet (60–90 cm) wide.

TEMPERATURE REQUIREMENTS: Zones 4–7.

POSITION: Average to humus-rich, moist but well-drained soil. Full sun to light shade. Drought-tolerant once established.

CULTIVATION: After flowering wanes, shear back flowering stems to promote fresh growth and renewed bloom. Plants seldom need division.

PROPAGATION: Divide in spring or fall. Take cuttings in late spring or early summer; remove the flower buds.

PEST AND DISEASE PREVENTION: No serious pests or diseases.

LANDSCAPE USE: Plant violet sages in borders or rock gardens with early summer perennials such as yarrows, lamb's-ears (*Stachys byzantina*), daylilies, coreopsis (*Coreopsis* spp.), and ornamental grasses.

CULTIVARS: 'Blue Queen' has violet-blue flowers and is 1½–2 feet (45–60 cm) tall. 'East Friesland' has purple-blue flowers on 1–1½-foot (30–45 cm) plants. 'Lubeca' has deep purple flowers. 'May Night' has violet-blue flowers on bushy plants.

Sanguinaria canadensis   Papaveraceae

BLOODROOT

Bloodroot is a bright, spring wildflower with a single, deeply cut, seven-lobed leaf that emerges wrapped around the single flower bud. Plants grow from a thick, creeping rhizome.

FLOWER COLOR: The snow white flowers have 8–11 narrow petals surrounding a cluster of yellow-orange stamens (male reproductive structures). Flowers last only a few days.

FLOWERING TIME: Early to midspring.

HEIGHT AND SPREAD: 4–6 inches (10–15 cm) tall; 6–8 inches (15–20 cm) wide.

TEMPERATURE REQUIREMENTS: Zones 3–9.

POSITION: Moist, humus-rich soil. Light to full shade. Spring sun is important but summer shade is necessary. During prolonged dry spells, plants go dormant with no ill effect.

CULTIVATION: Bloodroot foliage remains attractive all summer when ample moisture is available. Plants form dense clumps that can be divided.

PROPAGATION: Divide in late summer. Sow fresh seed outdoors in summer. Self-sown seedlings often appear.

PEST AND DISEASE PREVENTION: No serious pests or diseases.

LANDSCAPE USE: Plant bloodroot in woodland gardens with spring bulbs, wildflowers, hostas, and ferns. Use them as a groundcover under shrubs.

CULTIVARS: 'Multiplex' is a stunning, fully double form with long-lasting flowers.

Sanguisorba canadensis   Rosaceae

CANADIAN BURNET

The tall bottlebrushes of Canadian burnet bloom in late summer atop stout stems clothed in pinnately divided leaves with oblong leaflets. Plants grow from thick, fleshy roots.

FLOWER COLOR: The fuzzy, white flowers lack petals. They are tightly packed into dense spikes.

FLOWERING TIME: Late summer and early fall.

HEIGHT AND SPREAD: 4–5 feet (1.2–1.5 m) tall; 4 feet (1.2 m) wide.

TEMPERATURE REQUIREMENTS: Zones 3–8. Plants do not tolerate excessive summer heat.

POSITION: Evenly moist, humus-rich soil. Full sun to partial shade.

CULTIVATION: Mulch plants to help keep the soil cool and moist. Plants form stout clumps with age. Divide overgrown clumps.

PROPAGATION: Divide in spring. Sow seed outdoors in fall.

PEST AND DISEASE PREVENTION: No serious pests or diseases.

LANDSCAPE USE: Plant Canadian burnet at the rear of the border with phlox, monkshoods (*Aconitum* spp.), asters, boltonia (*Boltonia asteroides*), sedums, and ornamental grasses.

OTHER SPECIES:

S. obtusa, Japanese burnet, grows to just 3–4 feet (90–120 cm) with drooping rose pink flower clusters and blue-green leaves with rounded leaflets. Zones 4–8.

Santolina chamaecyparissus   Compositae

LAVENDER COTTON

Lavender cotton is a compact, semiwoody shrub with small, white, wooly, pinnately divided leaves topped with yellow flowers in summer. Plants grow from fibrous-rooted crowns.

FLOWER COLOR: The button-like yellow flowers are held above the foliage on thin stalks.

FLOWERING TIME: Summer.

HEIGHT AND SPREAD: 1–2 feet (30–60 cm) tall; 2 feet (60 cm) wide.

TEMPERATURE REQUIREMENTS: Zones 6–8.

POSITION: Average, well-drained soil. Full sun. Plants tolerate drought, poor soil, and salt.

CULTIVATION: Plants need winter protection in cold areas. Cut back in early spring to promote strong healthy growth.

PROPAGATION: Layer in spring. Take cuttings in summer.

PEST AND DISEASE PREVENTION: No serious pests or diseases.

LANDSCAPE USE: Use lavender cotton to edge walks and beds or to configure intricate knot garden designs. Combine it with other perennials that need good drainage like pinks (*Dianthus* spp.), rock cresses (*Arabis* spp.), and sedums.

OTHER SPECIES:
S. virens, green lavender cotton, is similar but has deep green foliage.

Saponaria x *lempergii*   Caryophyllaceae

SOAPWORT

Soapworts have mounds of flowers on sprawling stems with oval leaves. Plants grow from fibrous-rooted crowns. They are ideal for planting on walls or in rock gardens.

FLOWER COLOR: The 1-inch (2.5 cm) deep pink flowers have five squared petals.

FLOWERING TIME: Summer.

HEIGHT AND SPREAD: 4–6 inches (10–15 cm) tall; 12–14 inches (30–35 cm) wide.

TEMPERATURE REQUIREMENTS: Zones 5–8.

POSITION: Average, well-drained soil. Full sun to light shade.

CULTIVATION: Soapworts form broad clumps from creeping stems. Divide to control their spread. Cut back after flowering to encourage new growth.

PROPAGATION: Divide in spring or fall. Take cuttings in early summer.

PEST AND DISEASE PREVENTION: No serious pests or diseases.

LANDSCAPE USE: Plant soapworts along walks, along the edges of beds, at the front of borders, or in rock gardens.

CULTIVARS: 'Max Frei' is a compact grower with rich pink flowers.

OTHER SPECIES:
S. ocymoides, rock soapwort, is a sprawling plant with clusters of ¼-inch (6 mm) bright pink flowers. 'Rubra Compacta' forms tight mounds with deep pink to crimson flowers. Zones 3–7.
S. officinalis, bouncing bet, is a fast-spreading plant with 1–2½-foot (30–75 cm) stems and rounded clusters of pale pink flowers. Zones 2–8.

STRAWBERRY GERANIUM

PINCUSHION FLOWER

Strawberry geranium is not a true geranium but an attractive groundcover with round leaves that resemble bedding geraniums. The evergreen leaves are attractively veined with silver.

FLOWER COLOR: The small white flowers have five petals, two of which are longer than the others.

FLOWERING TIME: Spring.

HEIGHT AND SPREAD: 10–12 inches (25–30 cm) tall; 12 inches (30 cm) wide.

TEMPERATURE REQUIREMENTS: Zones 6–9.

POSITION: Moist, humus-rich soil. Partial to full shade.

CULTIVATION: Plants spread quickly to form dense, weed-proof mats. Plants are easily pulled if they spread out of bounds.

PROPAGATION: Remove and replant rooted offsets in spring or fall. Sow seed outdoors in fall.

PESTS AND DISEASE PREVENTION: No serious pests or diseases.

LANDSCAPE USE: Plant as a groundcover under flowering shrubs and small trees. In the shaded garden, use the silvery foliage to complement hostas, bulbs, wildflowers, and ferns. Plants perform admirably in pots.

CULTIVARS: 'Tricolor' has pink and cream variegation but is less hardy.

OTHER SPECIES:

S. x *urbium* (*S. umbrosa*), London pride, has toothed, spoon-shaped evergreen leaves and airy clusters of small pink flowers. Plants do not tolerate heat. Zones 6–8.

Pincushion flowers are old-fashioned perennials that are regaining the popularity they had in Victorian gardens. The stems are loosely clothed in lance-shaped to three-lobed leaves.

FLOWER COLOR: The unusual soft blue flowers are packed into flat, 2–3-inch (5–7.5 cm) heads. The flowers increase in size as they near the margins of the heads.

FLOWERING TIME: Summer.

HEIGHT AND SPREAD: 1½–2 feet (45–60 cm) tall; 1–1½ feet (30–45 cm) wide.

TEMPERATURE REQUIREMENTS: Zones 3–7.

POSITION: Average to humus-rich, moist but well-drained soil. Full sun to light shade. Sensitive to high temperatures. Will not tolerate wet soil.

CULTIVATION: Plants form good-sized clumps in 1–2 years. Divide if plants become overcrowded. Deadheading promotes continued bloom.

PROPAGATION: Divide in spring. Sow fresh seed outdoors in fall or indoors in late winter.

PEST AND DISEASE PREVENTION: No serious pests or diseases.

LANDSCAPE USE: Plant in groups to increase their visual impact. The airy flowers seem to dance above low, mounded plants like phlox, pinks (*Dianthus* spp.), and yarrows. They combine well with bee balms (*Monarda* spp.), daylilies, and columbines (*Aquilegia* spp.).

CULTIVARS: 'Alba' has white flowers. 'Butterfly Blue', of uncertain parentage, is long-blooming with lilac-blue flowers. 'Clive Greaves' has large lavender-blue heads. 'Miss Wilmot' is creamy white.

Sedum spectabile   Crassulaceae

SHOWY STONECROP

Showy stonecrops are late summer perennials with clusters of pink flowers atop thick stems clothed in broad gray-green leaves. Plants grow from fibrous-rooted crowns.

Hybrid 'Autumn Joy' sedum is a dependable performer for the late-season garden. The clustered green buds open to pink flowers that gradually age to deep red.

FLOWER COLOR: Small bright pink flowers are borne in 4–6-inch (10–15 cm) domed clusters. The pale green buds are attractive in summer and the brown seed heads hold their shape all winter.

FLOWERING TIME: Mid- to late summer.

HEIGHT AND SPREAD: 1–2 feet (30–60 cm) tall; 2 feet (60 cm) wide.

TEMPERATURE REQUIREMENTS: Zones 3–9. Plants are heat-tolerant.

POSITION: Average to humus-rich, well-drained soil. Full sun. Extremely drought-tolerant.

CULTIVATION: Clumps get quite full with age and may fall open. Divide overgrown plants.

PROPAGATION: Divide from spring to midsummer. Take cuttings of nonflowering shoots in summer. Sow seed in spring or fall.

PEST AND DISEASE PREVENTION: No serious pests or diseases.

LANDSCAPE USE: Plant in formal borders, informal gardens, and rock gardens. Combine with yarrows, purple coneflowers (*Echinacea* spp.), cranesbills (*Geranium* spp.), coreopsis (*Coreopsis* spp.), and ornamental grasses.

CULTIVARS: 'Brilliant' has rose pink flowers. 'Carmen' has carmine pink flowers.

HYBRIDS: Several hybrid cultivars are available. 'Autumn Joy' is a stout sedum similar to *S. spectabile* but more robust with darker flowers. 'Ruby Glow'

has 1-foot (30 cm) sprawling stems with purple-tinged leaves and ruby red flowers. 'Vera Jameson' is similar but has blue-gray leaves tinged purple and rose red flowers.

OTHER SPECIES:

S. aizoon, Aizoon stonecrop, is an upright grower with oval, toothed leaves and flat 3–4-inch (7.5–10 cm) clusters of yellow flowers. Zones 4–9.

S. alboroseum is similar to *S. spectabile* but less robust. 'Medio-variegatus' has leaves with creamy white variegation. Zones 5–9.

S. album, white stonecrop, is a creeping plant with lance-shaped evergreen leaves and 1–2-inch (2.5–5 cm) clusters of white flowers. Zones 3–9.

S. kamtschaticum, Kamschatka stonecrop, is a creeping plant with narrow, toothed evergreen leaves and flat clusters of yellow flowers. Zones 3–8.

S. maximum, stonecrop, is an upright plant with oval leaves and domed clusters of creamy rose flowers. The variety *atropurpureum* 'Honeysong' has deep purple leaves and rose pink flowers. Zones 3–8.

S. spurium, two-row sedum, is a creeper with rounded evergreen leaves and open clusters of pink flowers. 'Dragon's Blood' has red-tinged foliage and rose red flowers. 'Tricolor' has leaves variegated with pink, white and green. Zones 3–8.

S. ternatum, whorled stonecrop, is a low woodland plant with starry white flowers. Zones 4–8.

Smilacina racemosa	Liliaceae

SOLOMON'S PLUME

Solomon's plume is a showy woodland wildflower. The erect arching stems bear broad glossy green leaves arranged like ascending stairs. Plants grow from a thick, creeping rhizome.

FLOWER COLOR: Small, starry creamy white flowers are borne in terminal, plume-like clusters. Red berries ripen in late summer.

FLOWERING TIME: Spring.

HEIGHT AND SPREAD: 2–4 feet (60–120 cm) tall; 2–3 feet (60–90 cm) or more wide.

TEMPERATURE REQUIREMENTS: Zones 3–8.

POSITION: Evenly moist, humus-rich, neutral to acid soil in light to full shade. Plants burn in full sun.

CULTIVATION: Divide the tangled rhizomes if plants overgrow their position.

PROPAGATION: Divide in spring or fall. Sow fresh seed outdoors in fall.

PEST AND DISEASE PREVENTION: No serious pests or diseases.

LANDSCAPE USE: Plant Solomon's plumes in woodland gardens with hostas, bleeding hearts (*Dicentra* spp.), lungworts (*Pulmonaria* spp.), columbines (*Aquilegia* spp.), wildflowers, and ferns. Use them as an underplanting for shrubs and flowering trees.

OTHER COMMON NAMES: False Solomon's seal.

OTHER SPECIES:

S. stellata, starry Solomon's plume, has narrow blue-green foliage and small clusters of ¼-inch (6 mm) flowers. The attractive berries are green with deep purple stripes. Zones 2–7.

Solidago canadensis	Compositae

CANADA GOLDENROD

Canada goldenrod is a common roadside wildflower with plumed flower clusters and toothed, lance-shaped leaves. Plants grow from creeping rhizomes and can become invasive.

FLOWER COLOR: The small bright yellow flowers are grouped into large, plumed heads.

FLOWERING TIME: Late summer into fall.

HEIGHT AND SPREAD: 2–5 feet (60–150 cm) tall; 3–5 feet (90–150 cm) wide.

TEMPERATURE REQUIREMENTS: Zones 3–8.

POSITION: Average, moist to well-drained soil. Full sun to light shade.

CULTIVATION: Canada goldenrod spreads rapidly and needs frequent division.

PROPAGATION: Divide in spring or after flowering. Sow seed outdoors in fall. Take cuttings in early summer.

PEST AND DISEASE PREVENTION: No serious pests or diseases.

LANDSCAPE USE: Plant in formal or informal gardens, meadows, and prairie plantings. Combine with phlox, asters, sunflowers (*Helianthus* spp.), and gayfeathers (*Liatris* spp.). Contrary to popular belief, goldenrods do not cause hayfever. The culprit is ragweed, which blooms at the same time.

HYBRIDS: 'Baby Gold' is 2–2½ feet (60–75 cm) tall. 'Cloth of Gold' has pale yellow flowers on 1½–2-foot (45–60 cm) stems. 'Crown of Rays' has large flaring flower clusters. 'Goldenmosa' has drooping clusters of pale yellow flowers.

Stachys byzantina (syn. S. lanata)   Labiatae

LAMB'S-EARS

Lamb's-ears are eye-catching foliage plants with basal rosettes of elongated, densely white, wooly leaves. These sun-loving plants grow from slow-creeping stems.

FLOWER COLOR: Small, two-lipped rose purple flowers are carried on wooly flower stalks. Many people consider the flowers unattractive and remove them.

FLOWERING TIME: Early summer.

HEIGHT AND SPREAD: 6–15 inches (15 37.5 cm) tall; 12–24 inches (30–60 cm) wide.

TEMPERATURE REQUIREMENTS: Zones 4–8. Plants are sensitive to hot, humid weather.

POSITION: Well-drained, sandy or loamy soil. Full sun to light shade. Intolerant of heavy, soggy soil.

CULTIVATION: Lamb's-ears form dense broad clumps of tightly packed foliage. Divide overgrown clumps to control their spread.

PROPAGATION: Divide plants in spring or fall.

PEST AND DISEASE PREVENTION: In wet, humid weather rot may occur. Cut back affected plants. Proper siting is the best defense.

LANDSCAPE USE: Plant at the front of formal and informal gardens with irises, coral bells (*Heuchera* spp.), alliums (*Allium* spp.), yuccas, and sedums.

CULTIVARS: 'Primrose Heron' has soft, primrose yellow foliage in spring. 'Sheila McQueen' has larger, less-wooly leaves and grows well in warmer zones. 'Silver Carpet' is a neat, compact cultivar that is listed as nonflowering but it flowers in some gardens.

Stokesia laevis   Compositae

STOKE'S ASTER

Stoke's aster is attractive in foliage and flower. The broad, lance-shaped leaves are deep green with a white midvein. The leaves form a rosette from a crown with thick, fibrous roots.

FLOWER COLOR: The 2–3-inch (5–7.5 cm) daisy-like flowers have ragged blue rays and fuzzy white centers.

FLOWERING TIME: Summer.

HEIGHT AND SPREAD: 1–2 feet (30–60 cm) tall; 2 feet (60 cm) wide.

TEMPERATURE REQUIREMENTS: Zones 5–9.

POSITION: Average to humus-rich, moist but well-drained soil. Full sun to light shade. Established plants tolerate poor, dry soil.

CULTIVATION: Plants can grow undisturbed for many years. Divide in spring or fall as necessary.

PROPAGATION: Divide in early spring. Sow seed outdoors in fall or indoors in winter after stratification. To stratify, mix seed with moist peat moss or seed-starting medium in a plastic bag. Close the bag with a twist-tie and place it in the refrigerator for 4–6 weeks. Then sow the mixture as you would normal seed.

PEST AND DISEASE PREVENTION: No serious pests or diseases.

LANDSCAPE USE: Combine with verbenas (*Verbena* spp.), phlox, goldenrods (*Solidago* spp.), columbines (*Aquilegia* spp.), and ornamental grasses in formal and informal landscapes.

CULTIVARS: 'Alba' has white flowers. 'Blue Danube' has 5-inch (12.5 cm) lavender-blue flowers. 'Klaus Jelitto' has 4-inch (10 cm), deep blue flowers.

Thalictrum aquilegifolium   Ranunculaceae

COLUMBINE MEADOW RUE

Columbine meadow rue has billowy plumes crowning erect stalks clothed in intricately divided leaves that resemble those of columbines. Plants grow from fibrous-rooted crowns.

FLOWER COLOR: The ½-inch (1 cm) lavender or white flowers consist of many fuzzy stamens (male reproductive structures) in dense, branched clusters.

FLOWERING TIME: Late spring and early summer.

HEIGHT AND SPREAD: 2–3 feet (60–90 cm) tall; 1–2 feet (30–60 cm) wide.

TEMPERATURE REQUIREMENTS: Zones 5–8.

POSITION: Evenly moist, humus-rich soil. Full sun or partial shade. Plants tolerate wet soil.

CULTIVATION: Clumps spread slowly and seldom outgrow their position. Divide if necessary.

PROPAGATION: Divide in spring or fall. Sow seed outdoors in fall or indoors in early spring.

PEST AND DISEASE PREVENTION: No serious pests or diseases.

LANDSCAPE USE: Plant columbine meadow rue in formal or informal gardens. It performs well at pondside or along streams with irises, hostas, hibiscus (*Hibiscus* spp.), daylilies, and ferns.

CULTIVARS: 'Album' has white flowers. 'Atropurpureum' has violet flowers. 'Thundercloud' has deep purple flowers.

OTHER SPECIES:

T. flavum var. *glaucum,* dusty meadow rue, has blue-gray foliage and flattened heads of soft, sulfur yellow flowers on 3–5-foot (90–150 cm) stems. Zones 4–8.

Thermopsis caroliniana (syn *T. villosa*) Leguminosae

CAROLINA LUPINE

Carolina lupine produces upright flower spikes atop stout stems clothed in three-parted gray-green leaves. Plants grow from stout, fibrous-rooted crowns.

FLOWER COLOR: Lemon yellow pea-shaped flowers are tightly packed into 8–12-inch (20–30 cm) clusters.

FLOWERING TIME: Late spring or early summer.

HEIGHT AND SPREAD: 3–5 feet (90–150 cm) tall; 2–4 feet (60–120 cm) wide.

TEMPERATURE REQUIREMENTS: Zones 3–9. Heat-tolerant.

POSITION: Average to humus-rich, moist, acid soil. Full sun to light shade.

CULTIVATION: Clumps grow to shrub-like proportions but seldom need division if ample space is allotted. If foliage declines after bloom, cut it to the ground.

PROPAGATION: Take cuttings in early summer from sideshoots. Sow seed outdoors in fall. Sow seed indoors in early spring after soaking it in hot water for 12–24 hours.

PEST AND DISEASE PREVENTION: No serious pests or diseases.

LANDSCAPE USE: Plant toward the rear of the garden with peonies, willow blue star (*Amsonia tabernaemontana*), cranesbills (*Geranium* spp.), and other rounded or mounding plants. Lovely with shrubs or in meadows or lightly shaded wild gardens.

OTHER COMMON NAMES: Carolina thermopsis.

| *Tiarella cordifolia* | Saxifragaceae | *Tradescantia* x *andersoniana* | Commelinaceae |

FOAMFLOWER

COMMON SPIDERWORT

Foamflowers are elegant woodland wildflowers with fuzzy flowers and rosettes of triangular, three-lobed hairy leaves. Plants grow from fibrous-rooted crowns and creeping stems.

Common spiderworts have satiny flowers that open in the morning and fade in the afternoon. They are borne in clusters at the tips of the stems. Plants grow from thick, spidery roots.

FLOWER COLOR: The small, starry white flowers are borne in spike-like clusters. They are often tinged with pink.

FLOWERING TIME: Spring.

HEIGHT AND SPREAD: 6–10 inches (15–25 cm) tall; 12–24 inches (30–60 cm) wide.

TEMPERATURE REQUIREMENTS: Zones 3–8.

POSITION: Evenly moist, humus-rich, slightly acid soil. Partial to full shade.

CULTIVATION: Foamflowers spread by creeping stems to form broad mats. Divide plants to control their spread.

PROPAGATION: Remove runners in summer and treat them as cuttings if they lack roots of their own. Sow seed in spring.

PEST AND DISEASE PREVENTION: No serious pests or diseases.

LANDSCAPE USE: Foamflowers are consummate groundcovers. Their tight foliage mats discourage weeds under shrubs and flowering trees. In woodland gardens combine them with bulbs, ferns, and wildflowers like fringed bleeding heart (*Dicentra eximia*) and bloodroot (*Sanguinaria canadensis*), as well as hostas and irises.

VARIETIES: *T. cordifolia* var. *collina* (also listed as *T. wherryi*) is a clump-former with many pink-tinged flower spikes in each rosette.

FLOWER COLOR: The 1–1½-inch (2.5–3.5 cm) flowers have three rounded blue, purple, or white petals.

FLOWERING TIME: Spring and early summer.

HEIGHT AND SPREAD: 1–2 feet (30–60 cm) tall; 2 feet (60 cm) wide.

TEMPERATURE REQUIREMENTS: Zones 3–9.

POSITION: Moist but well-drained, average to humus-rich soil. Full sun to partial shade.

CULTIVATION: After flowering plants tend to look shabby. Cut them to the ground to encourage new growth. Plants in dry situations go dormant in summer.

PROPAGATION: Divide in fall. Self-sown seedlings often appear.

PEST AND DISEASE PREVENTION: No serious pests or diseases.

LANDSCAPE USE: Plant in informal gardens with bellflowers (*Campanula* spp.), columbines (*Aquilegia* spp.), hostas, and ferns. In formal gardens combine them with tulips and spring-blooming perennials.

CULTIVARS: 'Blue Stone' has rich medium blue flowers. 'James C. Weguelin' has sky blue flowers. 'Pauline' has orchid-pink flowers. 'Red Cloud' has maroon flowers. 'Zwanenberg Blue' is purple-blue.

Tricyrtis hirta   Liliaceae

COMMON TOAD LILY

Common toad lilies produce curious speckled flowers. The tall, arching stems are clothed in two-ranked, broadly lance-shaped, hairy leaves with prominent veins.

FLOWER COLOR: The purple-spotted white flowers face upward, with three petals and three petal-like sepals around a central column. The flowers are carried in the leaf axils on the upper one-third of the stem.

FLOWERING TIME: Late summer and fall.

HEIGHT AND SPREAD: 2–3 feet (60–90 cm) tall; 1–2 feet (30–60 cm) wide.

TEMPERATURE REQUIREMENTS: Zones 4–9.

POSITION: Evenly moist, humus-rich soil. Light to partial shade. Full sun will burn the foliage.

CULTIVATION: Plants spread by creeping stems to form handsome clumps that seldom need division. Plants often bloom in fall. In cooler zones plants may be damaged by frost just as they begin blooming.

PROPAGATION: Divide clumps in spring. Sow seed outdoors in fall.

PEST AND DISEASE PREVENTION: No serious pests or diseases.

LANDSCAPE USE: Common toad lilies are subtle and are best planted where they can be appreciated at close range. Large plants are effective with astilbes, hostas, ferns, and other woodland plants.

Uvularia grandiflora   Liliaceae

GREAT MERRYBELLS

Great merrybells is a graceful wildflower with nodding bell-shaped flowers on slender stalks clothed in gray-green leaves. Plants grow from rhizomes with brittle white roots.

FLOWER COLOR: The nodding lemon yellow flowers have three petals and three petal-like sepals that twist in the middle.

FLOWERING TIME: Spring.

HEIGHT AND SPREAD: 1–1½ feet (30–45 cm) tall; 1–2 feet (30–60 cm) wide.

TEMPERATURE REQUIREMENTS: Zones 3–8.

POSITION: Moist, humus-rich soil. Partial to full shade. Spring sun is important for bloom but summer shade is mandatory.

CULTIVATION: Great merrybells spread to form tight, attractive clumps. When flowers fade, the foliage expands to form an attractive summer-long groundcover.

PROPAGATION: Divide plants before flowering in early spring or fall.

PEST AND DISEASE PREVENTION: No serious pests or diseases.

LANDSCAPE USE: Plant in woodland gardens with wildflowers such as bloodroot (*Sanguinaria canadensis*), fringed bleeding heart (*Dicentra eximia*), and wild gingers (*Asarum* spp.). Ferns and hostas are also good companions.

OTHER COMMON NAMES: Large-flowered bellwort.

OTHER SPECIES:

U. sessilifolia, wild oats, is a slender, delicate plant with strawcolored flowers and narrow leaves. Zones 4–8.

Verbascum chaixii   Scrophulariaceae

NETTLE-LEAVED MULLEIN

Nettle-leaved mullein has thick flower spikes and stout stems with broadly oval, pointed leaves. The species has yellow flowers; the cultivar 'Album' has white flowers.

FLOWER COLOR: The small, five-petaled yellow flowers are tightly packed into dense clusters.

FLOWERING TIME: Summer.

HEIGHT AND SPREAD: 2–3 feet (60–90 cm) tall; 1–2 feet (30–60 cm) wide.

TEMPERATURE REQUIREMENTS: Zones 4–8.

POSITION: Average, well-drained soil. Full sun to light shade.

CULTIVATION: Established plants are quite attractive. Plants spread slowly and seldom need division.

PROPAGATION: Sow seed outdoors in fall or spring or indoors in spring. Take root cuttings in late winter or early spring. Plants often self-sow.

PEST AND DISEASE PREVENTION: No serious pests or diseases.

LANDSCAPE USE: Plant nettle-leaved mulleins in borders with fine-textured perennials like thread-leaved coreopsis (*Coreopsis verticillata*), cranesbills (*Geranium* spp.), and meadow rues (*Thalictrum* spp.). Combine them with mounded plants such as catmints (*Nepeta* spp.), and ornamental grasses in informal gardens.

CULTIVARS: 'Album' has white flowers with purple eyes.

OTHER SPECIES:

V. olympicum, olympic mullein, has broadly oval, pointed, silver gray hairy leaves and yellow flowers. Zones 6–8.

Verbena canadensis   Verbenaceae

ROSE VERBENA

Rose verbena has deeply lobed leaves and circular, flat flower clusters at the ends of the stems. Plants grow from fibrous-rooted crowns but also root along the trailing stems.

FLOWER COLOR: The tubular lavender to rose pink flowers have flat, five-petaled faces.

FLOWERING TIME: Late spring through fall.

HEIGHT AND SPREAD: 8–18 inches (20–45 cm) tall; 12–36 inches (30–90 cm) wide.

TEMPERATURE REQUIREMENTS: Zones 4–10.

POSITION: Poor to humus-rich, well-drained soil. Full sun. Plants are heat- and drought-tolerant.

CULTIVATION: Plants spread quickly to form broad clumps. Prune or divide plants that overgrow their position.

PROPAGATION: Take stem cuttings in summer.

PEST AND DISEASE PREVENTION: Powdery mildew may cause white blotches on the foliage. Spray infected plants with wettable sulfur to control the spread of the disease.

LANDSCAPE USE: Rose verbena is an excellent "weaver." Use it to tie mixed plantings together at the front of the border. The stems will cover bare ground between yuccas (*Yucca* spp.), mulleins (*Verbascum* spp.), and ornamental grasses.

HYBRIDS: A number of lovely hybrids are available in a full range of colors from white and yellow to pink, rose, red, lavender, and purple.

OTHER SPECIES:

V. bonariensis (syn. *V. patagonica*), Brazilian vervain, is an upright plant with sparse foliage and rounded clusters of violet flowers. Zones 7–9.

SPIKE SPEEDWELL

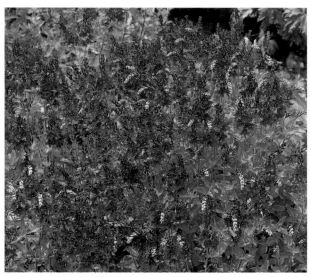

Spike speedwell has pointed flower clusters atop leafy stems. The opposite leaves are oval to oblong and clothed in soft hair. Plants grow from fibrous-rooted crowns.

FLOWER COLOR: The small, two-lipped pink, blue, or white flowers are tightly packed into erect spikes.

FLOWERING TIME: Summer.

HEIGHT AND SPREAD: 1–3 feet (30–90 cm) tall; 1½–2½ feet (45–75 cm) wide.

TEMPERATURE REQUIREMENTS: Zones 3–8.

POSITION: Average to humus-rich, moist, but well-drained soil. Full sun to light shade.

CULTIVATION: Plants grow slowly to form neat, attractive clumps. Cut plants back if they get rangy or to encourage fresh growth and continued bloom.

PROPAGATION: Divide in spring or fall. Take stem cuttings in late spring or early summer; remove any flower buds.

PEST AND DISEASE PREVENTION: No serious pests or diseases.

LANDSCAPE USE: Plant spike speedwells with summer perennials that need good drainage like yarrows, catmints (*Nepeta* spp.), sundrops (*Oenothera* spp.), and ornamental grasses. Their spiky forms are perfect for adding excitement to plantings.

CULTIVARS: 'Barcarolle' has rose pink flowers on 12–15-inch (30–37.5 cm) stems and gray-green leaves. 'Blue Fox' has lavender-blue flowers on 15–20-inch (37.5–50 cm) stems. 'Blue Peter' has dark blue flowers on 2-foot (60 cm) stems. 'Minuet' is a dwarf selection with rose pink flowers on 1–1½-foot (30–45 cm) stems. 'Snow White' has branching spikes

Hungarian speedwell is another showy species with short spikes of bright blue flowers. Combine it with other sun-loving summer bloomers like yarrows and daylilies.

of white flowers on 1½-foot (45 cm) stems.

OTHER SPECIES:

V. alpina, alpine speedwell, is an evergreen creeper with shiny oval leaves and spikes of dark blue flowers. 'Goodness Grows' is a floriferous, reblooming hybrid with deep blue flowers. Zones 3–8.

V. grandis is similar to *V. spicata* but has broader shiny green leaves. The variety *holophylla* has wide, somewhat heart-shaped leaves. 'Blue Charm' (also sold as 'Lavender Charm') has 6-inch (15 cm) spikes of rich lavender-blue flowers on bushy plants. 'Sunny Border Blue' is a long-blooming hybrid with deep navy blue flowers. Zones 4–8.

V. incana, wooly speedwell, is a 1–2-foot (30–60 cm) tall species with wooly silver gray leaves. 'Rosea' has pink-tinged flowers. 'Wendy' has lavender-blue flowers. Some selections listed under *V. spicata* may be hybrids with this species. Zones 3–8.

V. longifolia, long-leaved speedwell, is a showy species with 2–4-foot (60–120 cm) spikes of pale blue flowers and opposite to whorled, lance-shaped foliage. Zones 3–8.

V. teucrium, Hungarian speedwell, is a spreading species with bright blue spikes of ¼-inch (6 mm) flowers. 'Crater Lake Blue' has ultramarine flowers. Zones 3–8.

| *Viola odorata* | Violaceae | *Yucca filamentosa* | Liliaceae |

SWEET VIOLET

ADAM'S NEEDLE

Sweet violets are beloved for their delicate, fragrant, early-season flowers. They produce rosettes of heart-shaped leaves from creeping, fibrous-rooted rhizomes.

FLOWER COLOR: The deep purple or blue flowers have five petals. Two point upward and three point outward and down. The two outfacing petals have fuzzy beards.

FLOWERING TIME: Spring.

HEIGHT AND SPREAD: 2–8 inches (5–20 cm) tall; 4–8 inches (10–20 cm) wide.

TEMPERATURE REQUIREMENTS: Zones 6–9.

POSITION: Moist, humus-rich soil. Sun or shade. Widely tolerant of varying soil and moisture conditions.

CULTIVATION: Violets are prolific spreaders and make themselves at home in any garden.

PROPAGATION: Divide plants after flowering or in fall. Plants often self-sow.

PEST AND DISEASE PREVENTION: No serious pests or diseases.

LANDSCAPE USE: Violets form attractive groundcovers under shrubs and flowering trees. In informal gardens plant them with bulbs, wildflowers, hostas, and early-blooming perennials.

CULTIVARS: 'Deloris' has deep purple flowers. 'White Queen' has small white flowers.

OTHER SPECIES:

V. sororia, wooly blue violet, is similar but has hairier foliage. 'Freckles' has pale blue flowers flecked with purple. 'Priceana', the confederate violet, has white flowers with purple-blue centers. Zones 3–9.

Adam's needle produces tall, oval clusters of bell-like white flowers and rosettes of sword-shaped blue-green leaves. It grows from a woody crown with fleshy roots.

FLOWER COLOR: Nodding creamy white flowers have three petals and three petal-like sepals that form a bell.

FLOWERING TIME: Summer.

HEIGHT AND SPREAD: 5–15 feet (1.5–4.5 m) tall (5 feet [1.5 m] is average); 3–6 feet (90–180 cm) wide.

TEMPERATURE REQUIREMENTS: Zones 3–10.

POSITION: Average to humus-rich, well-drained soil. Full sun to light shade.

CULTIVATION: Plants thrive for years with little care. After flowering the main crown dies but auxiliary crowns keep growing.

PROPAGATION: Remove young sideshoots from the clump in spring or fall.

PEST AND DISEASE PREVENTION: No serious pests or diseases.

LANDSCAPE USE: Plant in dry borders or rock gardens as accents or in seaside gardens. Contrast the stiff foliage with soft or delicate plants like lamb's-ears (*Stachys byzantina*), sedums, and verbenas (*Verbena* spp.).

CULTIVARS: 'Bright Edge' has yellow-variegated leaves.

USDA
PLANT HARDINESS ZONE MAP

The map that follows shows the United States and Canada divided into 10 zones. Each zone is based on a 10°F (5.6°C) difference in average annual minimum temperature. Some areas are considered too high in elevation for plant cultivation and so are not assigned to any zone. There are also island zones that are warmer or cooler than surrounding areas because of differences in elevation; they have been given a zone different from the surrounding areas. Many large urban areas are in a warmer zone than the surrounding land.

Plants grow best within an optimum range of temperatures. The range may be wide for some species and narrow for others. Plants also differ in their ability to survive frost and in their sun or shade requirements.

The zone ratings indicate conditions where designated plants will grow well and not merely survive. Refer to the map to find out which zone you are in. In the "Plant by Plant Guide," starting on page 78, you'll find recommendations for the plants that grow best in your zone.

Many plants may survive in zones warmer or colder than their recommended zone range. Remember that other factors, including wind, soil type, soil moisture and drainage capability, humidity, snow, and winter sunshine, may have a great effect on growth.

Average annual minimum temperature (°F/°C)

Zone 1		Below -50°F/-45°C	Zone 6		0° to -10°F/-18° to -23°C
Zone 2		-40° to -50°F/-40° to -45°C	Zone 7		10° to 0°F/-12° to -18°C
Zone 3		-30° to -40°F/-34° to -40°C	Zone 8		20° to 10°F/-7° to -12°C
Zone 4		-20° to -30°F/-29° to -34°C	Zone 9		30° to 20°F/-1° to -7°C
Zone 5		-10° to -20°F/-23° to -29°C	Zone 10		40° to 30°F/4° to -1°C

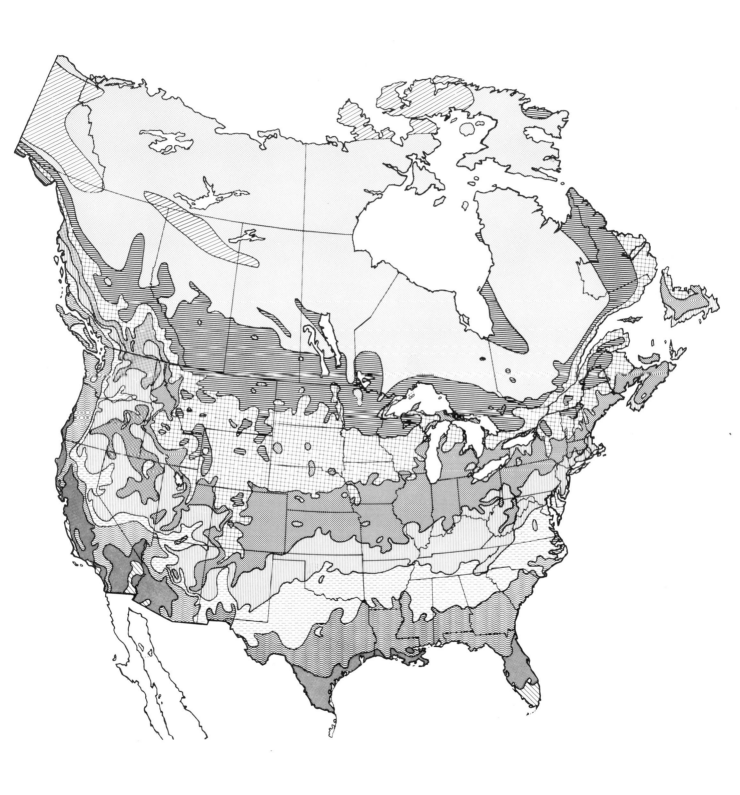

INDEX

The numbers in bold indicate main entries, and the numbers in italic indicate illustrations.

ACKNOWLEDGMENTS

Weldon Russell would like to thank Colonial Cottage Nursery, Kenthurst, New South Wales, Australia, for their assistance in the production of this book.

Photo Credits

Allan Armitage: pages 91 (left), 109 (right), 120 (right), 137 (right), and 146 (left).

Auscape: photographer Jerry Harpur: cover.

John Callanan: pages 80 (left), 81 (left), 83 (left), 85 (right), 86 (left and right), 92 (left and right), 93 (right), 97 (right), 99 (left), 102 (right), 106 (left and right), 112 (left and right), 114 (right), 115 (right), 124 (left), 132 (right), 133 (left), 137 (left), 144 (right), 148 (left), 151 (right), and 152 (left).

Bruce Coleman Ltd: photographer N. B. Blake: contents (bottom right); photographer Thomas Buchholz: page 58; photographer Jane Burton: page 67 (top right); photographer Patrick Clement: page 139 (left); photographer Eric Crichton: pages 12 and 56 (left); photographer R. Glover: page 59; photographer Dr. Frieder Sauer: page 67 (top left); photographer Kim Taylor: page 66 (bottom left); photographer R. Wanscheidt: page 35; photographer Peter Ward: page 65 (right).

Michael Dirr: pages 140 (right) and 150 (right).

Thomas Eltzroth: pages 6, 32, 80 (right), 82 (right), 84 (left), 85 (left), 87 (right), 88 (right), 89 (left), 90 (right), 91 (right), 93 (left), 94 (left), 99 (right), 100 (left), 103 (left and right), 104 (left and right), 108 (left), 110 (left and right), 111 (left and right), 114 (left), 117 (left and right), 118 (right), 121 (left), 122 (left and right), 123 (right), 126 (left), 127 (right), 129 (right), 130 (left and right), 131 (left), 135 (left and right), 136 (left and right), 138 (right), 143 (right), 147 (left and right), 149 (right), 151 left and 153 (left and right).

Derek Fell: back cover (center), pages 18 (top), 19, 44, 45 (top left, center, and right), 52 (bottom), 54, 55, 65 (center), 68 (bottom right), 73 (bottom), 95 (right), 98 (right), 105 (right), 109 (left), 131 (right), and 134 (right).

The Garden Picture Library: photographer Linda Burgess: pages 42, 56 (right), and 60 (bottom); photographer Tommy Candler: page 124 (right); photographer Brian Carter: pages 29, 67 (bottom left), 78, 101 (left), and 129 (left); photographer Tim Griffiths: page 17 (right); photographer Marijke Heuff: page 132 (left); photographer Michael Howes: page 18 (bottom); photographer Mayer Le Scanff: back cover (top); photographer Clive Nichols: page 145 (right); photographer Jerry Pavia: pages 50 and 57; photographer Clay Perry: page 5; photographer Brigitte Thomas: page 47 (bottom); photographer Didier Willery: page 14 (top); photographer Steven Wooster: pages 16 and 21.

Stirling Macoboy: page 94 (right).

Nancy J. Ondra: page 88 (left).

Photos Horticultural: endpapers, half title page, pages 2, 3, 8, 14 (bottom), 15, 17 (left), 20 (top and bottom), 22, 25 (left and right), 26, 27, 28, 30 (top and bottom), 31 (left and right), 34, 37 (top), 45 (bottom), 46, 47 (top), 52 (top), 53, 60 (top), 62, 63 (top), 64, 65 (left), 66 (top and bottom center), 67 (bottom center and right), 68 (top and bottom left), 69 (top and bottom left), 70, 73 (top), 75 (bottom), 83 (right), 84 (right), 87 (left), 89 (right), 90 (left), 95 (left), 96 (left and right), 98 (left), 107 (left and right), 108 (right), 113 (right), 115 (left), 116 (left and right), 123 (left), 126 (right), 133 (right), 134 (left), 138 (left), 139 (right), 140 (left), 141 (left and right), 145 (left), 149 (left), and 152 (right).

Rodale Stock Images: back cover (bottom), pages 63 (bottom) and 121 (right).

Tony Rodd: contents page (bottom left), pages 81 (right), 82 (left), 97 (left), 101 (right), 102 (left), 113 (left), 125 (left and right), 127 (left), 143 (left), 144 (left), 146 (right), and 150 (left).

Lorna Rose: page 128 (right).

Susan Roth: page 148 (right).

Anita Sabarese: page 100 (right).

John J. Smith: pages 118 (left) and 142 (left and right).

David Wallace: contents page (top left and top right), pages 11 (left and right), 36 (left and right), 37 (bottom), 48 (top left, center, right, bottom left, center, and right), 61, 72 (top left, right, bottom left, center, and right), 75 (top left, center, and right), 76 (top left, right, bottom left, and right), 105 (left), 119 (left and right), and 120 (left).

Weldon Russell: page 128 (left).

Weldon Trannies: pages 66 (bottom right), 68 (bottom center), and 69 (bottom center and right).